Norton Anthology of WESTERN MUSIC

SECOND EDITION

VOLUME II

Classic • Romantic • Modern

EDITED BY

CLAUDE V. PALISCA

Yale University

W • W • Norton & Company New York • London

Also available from Norton

An Anthology of Early Renaissance Music
Edited by Noah Greenberg and Paul Maynard

Anthology of Medieval Music
Edited by Richard H. Hoppin

The Norton Scores: An Anthology for Listening
Fourth Edition: Standard and Expanded
Edited by Roger Kamien

The Concerto, 1800–1900
Edited by Paul Henry Lang

The Symphony, 1800–1900
Edited by Paul Henry Lang

Anthology of Romantic Music
Edited by Leon Plantinga

Choral Music: A Norton Historical Anthology
Edited by Ray Robinson

Published simultaneously in Canada by Penguin Books Canada Ltd., 2801 John Street, Markham, Ontario L3R 1B4.
Printed in the United States of America.

The text of this book is composed in Times Roman,
with display type set in Bembo.
Composition by Vail-Ballou Press
of the Maple-Vail Book Group.

Second Edition

Library of Congress Cataloging in Publication Data

ISBN 0-393-95642-3 Vol. I
ISBN 0-393-95644-X Vol. II

W. W. Norton & Company, Inc., 500 Fifth Avenue, New York, N.Y. 10110
W. W. Norton & Company Ltd., 37 Great Russell Street, London WC1B 3NU

2 3 4 5 6 7 8 9 0

CONTENTS

CONCERTO

OPERA AND CANTATA

ROMANTIC

PIANO MUSIC

ORCHESTRAL MUSIC

Chamber Music

Lied

Opera

Choral Music

MODERN

Orchestral

Solo and Chamber Music

Song

Opera

PREFACE

The title of this anthology lacks one important qualifier: it is an *historical* anthology of western music. There is a wide difference between an historical anthology and one intended simply to supply a selection of music for study and analysis.

Historians cannot confine themselves to studying the great works that are the usual stuff of anthologies in splendid isolation. They are interested in products of the imagination great and small as they exist in a continuum of such works. Just as composers did not create in a musical void, standing aloof from the models of their predecessors and contemporaries, so the historically-oriented student and analyst must have the primary material that permits establishing historical connections. This anthology invites students and teachers to make such connections. It confronts, for example, important works and their models, pieces written on a common subject or built according to similar procedures or that give evidence of subtle influences of one composer's work on another's.

Most music before 1500 was composed on some pre-existent music, and there are numerous examples of this practice even after that date. Whenever possible in this anthology, the music that served to ignite a composer's imagination is provided. In one notable case a single chant gave rise to a chain of polyphonic elaborations. This is the Alleluia with verse, *Alleluia Pascha nostrum* (NAWM 16), elaborated by Léonin in organum purum with clausulae, refreshed with substitute clausulae by his successors; and both his and the new clausulae were turned into motets by adapting Latin or French texts to them or made fuller with new parts both with and without texts. (This Alleluia set, although different in content, format and realization, is itself modeled on similar sets on this chant devised by Richard Crocker and Karl Kroeger as local teaching aids, and I am indebted to them for the general idea and certain details.)

A similar chain of works are the masses built upon the melisma on the word *caput* in the Sarum version of the Antiphon, *Venit ad Petrum:* two are here given, the first by Obrecht, and the second by Ockeghem, each influencing the other (NAWM 40 and 41). It is instructive similarly to observe in Josquin's early motet, *Tu solus, qui facis mirabilia* (NAWM 32), the way he absorbed fragments of Ockeghem's arrangement of the song, *D'ung aultre amer* (NAWM 48), or to be able to refer to the *Benedictus* of Taverner's Mass, *Gloria tibi trinitas* (NAWM 42), the source of the famous subject, *In nomine,* when studying one of the many variations upon it, such as that by Christopher Tye (NAWM 65). The process of coloration and variation that produced Luys de Narváez's arrangement for vihuela (NAWM 49b) may be inferred from comparing it to the original polyphonic chanson *Mille regretz* by Josquin (NAWM 49a). A later example of this process, starting with a monodic model, may be found in the *Lachrimae* pavans of Dowland and Byrd (NAWM 102a and b) based on the well-known air, *Flow my tears,* by Dowland (NAWM 69). In the twentieth century the variation procedure is the structural principle for several excerpts, namely those by Strauss (NAWM 146), Schoenberg (NAWM 148), and Copland (NAWM 150). Arcadelt's parody in his Mass (NAWM 43) of Mouton's motet, *Noe, noe* (NAWM 34) may be assumed to be a tribute.

Subtler connections may be detected between Lully's overture to *Armide* (No. 75a) and the opening chorus of Bach's cantata, *Nun komm, der Heiden Heiland* (NAWM 90), between Gossec's *Marche lugubre* (NAWM 117) and the Funeral March from Beethoven's "Eroica" Symphony (NAWM 118), between the nocturnes of Field and Chopin (NAWM 125 and 126), or between Musorgsky's song *Bez solntsa* (NAWM 158) and Debussy's *Nuages* (NAWM 144).

Comparison of the musical realization of the same dramatic moments in the legend of Orpheus by Peri and Monteverdi (NAWM 71 and 72) reveal the latter's debts to the former. It is revealing to compare the settings of Mignon's song from Goethe's *Wilhelm Meister* by Schubert, Schumann, and Wolf (NAWM 133, 134, and 135).

Some of the selections betray foreign influences, as the penetration of Italian styles in England in Purcell's songs for *The Fairy Queen* (NAWM 76) or Humfrey's verse and anthem (NAWM 88). The crisis in Handel's career, brought on partly by the popularity of the ballad opera and the English audience's rejection of his own Italian *opera seria,* is documented in a scene from *The Beggar's Opera* (NAWM 81) and by the changes within his own dramatic *oeuvre* (NAWM 80, 82 and 89). The new Italian style to which he also reacted is exemplified by Pergolesi's *La serva padrona* (NAWM 121).

Some composers are represented by more than one work to permit comparison of early and late styles—Josquin, Monteverdi, Bach, Handel, Vivaldi, Haydn, Beethoven, Liszt, Schoenberg, Stravinsky—or to show diverse approaches by a single composer to distinct genres—Machaut, Dufay, Ockeghem, Arcadelt, Willaert, Monteverdi, Bach, Mozart.

A number of the pieces marked new departures in their day, for example Adrian Willaert's *Aspro core* from his *Musica nova* (NAWM 57), Viadana's solo concerto, *O Domine Jesu Christe* (NAWM 84), Rousseau's scene from *Le Devin du village* (NAWM 122), or C. P. E. Bach's sonata (NAWM 108). Other pieces were chosen particularly because they were singled out by contemporary critics, such as Arcadelt's *Ahime, dov'è 'l bel viso* (NAWM 56), hailed in 1549 by Bishop Cirillo Franco as a ray of hope for the future of text-expressive music; or Monteverdi's *Cruda Amarilli* (NAWM 67), dismembered by Artusi in his dialogue of 1600 that is at once a critique and a defense of Monteverdi's innovations; Caccini's *Perfidissimo volto* (NAWM 66), mentioned in the preface to his own *Euridice* as one of his pioneering attempts, or Cesti's *Intorno all'idol mio* (NAWM 74), one of the most cited arias of the mid-seventeenth century. Others are Lully's monologue in *Armide, Enfin il est en ma puissance* (NAWM 75b), which was roundly criticized by Rousseau and carefully analyzed by Rameau and d'Alembert; the scene of Carissimi's *Jephte* (NAWM 86), singled out by Athanasius Kircher as a triumph of the powers of musical expression; and the *Danse des adolescentes* in Stravinsky's *Le Sacre* (NAWM 147), the object of a critical uproar after its premiere.

Certain of the items serve to correct commonplace misconceptions about the history of music. Cavalieri's *Dalle più alte sfere* (NAWM 70) of 1589 shows that florid monody existed well before 1600. The movements from Clementi's and Dussek's sonatas (NAWM 109 and 110) reveal an intense romanticism and an exploitation of the piano that surpass Beethoven's writing of the same period and probably influenced it. The movement from Richter's String Quartet (NAWM 111) tends to refute Haydn's paternity of the genre. Sammartini's and Stamitz's symphonic movements (NAWM 113 and 114) show that there was more than one path to the Viennese symphony. The Allegro from Johann Christian Bach's E-flat Harpsichord Concerto (NAWM 119) testifies to Mozart's dependence (NAWM 120) on this earlier model. The scene from Meyerbeer's *Les Huguenots* (NAWM 139) is another seminal work that left a trail of imitations.

Most of the selections, however, are free of any insinuations on the part of this editor. They are simply typical, superlative creations that represent their makers, genres, or times outstandingly. Most of the *Ars nova* and many of the Renaissance works are in this category, as are a majority of those of the Baroque, Romantic, and Modern periods. My choices mark important turning points and shifts of style, historical phenomena that are interesting if not always productive of great music, new models of constructive procedures, typical moments in the work of individual composers, and always challenging exemplars for historical and structural analysis.

The proportion of space assigned to a composer or work is not a reflection of my estimation of his greatness, and, regretfully, numerous major figures could not be represented at all. In an anthology of limited size every work chosen excludes another of corresponding size that is equally worthy. Didactic functionality, historical illumination, intrinsic musical quality rather than ''greatness'' or ''genius'' were the major criteria for selection.

The inclusion of a complete Office (NAWM 4) and a nearly complete Mass (NAWM 3) deserves special comment. I realize that the rituals as represented here have little validity as historical documents of the Middle Ages. It would have been more authentic, perhaps, to present a mass and office as practiced in a particular place at a particular moment, say in the twelfth century. Since the Vatican Council, the liturgies printed here are themselves archaic formulas, but that fact strengthens the case for their inclusion, for opportunities to experience a Vespers service or Mass sung in Latin in their classic formulations are rare indeed. I decided to reproduce the editions of the modern chant books, with their stylized neumatic notation, despite the fact that they are not *urtexts,* because these books are the only resources many students will have available for this repertory, and it should be part of their training to become familiar with the editorial conventions of the Solesmes editions.

These volumes of music do not contain any commentaries, because only an extended essay would have done justice to each of the selections. By leaving interpretation to students and teachers, I hope to enrich their opportunities for research and analysis, for discovery and appreciation. Another reason for not accompanying the music with critical and analytical notes is that this anthology was conceived as a companion to Donald J. Grout's *A History of Western Music,* the Fourth Edition of which I revised. Brief discussions of every number in this collection will be found in that book: some barely scratch the surface, others are extended analytical and historical reflections. An index to these discussions by number in this anthology is at the back of each volume.

The anthology, it must be emphasized, was intended to stand by itself as a selection of music representing every important trend, genre, national school and historical development or innovation. It is accompanied by both records and cassettes.

The translations of the poetic and prose texts are my own except where acknowledged. They are literal to a fault, corresponding to the original line by line, if not word for word, with consequent inevitable damage to the English style. I felt that the musical analyst prefers precise detail concerning the text that the composer had before him rather than imaginative and evocative writing. I am indebted to Ann Walters for helping with some stubborn medieval Latin poems and to Ingeborg Glier for casting light on what seemed to me some impenetrable lines of middle-high German.

A number of research assistants, all at one time students at Yale, shared in the background research, in many of the routine tasks, as well as in some of the joys of discovery and critical selection. Robert Ford and Carolyn Abbate explored options in pre-Baroque and post-Classical music respectively during the selection phase. Gail Hilson Wolder and Kenneth Suzuki surveyed the literature on a sizeable number of the items, while Susan Cox Carlson contributed her expertise in early polyphony. Clara Marvin assisted in manifold ways in the last stages of this compilation.

My colleagues at Yale were generous with their advice on selections, particularly Elizabeth Keitel on Machaut, Craig Wright on Dufay, Leon Plantinga on Clementi, John Kirkpatrick on Ives, and Allen Forte on Schoenberg. Leeman Perkins' and Edward Roesner's suggestions after seeing preliminary drafts of the Medieval and Renaissance sections contributed to rounding out those repertories. I am also indebted to Paul Henry Lang for his reactions to the classic period choices and to Christoph Wolff for those of the Baroque period.

The Yale Music Library was the indispensable base of operations, and its staff a prime resource for the development of this anthology. I wish to thank particularly Harold Samuel, Music Librarian, and his associates Alfred B. Kuhn, Kathleen J. Moretto, Karl W. Schrom, Kathryn R. Mansi, and Deborah Miller for their many favors to me and my assistants.

Most of all I have to thank Claire Brook, whose idea it was to compile an anthology to accompany the Third and Fourth Editions of *A History of Western Music*. Her foresight, intuition, and creative editorial style gave me confidence that somehow within a short space of time this complex enterprise would unfold. Thanks to the efforts of her assistant, Ray Morse, we were able to achieve the goal of bringing out the anthology with the accompanying text.

From my first association with this project, Professor Grout's text set a standard of quality and scope that was my constant challenge and inspiration. He accepted the idea of the anthology with enthusiasm and subordinated proprietary and justly prideful feelings to a pedagogical ideal. For this, the users of these tools and I owe him a great debt, particularly since this coupling of text and anthology has already achieved a measure of the success that his book has enjoyed.

W. W. Norton and I are grateful to the individuals and publishers cited in the footnotes who granted permission to reprint, re-edit or adapt material under copyright. Where no modern publication is cited, the music was edited from original sources.

Claude V. Palisca
Hamden, Connecticut

107

Domenico Scarlatti (1685–1757)

Sonata in D Major, K. 119 (1749)

Reprinted by permission from *Sixty Sonatas,* edited by Ralph Kirkpatrick (New York, © 1953), Vol. I, pp. 62–65. Scarlatti's sonatas are identified by the numbers given in Kirkpatrick, *Domenico Scarlatti* (Princeton, 1953), "Catalogue of Sonatas," pp. 442 ff.

Veloce
30
il primo tempo
36
45
Tremulo nell' A la mi re
54
63
R
R
72

80
88
96
106
116
126
135

144
154
163
L
172
181
R R
L L
L L
190
R R
k
199

108

Carl Philipp Emanuel Bach (1714–88)
Sonata IV in A Major, Wq. 55/4: Poco adagio (second movement)

C. P. E. Bach, *Sechs Clavier-Sonaten für Kenner und Liebhaber* (Leipzig, 1779). Bach's sonatas are identified by the numbers in Alfred Wotquenne, *Thematisches Verzeichnis der Werke Ph. E. Bachs* (Leipzig, 1905). Reprinted from *Sechs Claviersonaten: Erste Sammlung*, edited by Lothar Hoffmann-Erbrecht (Leipzig, n.d.), pp. 24–36.

ten.
ten.
12
17
21

25
ten.
ten.
29

109

Muzio Clementi (1752–1832)
Sonata in G Minor, Op. 34, No. 2 (1795): Largo e' sostenuto—Allegro con fuoco (first movement)

Reprinted from *Deux grandes Sonates pour Clavecin ou Forté-Piano, Oeuvres trente-quatre ou trente-huit,* (Paris, Sieber, (180-).

30
rinf
fz.
rinf
40
fz
P
con espress
cres
PP
cres
FF
F
fz.
fz.
52
fz.
rinf
rinf
FF
fz. dimin. P
PP
F
fz.
65
fz.
fz.
fz.
dol.
fz.

F
fz.
fz.
fz.
fz.
dol.
77
P
cres
F
V.S.
1418
F
fz.
dimin.
P
dol.
91
cres
F
P
dol.
FF
102
fz.
fz.
fz.
F
fz.
fz.
fz.

fz.
F
ten
dimin
P
115
FF
dimin.
PP
Legato
Largo
dim.
130
cres
Tempo I°
140
FF

151
rinf
fz.
fz.
FF
V.S.
161
rinf
fz.
P
rinf
fz.
P
con espres.
cres
PP
cres
fz.
fz.
174
fz.
fz.
fz.
FF
P
F
rinf
F
184
rinf
rinf
FF

dimin.
cres
P
cres
196
F
FF
rinf
rinf
P
207
PP
218
FF
fz.
fz.
VS
cres
P

228
F
fz.
fz.
rinf
fz
233
con espress.
P
FF
fz.
P
FF
fz.
244
F
F
fz.
fz.
rinf
rinf
253
con espress.
F
fz.
FF

263
fz
dimin.
P
PP
F
F
fz.
272
FF
fz.
fz.
fz.

JAN DUSSEK (1760–1812)
Sonata in E flat, Op. 44, "Les Adieux" (pub. 1800): Grave—Allegro moderato (first movement)

Reprinted from *Sonatas for Piano,* edited by Jan Racek and Václan Jan Sýkora, Vol. III (Prague, 1962), pp. 20–50. Reprinted by permission.

*) orig.  etc. sempre

dim.
ff
p
pp
sf

*) orig. 

ff
80
sf
con passione
[mf] dolce
85
90
[cresc.]
[f]
tr
p
95
scherzando

con passione
dim.
dim.
dim.
sotto voce

dim.

145
ff
150
il più f possibile
155
sf
dim.
[cresc.]
ff
p
160
p
poco a poco cresc.

165
f
170
rall.
sf
dim.
[a
p
tempo]
ff
p
ff
175
ff
180
sf
sf
sf
185
sf

sf
dim.
sf
190
p
pp
p
195
p
pp
200
f
[fp]
p
205
ff
210
sf

215
[mf] dolce
[cresc. poco a poco]
220
[f]
tr
pp
225
scherzando
230
pp
235
[mf]
[pp]

*) orig.:

III

Franz Xaver Richter (1709–89)
String Quartet in B-flat Major, Op. 5, No. 2 (1768): Fugato presto (third movement)

Reprinted from *Denkmäler deutscher Tonkunst.* Series 2: *Denkmäler der Tonkunst in Bayern.* Jahrg. 15, Vol. I. edited by Hugo Riemann (Leipzig, 1914), pp. 18–21. Reprinted by permission of Breitkopf & Härtel, Wiesbaden.

34
Pia
Pia
Pia
For
For
For
For
MF
MF
MF
For
For
For
For
56
Dol
Dol
Dol
Dol
For
For
For
For
MFor
MFor
For
For
For
For
76

107
Pia
For
MFor
127
tr

147
Pia
Pia
Pia
Pia
For
Dol
MFor
Dol
For
MFor
Dol
MFor
For
Dol
171
For
MFor
For
For
For
MFor
For
For
For
Dol
Dol
Dol
Ten
192
For
For
For
For
Fine.

112

Ludwig van Beethoven (1770–1827)
String Quartet in C-sharp Minor, No. 14, Op. 131 (1826)

a) Adagio ma non troppo e molto espressivo (first movement)

Complete String Quartets (New York: Dover, 1975), pp. 119–26, reprinted from the Breitkopf & Härtel *Complete Works* Edition (Leipzig, n.d.)

27
cresc.
45
cresc.
più cresc.
60
dim.
p dolce cresc.

dolce
77
cresc.
p
94
sf
f

b) Allegro molto vivace (second movement)

25
cresc.
p
dim.
43
più p
pp
in tempo
poco rit.
60
f
sf

sf
p
cresc.
p express.
poco rit.
in tempo
93
f

109
dim.
più p
pp
cresc.
131
148
p espress.
poco rit.

in tempo
cresc.
181
mezza voce

113

Giovanni Battista Sammartini (ca. 1700–75)

Symphony in F Major, No. 32 (before 1744): Presto (first movement)

The symphonies are identified through the numbering in Newell Jenkins and Bathia Churgin, *Thematic Catalogue of the Works of Giovanni Battista Sammartini* (Cambridge: Harvard University Press for the American Musicological Society, 1976). Reprinted by permission of the publishers from *The Symphonies of G. B. Sammartini*, Vol. I: *The Early Symphonies*, edited by Bathia Churgin (Harvard Publications in Music, 2). Cambridge, Mass.: Harvard University Press, © 1968 by the President and Fellows of Harvard College.

8
[f]
[f]
[f]
f
[p]
[p]
[p]
p
12
[f]
[f]
[f]
f
17
20

*m. 35: In mm. 35-36, the octave skips in the manuscript are reversed, starting with the upper octave and descending.

114

Johann Anton Wenzel Stamitz (1717–57)
Sinfonia in E-flat Major
(*La Melodia Germanica* No. 3) (1754–55):
Allegro assai (first movement)

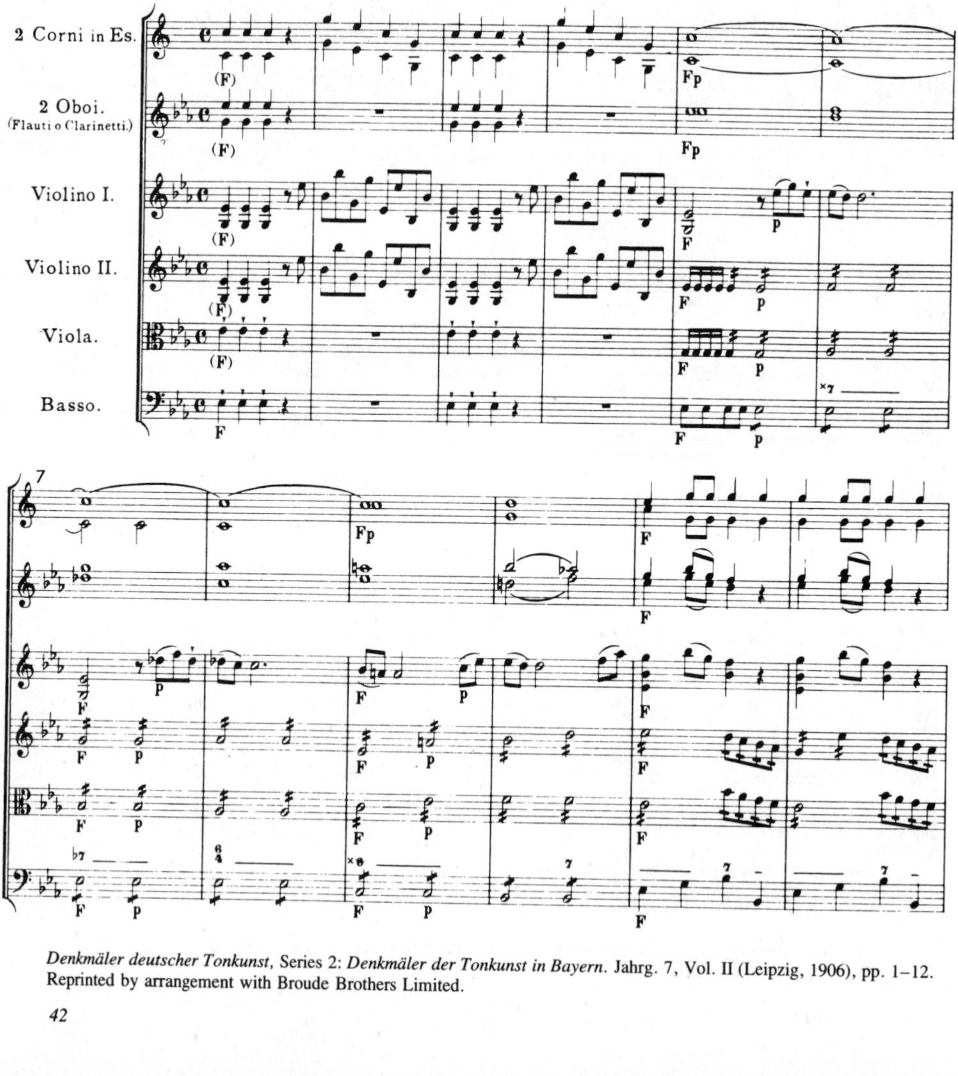

Denkmäler deutscher Tonkunst, Series 2: *Denkmäler der Tonkunst in Bayern*. Jahrg. 7, Vol. II (Leipzig, 1906), pp. 1–12.
Reprinted by arrangement with Broude Brothers Limited.

(decres)
(decres)
pp
19
cres
crescendo
rinf
FF

28
cres
cres
crea
cres
F
F
FF
FF
FF
F
F
p
p
p
p
36
p
p
Fp
Fp
F
p
F
p
F
p
F
p

Fp
Soli
48

63
a 2.
p
cres
pp
F
FF
75

86
(cres)
(cres)
(cres)
(cres)
FF
FF
FF
FF
FF

96
Soli
109

p
F
p
F
p
F
p
F
p
125
p
cres
p
cres
pp
cres
F
p
cres
p
cres
rinf
p
F
FF
p
pp
FF
p
pp
FF
p
F
FF
p
F
p
FF
p
F
p
FF
p
F
p

137
a 2.
FF

115

FRANZ JOSEPH HAYDN (1732–1809)
Symphony No. 7 in C Major, "Midi" (Hoboken I:7; 1761)

a) Adagio-Allegro (first movement)

The numbering of Haydn's symphonies follows A. von Hoboken's *Thematisches-bibliographisches Werkverzeichnis* (Mainz, 1957, 1971). Reprinted from *Joseph Haydn, Critical Edition of the Complete Symphonies,* edited by H. C. Robbins Landon, Vol. I, pp. 157–80. Reprinted by permission of Ludwig Doblinger (B. Herzmansky), Vienna.

8
p
f
[f]

11 Allegro
Allegro

17
a2

22
a2
a2
Solo
p
Solo
p
p

*) Esterházy - Archiv

38
[p]
p
tr
43

48
(Solo)
53
tr
[tr]
f
[f]
(Tutti)
Tutti

58
a 2
1.
2.
62
[p]
a 2
[p]
Solo
tr
p
Solo
p
[p]
Solo)
[p]

68
[p]
(Tutti)
[Tutti]
74
(Solo)
[Solo]
[Tutti]

*) Esterházy - Archiv

91
f
p

96
tr
p

*) Autograph, Esterhazy-Archiv

113
[Solo]
[p]
[p]
(Solo)
[Solo]
(p)

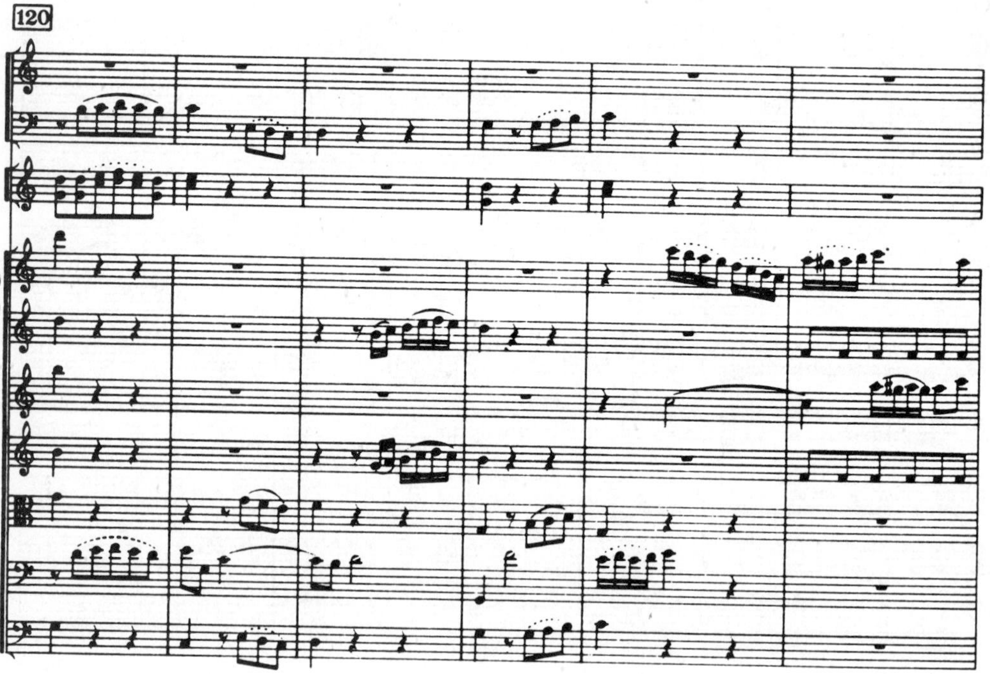
120

126
[p]
[Tutti]
132
[Solo]

138
a 2
tr
f
(Tutti)
144
a 2

b) Adagio-Recitativo (second movement excerpt)

8
pp
p
p
p
p
p
10
f
(Allegro)
f
f
f
f
13
Allegro
a2
f
f
f
f
f
f

*) Ausführung / *execution*

116

Franz Joseph Haydn

Symphony No. 77 in B-flat Major (Hoboken I:77; 1782): Finale, Allegro spiritoso (fourth movement)

For an explanation of the numbering see page 51. Reprinted from *Ibid.*, Vol. 8 (Vienna, 1966), pp. 188–203.

15
15
fz
p
fz
p
fz
p
fz
[p]
fz
p
fz
p
p

22
22
fz
[p]
fz
[p]
fz
p
fz
[p]

29
29
fz
[p]
p

36
36
fz
p
[fz]
[p]

42
42

48
f
f
[Tutti]
f
f
48
f
[f]
[f]
f

54
54

60
60

65
a 2
65

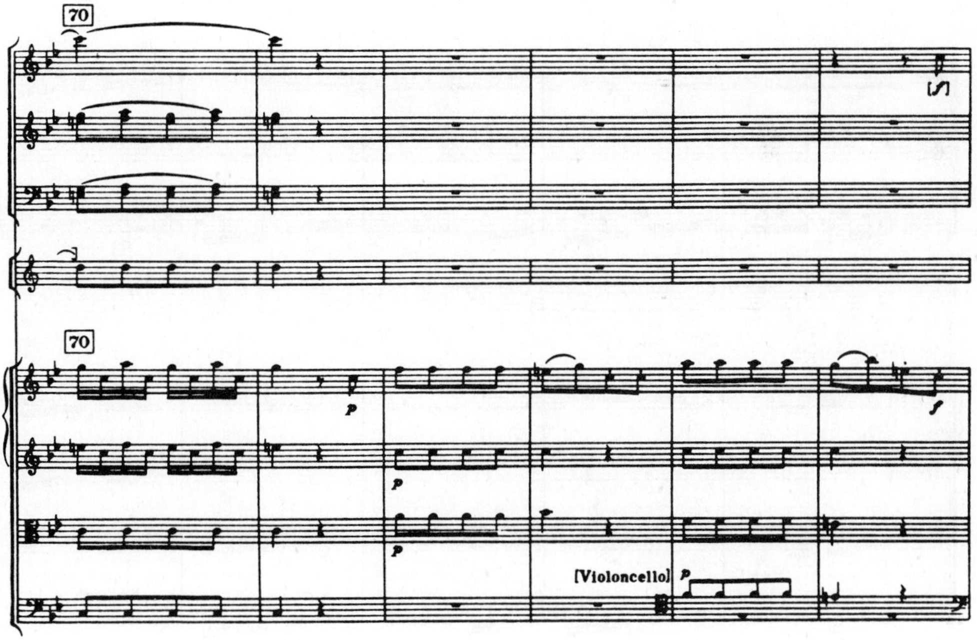
70
[f]
70
p
p
p
f
[Violoncello]
p

*) Pausen } in Esterházy-Archiv, British Museum
Rests

86
a 2
p
86
p
p
[Vlc.]
p
p
[Basso]

91
pp
pp
[Solo]
p
pp
91
p
p

99
[f]
[f]
[Tutti]
[f]
[f]
f
99
f
f
f
[Violoncello]
[Tutti]
f

104
104

109
109

114
114

119
119

124
124

129
Recapitulation

135

*) Pausen / Rests } in Esterházy-Archiv

155
f
f
155
fz
[p]
f
[fz]
[p]
f
[fz]
[p]
p
fz
[p]

162
f
f
162
[f]
f

167
[a 2]
167
p
p
p
[fp]

174
p
p
[Solo]
p
p
174

*) Esterházy-Archiv *ff* {von Haydns Hand / in Haydn's hand

Fine

117

François Joseph Gossec (1734–1829)

Marche lugubre (1790)

Scored from printed parts in Paris, B. N., Dépt. de la Musique.

a2

25
30
a2

35
40
45
a2

118

Ludwig van Beethoven

Symphony No. 3 in E-flat Major, "Eroica" (1803–04): *Marcia funebre* (second movement)

12
A
cresc.
decresc.
1.
p cresc.
espressivo decresc.

20
espressivo decresc.

33
cresc.
p cresc.
40

47
cresc.
decresc.
B
55
a 2

63
Maggiore
sf
f
p
71
cresc.

76
C
82
cresc.

87
sempre p
sempre p
92
cresc.
cresc.
cresc.
cresc.
cresc.
cresc.
cresc.
cresc.
cresc.
cresc.
sempre più f

97
Minore
f cresc.
ff
sf
fp
cresc.
p
sotto voce
sotto voce
sotto voce
106
p

114
a 2
122

129
D
136

143
a 2
a 2
tr
tr
150 E
decresc.
sotto voce

162
sf
ff
167
decresc.
p

172
F
p
177
cresc.
decresc.
p

183
cresc.
191
cresc.

195
G
cresc.
p
f
199
a 2
sf

203
decresc.
207
H
cresc.
decresc.

214
pp
sf cresc.
cresc.

221
p cresc.
cresc.
pp
p
decresc.

232
p cresc.
decresc.
espressivo
espressivo
decresc.
pp
pp
cresc.
decresc.
cresc.
decresc.
cresc.
decresc.
cresc.
decresc.
cresc.
decresc.
238
pp
pp
sf
sf
sf
sf
sf
p
pp
sotto voce
sempre piu p
pp
f
pp
f
pp
f
pizz.
arco
f
decresc.
p
pizz.
arco
f
decresc.
p

119

JOHANN CHRISTIAN BACH (1735–82)
Concerto for Harpsichord or Piano and Strings in E-flat Major, Op. 7, No. 5: (first movement)

Cadenza is omitted. Reprinted from *Konzert für Cembalo (oder Klavier)*, edited by Christian Döbereiner (Frankfurt, 1927), pp. 3–19, 22. Reprinted by permission.

f
f
f
f
16
A
dim.
marc.

25
segue
35
segue

cresc.
cresc.
cresc.
44
Solo

55
B
64

cresc.
f
tr
mf
legato
72
p
dim.
pp

80
tr
poco a poco cresc.
C
f
p
86
pp
cresc.

93

99
cresc.
poco a poco
cresc.
105
5
Tutti
Tutti
segue
segue
Accompagnamento

115
Solo
2 tranquillo
p Portato
f
p
pp
mf Portato
dim.
tr

123
pp
poco f
p
cresc.
mf
dim.
tr
f
mp
131
D

137
4
poco a poco cresc.
poco a poco cresc.
poco a poco cresc.
tr
poco a poco cresc.
4

143
Cadenza ad libitum
151

E
162
poco a poco cresc.

170
cresc.
178

184
cresc.
p cresc.
mf cresc.
f cresc.
mf cresc.
poco a poco cresc.

190
allargando
f cresc.
ff
ff
f cresc.
ff
allargando
f
Cadenza ad libitum
Tutti
f
f
segue
f
Tutti
f
196
tr
p
tr
mf
p
6
pp

f
f
mf
f
tr
mf
f

120

WOLFGANG AMADEUS MOZART (1756–91)
Piano Concerto in A Major, K. 488 (1786): Allegro (first movement)

Reprinted by permission of Bärenreiter-Verlag, Kassel, Basel, Tours, London from: *Neue Mozart Ausgabe,* Serie V, Werkgruppe 15, Band 7, edited by Hermann Beck (Kassel, 1959), pp. 3–34.

17
a 2

23

28
p
p
p

33
p
Violoncelli
Vc. e B.
p

40
46

52
p
cresc.
f

57
p

63
70

76
80
f
a 2

85
p
p
p
p

89
tr

93
sf
p
96
f

112
p
p
p
116

120

124

128

131

134
a 2
tr
138

143
150
154

159

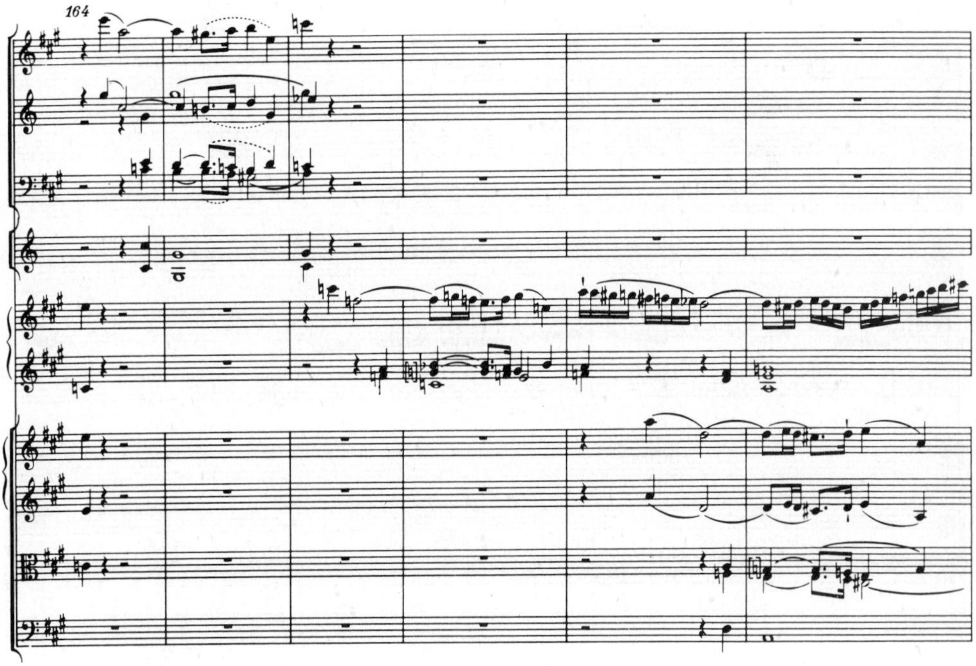
164

170
173

176
180

184
188

193
6
197
p
p
p
p

203
209

213
f
a 2
p

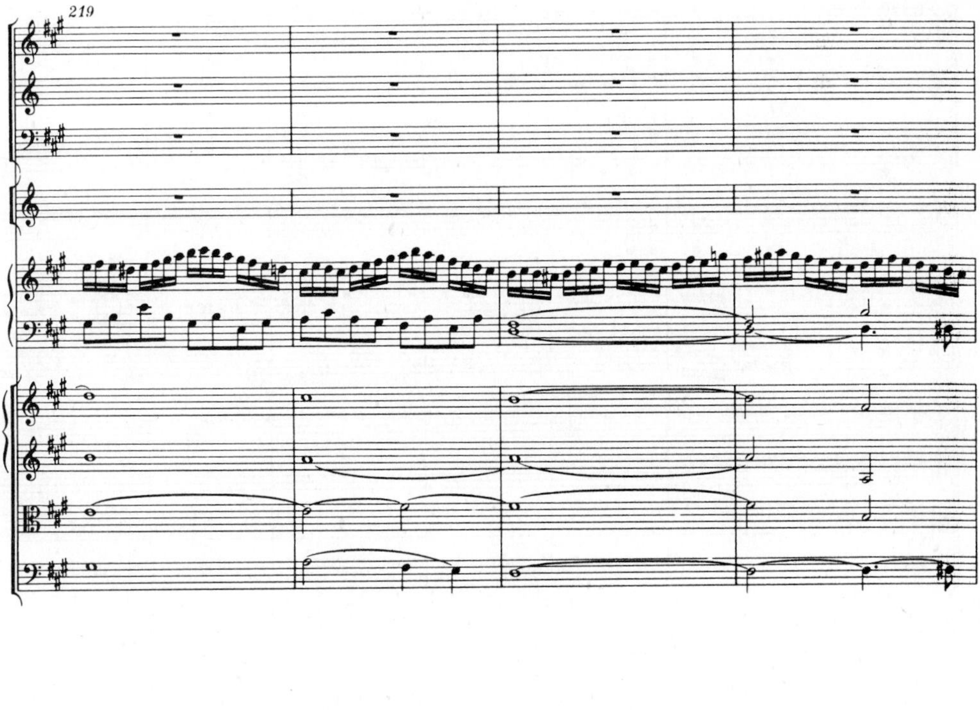
219

223
227

233

239

244
p
248

252

256

260
tr

268

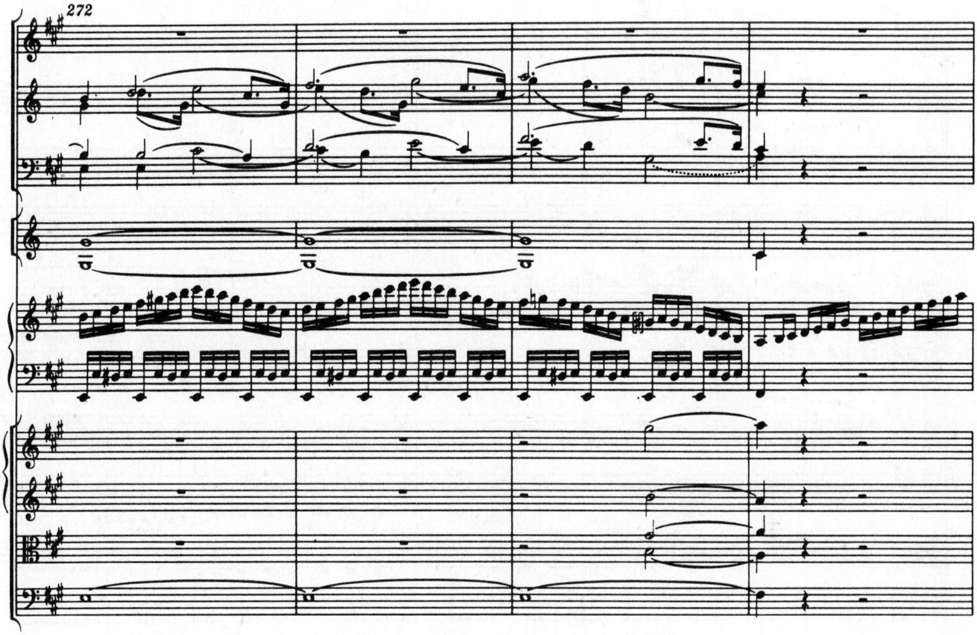
272

276
3

280
f
f
cresc.
tr
cresc.
cresc.
cresc.
cresc.

284
a 2
f
f
f
f

290
p
f

Cadenza
[4]
[6]
[10]
tr

[15]
[19]
[24]
[27]
298

304
310

121

GIOVANNI BATTISTA PERGOLESI (1710–36)

La serva padrona (1733): *Ah quanto mi sa male—Son imbrogliato io*

Serpina
Uberto
Serpina
U.
da - re! Vuol ve-de - re il mio spo - so? Sì, l'av-rei ca - ro. Io man-de -
Cemb.
Vlc. e Cb.
Uberto
Serpina
(esce)
(ab)
10
S.
rò per lu - i: già in stra-da ei si trat - tien. Va! Con li-cen - za.
Uberto
Or in - do - vi - no, chi sa - rà co - stu - i! For - se la pe - ni -
U.
ten - za fa - rá co - sì di quant' el - la ha fat - to al pa - dro - ne. Se
15
ver, co - me mi di - ce, un tal ma - ri - to la ter -

U.
rà fra la ter-ra ed il ba - sto - ne. Ah, po - ve - ret - ta
Cemb.
Vlc. e Cb.
6
Vl.I
Vl.II
Vla.
(p)
U.
P.
le - i! Per al - tro io pen-se-rei... Ma el - la è
6
Pfte.
p
20
ser - va... Ma il pri - mo non sa - re - sti...

Vl.I
Vl.II
Vla.
U.
P.
Dun-que, la spo-se-re-sti?
Ba-sta!
Eh! no, no, non
Cemb.
Vlc.
e Cb.
si - a!
Su, pen-sie-ri ri-bal-di,
an-da-te vi-a!
Pia-no!
Io
me l'ho al-le -

Vl.I
Vl.II
Vla.
U.
P.
va ta, sò poi com'el - la è na-ta...Eh! Che sei mat-to! Pia - no di grazia,
Cemb.
Vlc. e Cb.
eh non pen-sa-re af - fat - to! Ma io ci ho pas-sio - ne, e
pur? Quel - la me-schi - na..e tor - na... Oh Dio' e-siam da

ARIA
Allegro

Vl.I
Vl.II
Vla.
Uberto
Son imbro-glia - to i - o già, son im-bro-glia - to i - o
Cemb.
Vlc. e Cb.
(p)
Vl.I
Vl.II
Vla.
U.
già, son im-bro - glia - to i - o già! Ho un cer - to che nel
Cemb.
Vlc. e Cb.
Vl.I
Vl.II
Vla.
U.
co - re, che dir per me non so, non so, s'è a -
Cemb.
Vlc. e Cb.

Vl.I
Vl.II
Vla.
U.
mo - re s'è a - mo - re, o s'è pie - tà, pie -
Cemb.
Vlc. e Cb.
tà? Sent' un che poi mi di - ce, mi di - ce, mi
di - ce: U - ber - to, pen - sa a te, pen -

Vl.I
Vl.II
Vla.
U.
sa a te!
Ho un cer - to che nel
Cemb.
Vlc. e Cb.
co - re, che dir per me non so, non so, s'è a -
mo-re o s'è pie - tà? Per me... non so... ho un
*)

Vl.I
Vl.II
Vla.
U.
cer-to che sì...
non so che dir, che dir non
Cemb.
Vlc. e Cb.
f
so, non so che dir, per me non so, son im-bro-glia -
- to, im - bro - glia-to i-o già! Sent'-un che poi mi

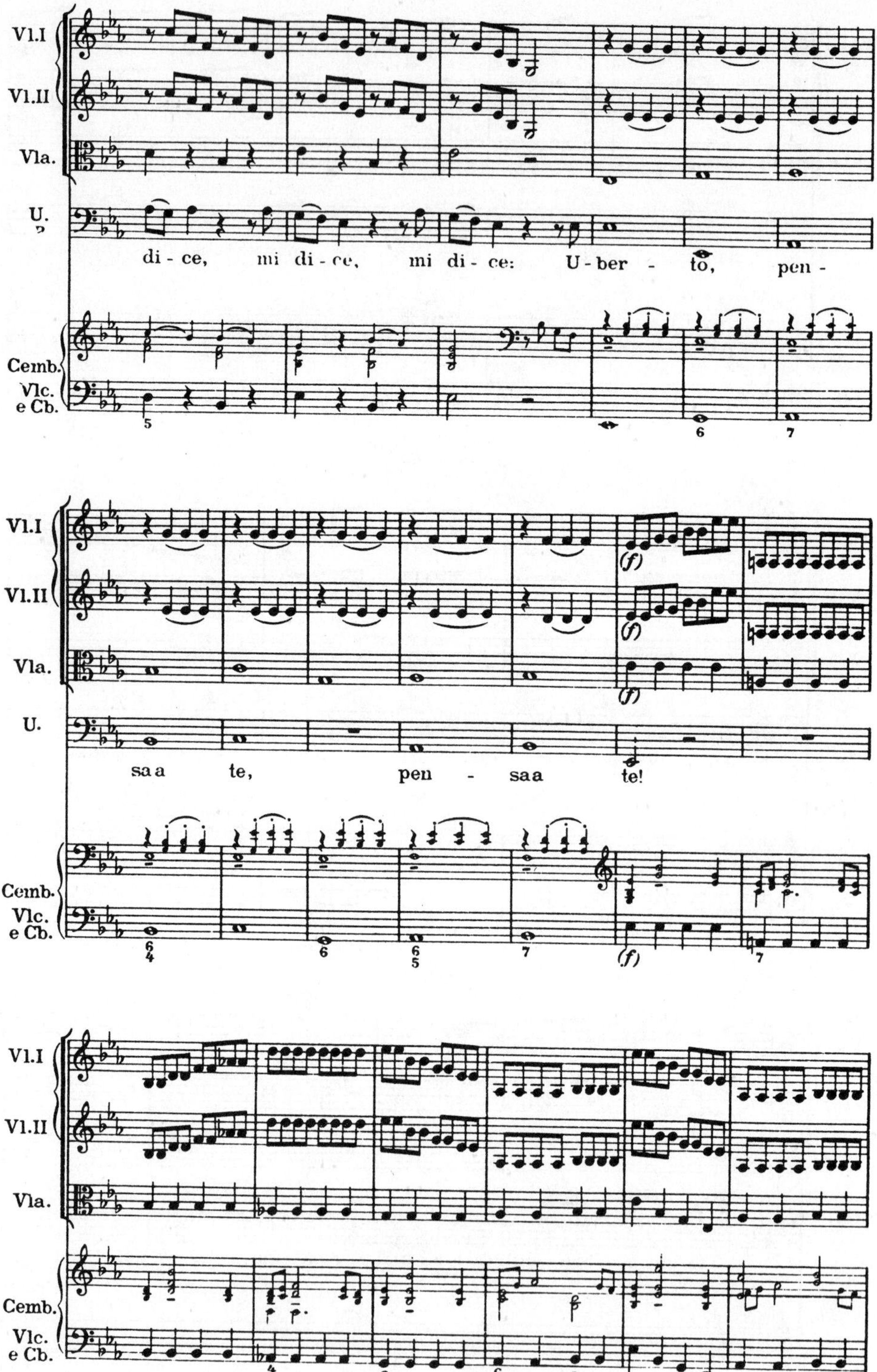
Vl.I
Vl.II
Vla.
U.
di - ce, mi di - ce, mi di - ce: U - ber - to, pen -
sa a te, pen - sa a te!
Cemb.
Vlc. e Cb.
(f)

Fine
Vl.I
Vl.II
Vla.
Uberto
U.
Io sto fra il sì e il no, fra il vo-glio e fra il non
Cemb.
Vlc. e Cb.
dim.
(p)
vo-glio, e sem-pre più m'im-bro-glio, più m'im-bro-glio, più m'im-
bro-glio. Ah! mi-se-ro in-fe-li-ce, che

UBERTO (aside)

Ah, quanto mi sa male	Ah, it doesn't feel right–
Di tal risoluzione;	this resolution;
Ma n'ho colpa io?	but is it my fault?

SERPINA (aside)

Dì pur fra te che vuoi;	Tell yourself what you want,
Che ha da riuscir la cosa a modo mio.	because this affair will end my way.

UBERTO

Orsù, non dubbitare	Come now, do not doubt
Che di te mai non mi saprò scordare.	that I could ever disagree with you.

	SERPINA
Vuol vedere il mio sposo?	Do you want to see my groom?
	UBERTO
Sì, l'avrei caro	Yes, I would love to.
	SERPINA
Io mandarò per lui: Giù in strada ei si trattien.	I shall send for him. He is waiting down in the street.
	UBERTO
Va.	Go ahead.
	SERPINA
Con licenza . . . . *(parte)*	With your permission . . . . *(leaves)*
	UBERTO
Or indovino, chi sarà costui! Forse la penitenza farà così. Di quant'ella ha fatto al padrone; S'è ver, come mi dice, un tal marito	Now I can guess who it will be. This will be her penance perhaps. He will do to her what she did to me. If what she told me is true, a husband like that
La terrà fra la terra ed il bastone. Ah, poveretta lei! Per altro io penserei . . . Ma ella è serva . . . Ma il primo non saresti . . . Dunque, la sposeresti? Basta . . . oh! no, no, non sia. Su, pensieri ribaldi, andate via! Piano, io me l'ho allevata: Sò poi com'ella è nata . . . Eh! Che sei matto! Piano di grazia, Eh non pensare affatto. Ma io ci ho passione, e pur . . . Quella meschina . . . Eh torna . . . Oh Dio! . . . e siam da capo . . . Oh . . . che confusione!	would keep her between the earth and a stick. Poor thing, she is. Otherwise I would think of . . . but she is a servant . . . but I would not be the first . . . . Would you marry her, then? Enough . . . oh no, no, it cannot be. Rascally thoughts, go away! Easy, I raised her for myself. I know how she was born . . . . How crazy you are! Easy now, please, think no more about it. Still, I feel a passion for her . . . that wretched creature . . . . And yet . . . . Oh God! . . . are we beginning all over? Oh! . . . what confusion!
Son imbrogliato io già, Ho un certo chè nel core, Che dir per me non so, S'è amore o sè pietà. Sent'un che poi mi dice: Uberto, pensa a te. Io sto fra il sì e 'l no, Fra il voglio e fra il non voglio, E sempre più m'imbroglio, Ah misero infelice, Che mai sarà di me!	I am all mixed up. I have a certain something in my heart. Truly, I cannot tell whether it's love or pity. I hear a voice that tells me: Uberto, think of yourself. I am between yes and no, between wanting and not wanting, and I get more confused all the time, unhappy fellow. What will ever become of me?

G. A. FEDERICO

Jean-Jacques Rousseau (1712–78)

Le Devin du village (1752): Scene 1, Air, *J'ai perdu tout mon bonheur*

Reprinted from *Le Devin du Village,* edited by Charles Chaix (Geneva: Édition Henn, c1924), pp. 11–17.

lin me dé - lais - se Co - lin me dé - lais - se.
doux.
f p
f 3 f
f
23
J'ai per - du mon ser-vi - teur j'ai per -
doux
f p
tr
du tout mon bonheur. Co lin me dé - lais-se. Co-lin me dé -
ff
p
ff
p
33
tr
laisse. hé-las!
f
doux.f
doux.f
f
doux.

il a pu chan-ger!
je voudrais n'y plus songer.
hé - las! hé - las!
hé - las! hélas!
doux
il a pu chan-ger,
je vou-drais n'y plus son-ger.
hé -
53
las! hé - las!
j'y son-ge sans ces-se j'y son - ge sans ces -

se
un peu f
doux
f
j'ai per - du mon ser - vi - teur; j'ai per - du tout mon bon - heur. Co -
doux
doux
f
p
lin me dé - lais - se Co - lin me dé - lais - se
f
doux
72
j'ai per - du mon ser vi - teur; j'ai per -
Très doux
doux
du tout mon bon - heur. Co - lin me dé - lais-se Co - lin me dé -
tr
ff
p
ff

82
tr
lai - se.
f
doux
doux
doux
f
Récit.
Il m'ai - mait au - tre - fois et ce fut mon mal - heur. . . .
89 Ferme
mais quelle est donc cel - le qu'il me pré - fè - re?
(Ironie et dépit)
elle est donc bien char -
animé
man - te! Impruden - te ber - gè - re,
ne crains tu point les maux que j'éprouve en ce
93
(Douleur)
(Menace)
jour? Co - lin a pu chan - ger; tu peux avoir ton tour. . .
que me sert d'y rêver sans

(douleur tendre)
ces-se? Rien ne peut gué-rir mon a-mour et tout aug-men-te ma tris-
99
tes-se.
f
J'ai per-du mon ser-vi-teur; j'ai per-du tout mon bon-
p
f
p
106
heur. Co-lin me dé-lais-se, Co-lin me dé-
tr
ff
p
ff
p
lais-se.
tr
f
doux
f
doux
f

113
doux
ff
p
tr
f
Recit.
(reflexion douce)
(reflexion triste)
Je veux le ha-ir; je le dois... peut-être il m'aime en - cor... pour quoi me fuir sans
p
119
(avec douceur)
(débité)
ces - se? Il me cher - chait tant au-tre - fois. Le de-vin du can -
(tendrement)
f
ton fait i - ci sa de-meu-re: il sait tout; il sau-ra le sort de mon a -

123
(débité)
tr
mour. Je le vois et je veux m'é-clair - cir en ce jour.

COLETTE

J'ai perdu tout mon bonheur,
J'ai perdu mon serviteur.
Colin me délaisse.
Hélas! il a pu changer!
Je voudrais n'y plus songer.
J'y songe sans cesse.

I have lost all my happiness,
I have lost my servant.
Colin forsakes me.
Alas, he could have changed.
I would rather stop dreaming about it.
Yet I dream about it incessantly.

(*Récit*).

Il m'aimait autrefois, et ce fut mon malheur . . .
Mais quelle est donc celle qu'il me préfère?
Elle est donc bien charmante!
Imprudente bergère,
Ne crains tu point les maux
Que j'éprouve en ce jour?
Colin a pu changer; tu peux avoir ton tour . .
Que me sert d'y rêver sans cesse?
Rien ne peut guérir mon amour
Et tout augmente ma tristesse.
J'ai perdu mon serviteur . . . etc.
Je veux le haïr; je le dois . . .
Peut-être il m'aime encor . . .
Pourquoi me fuir sans cesse?
Il me cherchait tant autrefois.
Le devin du canton fait ici sa demeure:
Il sait tout; il saura le sort de mon amour.
Je le vois et je veux m'eclaircir en ce jour.

He loved me once, and this was my bad luck . . .
But who, then, is she whom he prefers?
She must be very charming!
Imprudent shepherdess,
do you not fear at all the misfortunes
that I am experiencing today?
Colin could have changed; you may have your turn . . .
What good does it do to dream about it incessantly.
Nothing can cure my love
and everything increases my sorrow.
I have lost all my happiness . . . etc.
I want to hate him: I must do it . . .
Perhaps he loves me still . . .
Why do I flee incessantly?
He used to look for me once.
The soothsayer of the canton makes his home here.
He knows all; he will know the fate of my love.
I see him, and I want this clarified today.

Libretto by the composer

123

Christoph Willibald Gluck (1714–87)

Orfeo ed Euridice (1762): Act II, Scene 1 (excerpt)

Ballo

Reprinted by permission of Bärenreiter-Verlag, Kassel, Basel, Tours, London from *Sämtliche Werke,* Abteilung I, Bd. I, edited by A. A. Abert and Ludwig Finscher (Kassel, 1963), pp. 55–75.

21
Harpa
Violino I
pizz.
Violino II
(pizz.)
Viola
(pizz.)
Orchestra II
(Cembalo)
Violoncello e Basso
pizz.

Coro

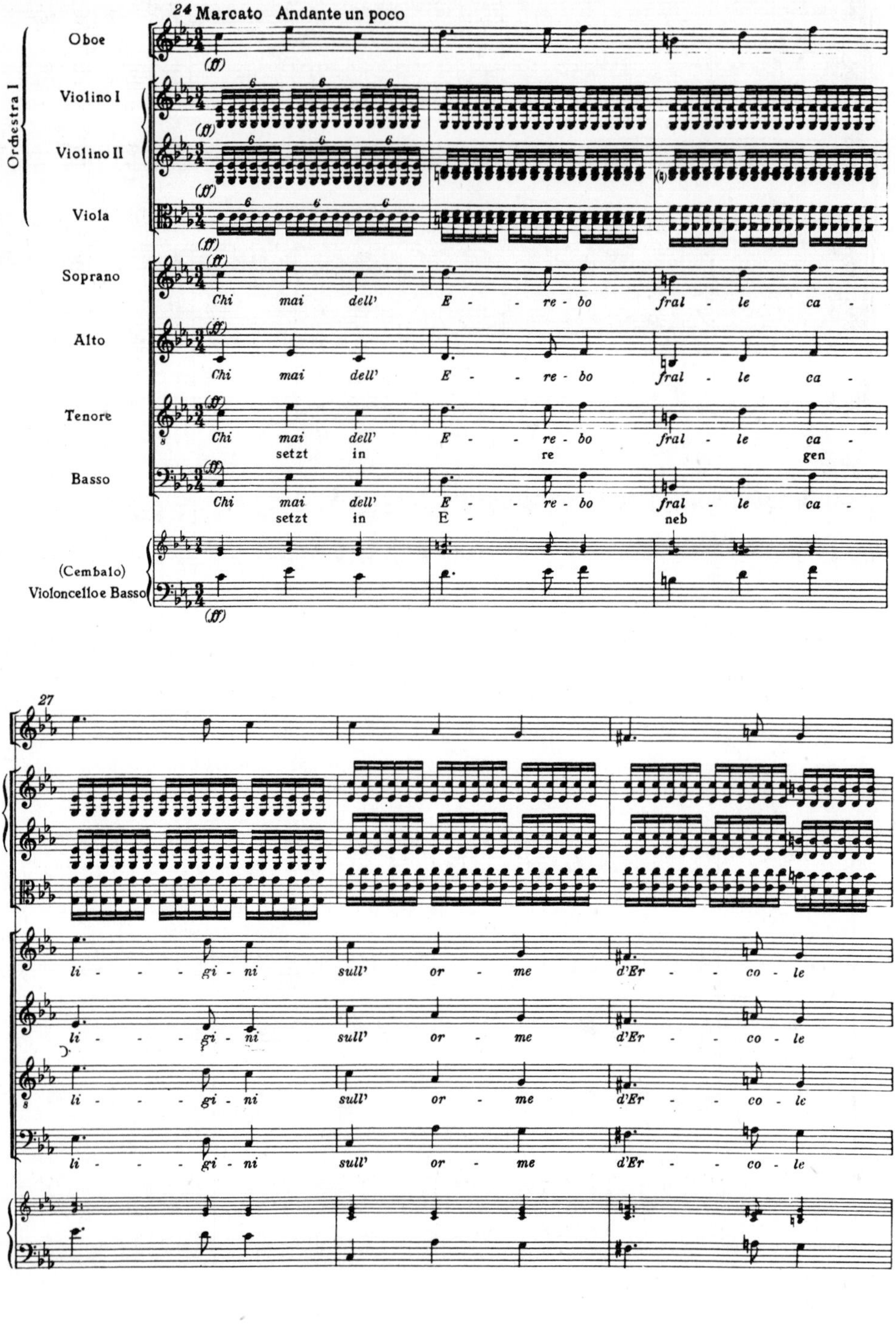
24 Marcato Andante un poco
Orchestra I
Oboe
Violino I
Violino II
Viola
Soprano
Alto
Tenore
Basso
(Cembalo)
Violoncello e Basso
(ff)
Chi mai dell' E - - re - bo fral - le ca -
setzt in re gen
setzt in E - neb
27
li - - - gi - ni sull' or - me d'Er - - co - le

30
e di Pi - ri - to - o con - du - ce il piè?
e di Pi - ri - to - o con - du - ce il piè?
e di Pi - ri - to - o con - du - ce il piè?
e di Pi - ri - to - o con - du - ce il piè?

Ballo

34 Presto
Violino I
(f)
Violino II
(f)
Viola
(f)
(Cembalo)
Violoncello e Basso
(f)

38
42
46

Coro

51 Andante
Oboe
Violino I
Violino II
Viola
Soprano
Alto
Tenore
Basso
(Cembalo)
Violoncello e Basso
(ff)
Chi mai dell' E - - - re - bo fral - le ca -

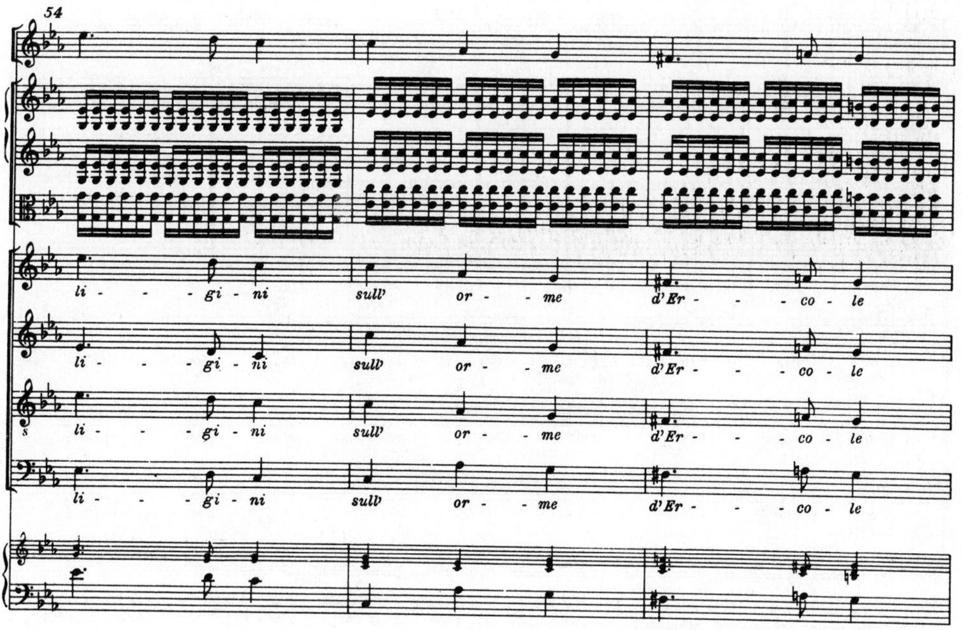
54
li - - - gi - ni sull' or - - me d'Er - - - co - le

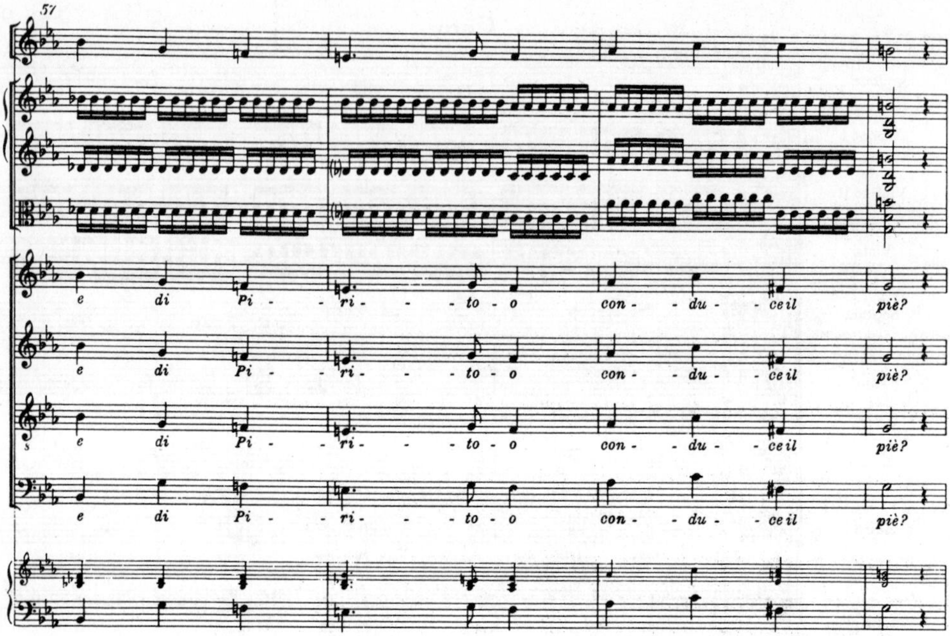
57
e di Pi - ri - - to - o con - du - ce il piè?
e di Pi - ri - - to - o con - - du - ce il piè?
e di Pi - ri - - to - o con - du - ce il piè?
e di Pi - ri - - to - o con - du - ce il piè?

61
D'or - ror l'in - gom - - bri - no le fie - re Eu -
D'or - - ror l'in - gom - bri - no le fie - re Eu -
In -
D'or - ror l'in - gom - bri - no le fie - re Eu -
D'or - ror l'in - gom - bri - no le fie - re Eu -
Un -
6 6 6

64
(poco f)
poco f
poco f
(poco f)
me - ni - di, e lo spa - ven - ti - no gli ur - li di
me - ni - di, e lo spa - ven - ti - no gli ur - li di
me - ni - di, e lo spa - ven - ti - no gli ur - li di
me - ni - di, e lo spa - ven - ti - no gli ur - li di,
poco f

68
Cer - be - ro, se un dio non è! E lo spa -
Cer - be - ro, se un dio non è! E lo spa -
Cer - be - ro, se un dio non è! E lo spa -
Cer - be - ro, se un dio non è! E lo spa -

72
ven - - - ti - no gli ur - li di Cer - - - be - ro, se un dio non
ven - - - ti - no gli ur - li di Cer - - - be - ro, se un dio non
ven - - - ti - no gli ur - li di Cer - - - be - ro, se un dio non
ven - - - ti - no gli ur - li di Cer - - - be - ro, se un dio non

76
(ff)
ff
ff
(ff)
è!
è!
è!
è!
ff

79
(mf)
mf
(mf)
mf
(mf)
D'or - ror l'in - gom - - bri - no
(mf)
D'or - ror l'in - gom - bri - no
(mf)
D'or - ror l'in - gom - bri - no
(mf)
D'or - ror l'in - gom - bri - no
mf

83
le fie - re Eu - me - - ni - di, e lo spa - ven - - ti - no
le fie - re Eu - me - ni - di, e lo spa - ven - ti - no
le fie - re Eu - me - ni - di, e lo spa - ven - - ti - no
le fie - re Eu - me - ni - di, e lo spa - ven - - ti - no

Segue il Ballo, girando intorno ad Orfeo per spaventarlo.

Ballo

111
Harpa
(p)
Orchestra II
Violino I
(pizz.)
(p)
Violino II
(pizz.)
(p)
Viola
(pizz.)
(p)
Violoncello e Basso
(pizz.)
(p)
Orchestra I
Cornetto
Trombone I, II
Violino I
Violino II
ORFEO
Deh pla-
Soprano
Alto
Tenore
Basso
(Cembalo)
Viola col Basso, Violoncello
*)
p

114
f
(f)
(a2)
ca - te - vi con me,
Fu - rie,
lar - ve,
Nò!
Nò!

118
(f)
(f)
(f)
(f)
om - bre sde - gno - se! Vi ren - da al-men pie - to - se il mio bar - ba - ro do-
Nò!
Nein!
Nò!
Nein!
Nò!
Nein!
Nò!
Nein!
(f)

123
(f)
(f)
(f)
(f)
lor, vi ren-da al-men pie-to-se il mio bar-ba-ro— do-lor!
Nò!
Nò!
Nò!
Nò!
(f)

128
(p)
(f)
Deh — pla - ca - te - vi, pla - ca - te - vi con
Nò!
Nò!

133
(a 2)
(f)
me! Fu - rie, lar - ve, om - bre sde - gno - se! Vi
Nò!

138
(f)
(f)
(f)
(f)
ren - da al - men pie - to - se il mio bar - ba - ro do - lor! Fu - rie,
Nò!
Nò!
Nò!
Nò!
(f)

143
(f)
lar - ve, om - - bre sde - gno - se! Vi ren - da al - men pic - to - se il mio
Nò! Nò! Nò!
Nò! Nò! Nò!
Nò! Nò! Nò!
Nò! Nò! Nò!
(f) (f) (f)

148
bar - ba - ro do - lor, il mio bar - - ba - ro do - - lor!

CHORUS

Chi mai dell'Erebo	Who from Erebos
Fralle caligini	through the dark mists,
Sull'orme d'Ercole	in the footsteps of Hercules
E di Piritoo	and of Peirithous
Conduce il piè?	would ever set forth?
D'orror l'ingombrino	He would be blocked with horror
Le fiere Eumenidi,	by the fierce Eumenides
E lo spaventino	and frightened by
Gli urli di Cerbero,	the shrieks of Cerberus,
Se un dio non è.	unless he were a god.

ORPHEUS

Deh, placatevi con me.	Please, be gentle with me.
Furie, Larve, Ombre sdegnose!	Furies, specters, scornful phantoms!

CHORUS

No! . . . No! . . .	No! . . . No! . . .

ORPHEUS

Vi renda almen pietose	Let it at least make you merciful,
Il mio barbaro dolor!	my cruel pain!

Libretto by RANIERO DE' CALZABIGI

124

Wolfgang Amadeus Mozart

Don Giovanni, K. 527 (1787); Act I, Scene 5

a) No. 3, Aria: *A chi mi dice mai*

10
Clar. (in Si♭)
Fag.
Cor. (in Mi♭)
V. I
V. II
Va.
D. E.
Vc. e B.
DONNA ELVIRA
Ah chi mi di - ce ma - i quel
15
a 2
bar - ba - ro dov' è, che per mio scor - no a - ma - i, che

19
Clar. (in Sib)
Fag.
Cor. (in Mib)
V. I
V. II
Va.
D. E.
mi man - cò di fè, che mi man-cò di fè?
Vc. e B.
crescendo
24
Ah se ri - tro - vo l'em-pio, e a me non tor - na an-
sfp

30
Clar. (in Sib)
Fag.
Cor. (in Mib)
V. I
V. II
Va.
D. E.
Vc. e B.
cresc.
fp
f
cor, vo' far - ne or-ren - do scem-pio, gli vo' ca-va - re il cor, gli vo' ca - va - re il
37
p
DON GIOVANNI
D. G.
cor, vo' far - ne orren - do scem-pio, gli
U - di-sti! qualche bel-la dal va-go abban-do-na-ta.

44
Clar. (in Sib)
Fag.
Cor. (in Mib)
V. I
V. II
Va.
D. E.
vo' ca-va - re il cor,
gli vo' ca - va - re il cor, sì,
D. G.
Po - ve-ri - na, po - ve-ri-na!
Vc. e B.
51
a 2
gli vo' ca-va - re il cor.
Cerchiam di con-so - la - re il suo tor - men-to.
L.
LEPORELLO
Co-sì ne con-so-lò mille e ot - to -

57
Clar. (in Sib)
Fag.
a 2
Cor. (in Mib)
V. I
V. II
Va.
D. E.
Ah chi mi di - ce ma-i quel bar - ba-ro dov' è, che
L.
cen-to.
Vc. e B.

63
Clar. (in Sib)
crescendo
Fag.
a 2
crescendo
Cor. (in Mib)
crescendo
V. I
crescendo
V. II
crescendo
Va.
crescendo
D. E.
per mio scor - no a-ma - i, che mi man - cò di fè, che
Vc. e B.
crescendo

67
Clar. (in Sib)
Fag.
a 2
Cor. (in Mib)
V. I
V. II
Va.
D. E.
Vc. e B.
f
p
f p
sfp
— mi man-cò di fè?
Ah se ri - tro - vo l'em-pio,

73
Clar. (in Sib)
Fag.
Cor. (in Mib)
V. I
V. II
Va.
D. E.
Vc. e B.
cresc.
fp
sfp
e a me non tor - na an-cor, vo' far - ne or-ren - do scem-pio, gli

79
Clar. (in Sib)
Fag.
Cor. (in Mib)
V. I
V. II
Va.
D. E.
vo' ca-va - re il cor,
gli vo' ca-va - re il cor, sì,
gli vo' ca-
DON GIOVANNI
D. G.
Po-ve - ri-na, po-ve - ri-na!
Vc. e B.
87
va - re il cor,
gli vo' ca-va-
Cerchiam di con-so - la - re il suo tor - men-to.
LEPORELLO
L.
Co-sì ne con-so - lò mille e ot - to - cen-to.

*) Vorschlag zur eventuellen Auszierung der Fermate:

Recitative: *Chi è là*

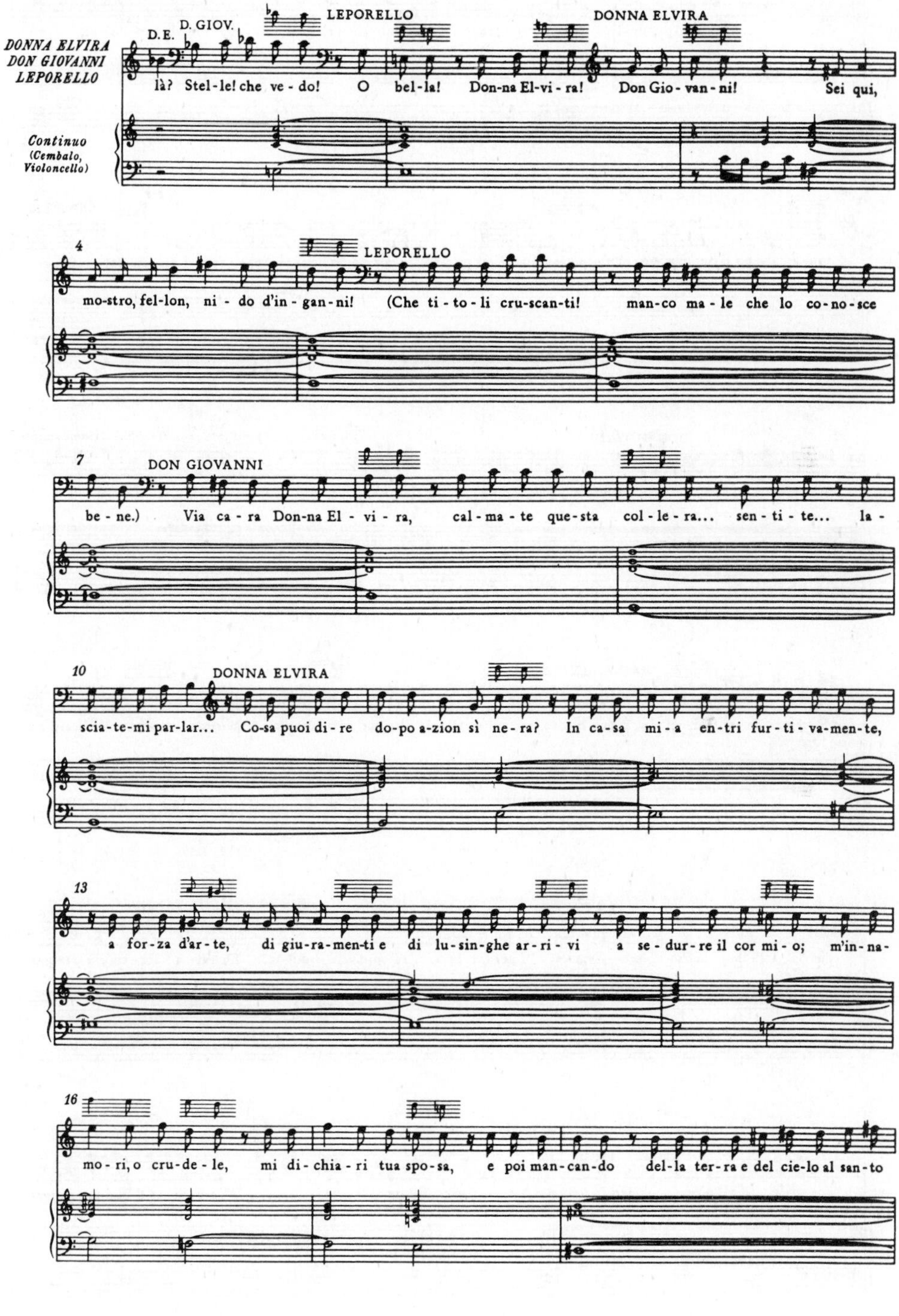
DONNA ELVIRA
DON GIOVANNI
LEPORELLO
Continuo (Cembalo, Violoncello)
D. E.
D. GIOV.
LEPORELLO
DONNA ELVIRA
là? Stel-le! che ve-do! O bel-la! Don-na El-vi-ra! Don Gio-van-ni! Sei qui,
mo-stro, fel-lon, ni-do d'in-gan-ni! (Che ti-to-li cru-scan-ti! man-co ma-le che lo co-no-sce
DON GIOVANNI
be-ne.) Via ca-ra Don-na El-vi-ra, cal-ma-te que-sta col-le-ra... sen-ti-te... la-
DONNA ELVIRA
scia-te-mi par-lar... Co-sa puoi di-re do-po a-zion sì ne-ra? In ca-sa mi-a en-tri fur-ti-va-men-te,
a for-za d'ar-te, di giu-ra-men-ti e di lu-sin-ghe ar-ri-vi a se-dur-re il cor mi-o; m'in-na-
mo-ri, o cru-de-le, mi di-chia-ri tua spo-sa, e poi man-can-do del-la ter-ra e del cie-lo al san-to

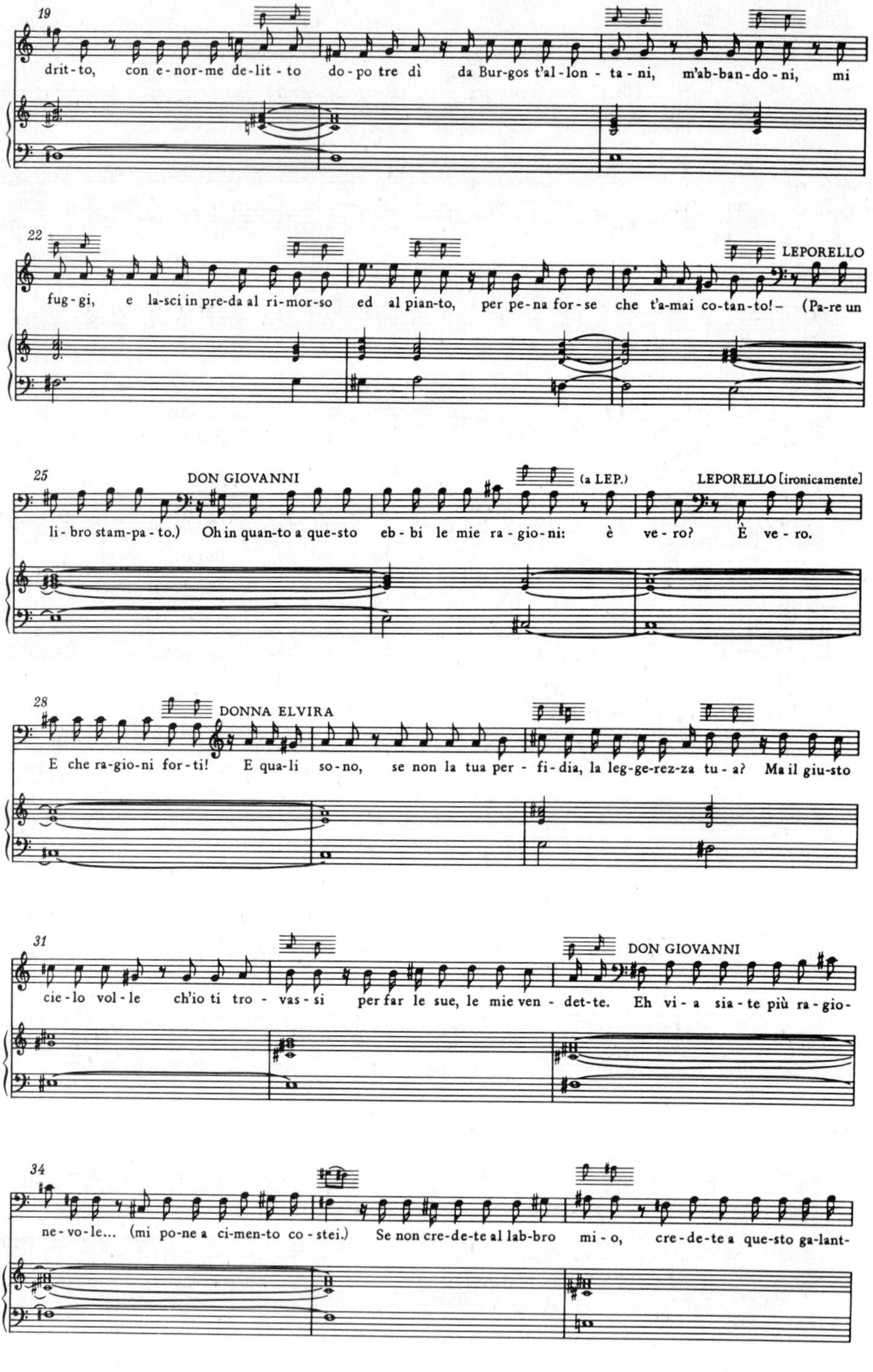
19
drit-to, con e-nor-me de-lit-to do-po tre dì da Bur-gos t'al-lon-ta-ni, m'ab-ban-do-ni, mi
22
fug-gi, e la-sci in pre-da al ri-mor-so ed al pian-to, per pe-na for-se che t'a-mai co-tan-to! –
LEPORELLO
(Pa-re un
25
li-bro stam-pa-to.)
DON GIOVANNI
Oh in quan-to a que-sto eb-bi le mie ra-gio-ni:
(a LEP.)
è ve-ro?
LEPORELLO [ironicamente]
È ve-ro.
28
E che ra-gio-ni for-ti!
DONNA ELVIRA
E qua-li so-no, se non la tua per-fi-dia, la leg-ge-rez-za tu-a? Ma il giu-sto
31
cie-lo vol-le ch'io ti tro-vas-si per far le sue, le mie ven-det-te.
DON GIOVANNI
Eh vi-a sia-te più ra-gio-
34
ne-vo-le... (mi po-ne a ci-men-to co-stei.) Se non cre-de-te al lab-bro mi-o, cre-de-te a que-sto ga-lant-

37
LEPORELLO
DON GIOVANNI forte
LEPORELLO piano
D. GIOV. forte
uo - mo. (Sal - vo il ve - ro.) Via dil - le un po - co... E co - sa de - vo dir - le? Sì
39
D. ELV. (a LEP.)
(In questo fra tempo D. G. fugge.)
LEPORELLO
sì, dil - le pur tut - to. Eb - ben, fa pre - sto... Ma - da - ma... ve - ra - men - te... in que - sto
42
DONNA ELVIRA (a LEP.)
mon - do con - cios - sia co - sa quan - do fos - se che il qua - dro non è ton - do... Scia - gu -
44
[verso DON GIOVANNI, che non crede partito]
ra - to, co - sì del mio do - lor gio - co ti pren - di? Ah voi... stel - le! l'i - ni - quo fug -
47
LEPORELLO
gì! mi - se - ra me! do - ve, in qual par - te... Eh, la - scia - te che va - da: e - gli non mer - ta
50
DONNA ELVIRA
LEPORELLO
che di lui ci pen - sia - te... Il scel - le - ra - to m'in - gan - nò, mi tra - dì! Eh con - so - la - te - vi; non sie - te

53
voi, non fo - ste, e non sa - re - te né la pri - ma, né l'ul - ti - ma; guar - da - te
56
que - sto non pic - ciol li - bro: è tut - to pie - no dei no - mi di sue bel - le; o - gni
58
vil - la, o - gni bor - go, o - gni pa - e - se è te - sti - mon di sue don - ne - sche im - pre - se.
attacca

b) *No. 4, Aria:* Madamina! Il catalogo è questo

Allegro
Flauto I, II
Oboe I, II
Fagotto I, II
Corno I, II in Re/D
Violino I
p
Violino II
p
Viola I, II
p
LEPORELLO
Ma - da - mi - na, il ca - ta - lo - go è que - sto del - le
Continuo (Cembalo, Violoncello)
*)
Violoncello è Basso
p

*) Vgl. Vorwort.

6
V. I
V. II
Va.
L.
bel-le che a-mò il padron mi-o, un ca-ta-lo-go e-gli è che ho fatt' i-o, os-ser-va-te, leg-
Vc. e B.
12
Fl.
Fag.
Cor. (in Re)
V. I
V. II
Va.
L.
ge-te con me, os-ser-va-te, leg-ge-te con me.
Vc. e B.
17
Fl.
Ob.
Fag.
Cor. (in Re)
V. I
V. II
Va.
L.
In I-ta-lia sei-cen-to e qua-ran-ta,
Vc. e B.

*) Vorschlag zur eventuellen Auszierung der Fermate:

35
Fl.
Ob.
Fag.
Cor. (in Re)
V. I
V. II
Va.
L.
Vc. e B.
a 2
p
tre, mil-le e tre. V'han fra que-ste con-ta - di-ne,
Violonc.
Tutti Bassi
40
ca-me-rie-re e cit-ta - di-ne, v'han con-tes-se, ba-ro - nes-se, mar-che-sa-ne, prin-ci-

45
Fl.
Ob.
Fag.
Cor. (in Re)
V. I
V. II
Va.
L.
Vc. e B.
a 2
cre - - - scendo
f
p
pes-se, e v'han don-ne d'o-gni gra-do, d'o-gni for-ma, d'o-gni e-tà, d'o-gni for-ma, d'o-gni e-tà.
50
Imo
In I-ta-lia sei-cen-to e qua-ran-ta, in La-

55
1mo
Fl.
Ob.
Fag.
a 2
Cor. (in Re)
V. I
V. II
Va.
L.
ma - gna duecen - to e trent' u - na, cen - - - to in Fran - cia, in Tur-
Vc. e B.
60
1mo
Fl.
Ob.
p
sfp
Fag.
a 2
p
sfp
Cor. (in Re)
a 2
a 2
p
sfp
V. I
sfp
V. II
sfp
Va.
sfp
L.
chia no - vant' u - na, ma, ma—, ma in I - spag - na, ma in I - spag - na son già mil - le e tre,
Vc. e B.
sfp

68
Fl.
Ob.
Fag.
Cor. (in Re)
V. I
V. II
Va.
L.
Vc. e B.
a 2
Violoncello
Tutti Bassi
mil-le e tre, mil-le e tre. V'han fra que-ste con-ta - di-ne, ca-me-rie-re e cit-ta -

73
Fl.
Ob.
Fag.
Cor. (in Re)
V. I
V. II
Va.
L.
Vc. e B.
a 2
crescendo
di-ne, v'han contes-se, ba-ro - nes-se, mar-che-sa-ne, prin-ci - pes-se, e v'han don-ne d'o-gni gra-do, d'o-gni for-ma, d'o-gni e -

77
Fl.
Ob.
Fag.
a 2
Cor. (in Re)
V. I
V. II
Va.
L.
tà, d'o - gni for - ma, d'o - gni e - tà, d'o - gni
Vc. e B.
81
Andante con moto
crescendo
forma, d'o - gni e - tà.
Nel - la bion-da e - gli ha l'u - san-za

89
Fl.
Ob.
Fag.
Cor. (in Re)
V. I
V. II
Va.
L.
Vc. e B.
a 2
f
di lo - dar la gen - ti - lez - za, nel - la bru - na la co -
96
Fl.
Ob.
Fag.
Cor. (in Re)
V. I
V. II
Va.
L.
Vc. e B.
a 2
Imo
p
stan - za, nel - la bian - ca la dol - cez - za. Vuol d'in -

102
Imo
Fl.
Ob.
Fag.
Cor. (in Re)
V. I
V. II
Va.
L.
Vc. e B.
crescendo
cresc.
f
p
ver - no la gras-sot - ta, vuol d'e-sta - te la ma-grot-ta; è la
107
Fl.
Ob.
Fag.
Cor. (in Re)
V. I
V. II
Va.
L.
Vc. e B.
cresc.
crescendo
f
p
gran - de ma - e - sto - sa, è la gran - - de

*) Vorschlag zur eventuellen Auszierung der Fermate: 

120
Fl.
Ob.
Fag.
Cor. (in Re)
V. I
V. II
Va.
L.
Vc. e B.
ci - na è o-gnor vez - zo - sa, è ognor vez - zo - sa, è ognor vez - zo - sa... Del - le vec-chie fa con-

127
Fl.
Ob.
Fag.
Cor. (in Re)
V. I
V. II
Va.
L.
Vc. e B.
qui - sta pel pia - cer di por - le in li - sta; ma passion predomi - nan - te

134
Fl.
Ob.
Fag.
Cor. (in Re)
V. I
V. II
Va.
L.
Vc. e B.
Imo
tr
mfp
mfp
— è la gio-vin prin-ci-pian-te.
Non si pic - ca se sia

138
Fl.
Ob.
Fag.
Cor. (in Re)
V. I
V. II
Va.
L.
Vc. e B.
Imo
tr
crescendo
cresc.
f
mfp
mf
ric - ca, se sia brut - ta, se sia bel - la, se sia ric-ca, brut-ta, se sia bel - la:

*) Zu einem im Autograph nach T. 153 gestrichenen Takt vgl. Krit. Bericht.

158
Fl.
Ob.
Fag.
Cor. (in Re)
V. I
V. II
Va.
L.
fa, voi sa-pe-te, voi sa-pe-te quel che fa, quel che fa, quel che
Vc. e B.
mf
p
Imo

166
Fl.
Ob.
Fag.
Cor. (in Re)
V. I
V. II
Va.
L.
[Parte]
fa, voi sa-pe-te quel che fa.
Vc. e B.
Imo
a2
f

DONNA ELVIRA

Ah, chi mi dice mai,
Quel barbaro dov'è,
Che per mio scorno amai,
Che mi mancò di fè,
Ah, se ritrovo l'empio,
E a me non torna ancor,
Vo' farne orrendo scempio,
Gli vo' cavare il cor.

Ah, who will ever tell me
where that barbarian is,
whom, to my shame, I loved,
who failed to keep faith?
Ah, if I ever find the scoundrel,
and to me he does not return,
I shall brutally slaughter him.
I shall take out his heart.

DON GIOVANNI
(*to Leporello*)

Udisti? Qualche bella
Dal vago abbandonata.
Poverina! poverina!
Cerchiam di consolare il suo tormento.

Did you hear? Some beauty
by her lover abandoned.
Poor girl! Poor girl!
Let us try to console her torment.

LEPORELLO
(*aside*)

Così ne consolò mille e ottocento.

Thus he consoled a thousand and eight hundred.

DON GIOVANNI

Signorina! Signorina!

Signorina, Signorina!

DONNA ELVIRA

Chi è là?

Who goes there?

DON GIOVANNI

Stelle! che vedo!

Heavens! Whom do I see?

LEPORELLO
(*aside*)

O bella! Donna Elvira!

O this is nice! Donna Elvira!

DONNA ELVIRA

Don Giovanni!
Sei quì, mostro, fellon, nido d'inganni!

Don Giovanni!
You're here, monster! Felon, nest of deceits!

LEPORELLO
(*aside*)

Che titoli cruscanti!
Manco male che lo conosce bene.

Such Tuscan insults!
At least you know him well.

DON GIOVANNI

Via, cara Donna Elvira,
Calmate questa collera . . .
Sentite . . . lasciatemi parlar.

Now, dear Donna Elvira,
calm your anger . . .
Listen . . . let me speak.

DONNA ELVIRA

Cosa puoi dire, dopo azion si nera?
In casa mia entri furtivamente,
A forza d'arte,

What can you say, after such a black deed?
You entered my house furtively
through trickery.

Di giuramenti e di lusinghe arrivi
A sedurre il cor mio:
M'innamori, o crudele,
Mi dichiari tua sposa,
E poi mancando della terra e del cielo
Al santo dritto,
Con enorme delitto
Dopo tre dì da Burgos t'allontani.
M'abbandoni, mi fuggi
E lasci in preda al rimorso ed al pianto,
Per pena forse che t'amai cotanto.

With oaths and flattery you succeded
in seducing my heart.
I fell in love.
You proclaimed me your bride,
and without earthly or heavenly writ
or legality,
with high crime, rather,
after three days you left Burgos.
You abandoned me; you fled
and left me a prey to remorse and to tears,
as penance, perhaps, for loving you so.

LEPORELLO
(*aside*)

Pare un libro stampato!

She sounds like a printed book.

DON GIOVANNI

Oh in quanto a questo, ebbi le mie ragioni!

As far as that's concerned, I had my reasons.

(*to Leporello*)

È vero.

It's true.

LEPORELLO

È vero, e che ragioni forti!

It's true, and what good reasons!

DONNA ELVIRA

E quali sono, se non per la tua perfidia,
La leggerezza tua?
Ma il giusto cielo volle ch'io ti trovassi,
Per far le sue, le mie vendette.

And what were they, if not your perfidy,
your trifling?
But the just heavens willed that I should find you
to have both its and my revenge.

DON GIOVANNI

Eh via, siate più ragionevole!
(Mi pone a cimento costei!)
Se non credete al labbro mio,
credete a questo galantuomo.

Now, now, be more reasonable.
(She pins me to the wall, this one.)
If you do not believe it from my lips,
believe this gentleman.

LEPORELLO

(Salvo il vero)

(Except for the truth.)

DON GIOVANNI
(*loudly*)

Via, dille un poco . . .

Go on, tell her something . . .

LEPORELLO
(*softly*)

E cosa devo dirle?

And what should I tell her?

DON GIOVANNI
(*loudly*)

Sì, sì, dille pur tutto.

Yes, yes, tell her everything.

	DONNA ELVIRA
Ebben, fa presto . . .	Well, hurry up . . .
	DON GIOVANNI
	(*flees*)
	LEPORELLO
Madama . . . veramente . . . in questo mondo Conciossia cosa quando fosse Che il quadro non è tondo.	Madam . . . truthfully . . . in this world notwithstanding that a square is not a circle.
	DONNA ELVIRA
Sciagurato! così del mio dolor gioco ti prendi?	Scoundrel! thus of my anguish you jest?
	(*to Don Giovanni, who, she thinks, has not left*)
Ah voi . . . stelle! l'iniquo fuggi!	Ah, you . . . heavens! You, the guilty one, flees.
Misera me! dove? in qual parte . . .	Poor me! Where? In what direction?
	LEPORELLO
Eh lasciate che vada; egli non merta Che di lui ci pensiate.	Let him go; he does not deserve that you should think of him.
	DONNA ELVIRA
Il scellerato m'ingannò, mi tradì!	The rascal deceived me, he betrayed me.
	LEPORELLO
Eh, consolatevi: non siete voi, Non foste, e non sarete né la prima Né l'ultima: guardate questo non picciol libro; È tutto pieno dei nomi di sue belle; Ogni villa, ogni borgo, ogni paese È testimon di sue donnesche imprese.	Oh, console yourself: you are not, were not the first, and will not be the last. Look at this little book; It is full of the names of his conquests; every village, every suburb, every country is a testimony to his womanizing.
Madamina! Il catalogo è questo Delle belle che amò il padron mio; Un catalogo egli è che ho fatt'io; Osservate, leggete con me! In Italia seicento e quaranta, In Almagna due cento e trent'una, Cento in Francia, in Turchia novant'una, Ma in Ispagna son già mille e tre. V'han fra queste contadine, Cameriere, cittadine, V'han contesse, baronesse, Marchesane, principesse, E v'han donne d'ogni grado, D'ogni forma, d'ogni età. In Italia . . . Nella bionda egli ha l'usanza Di lodar la gentilezza, Nella bruna la costanza, Nella bianca la dolcezza;	Madamina, This is the catalog of the beauties that my lord loved; it is a catalog that I made myself. Observe! Read with me. In Italy, six hundred forty, in Germany two hundred thirty-one, a hundred in France, in Turkey ninety-one, but in Spain there are a thousand and three. Among these there are farm girls, maids, city girls, there are countesses, baronesses marchionesses, princesses, and there are women of every rank, every shape, and every age. In Italy . . . In a blonde he usually praises her gentility, in a brunette her constancy, in the white-haired, sweetness;

Vuol d'inverno la grassotta,	he wants, in winter, a plump one,
Vuol d'estate la magrotta;	he wants in summer a rather thin one;
E' la grande maestosa;	and the large one is majestic;
La piccina è ognor vezzosa.	the petite one is always charming.
Delle vecchie fa conquista	Of the old he makes a conquest
Pel piacer di porle in lista;	for the pleasure of adding them to the list;
Ma passion predominante	but his dominant passion
È la giovin principiante;	is the young beginner.
Non si picca se sia ricca,	He is not bothered if she is rich,
Se sia brutta, se sia bella,	if she's ugly, if she's pretty,
Purchè porti la gonnella:	as long as she wears a skirt.
Voi sapete quel che fa.	You know what it is he does.

Libretto by LORENZO DA PONTE

125

John Field (1782–1837)

Nocturne in A Major, No. 8 (1811–15)

This composition was first published in a longer version (96 measures) as a *Pastorale* in the *Second Divertimento for Piano with Accompaniment of a String Quartet* (Moscow, *ca.* 1811; London, *ca.* 1811–12). In 1815 it appeared in the present version as the first of three *Romances for Piano* (Leipzig, 1815), eventually becoming one of the *Nocturnes,* usually called No. 8, but actually No. 9 (see Cecil Hopkinson, *A Bibliographical Thematic Catalogue of the Works of John Field,* London, 1961, p. 33). Reprinted from *Nocturnes,* rev. by Louis Koehler (Frankfurt, etc., Peters n.d., pl. no. 6515), pp. 28–31.

con tenerezza
21
dolce
sotto voce
dim.
leggiero
mf
26
leggiero

30
dolce
sotto voce
dim.
mf
Ped.
cresc.
35
dim.
pp
mf
tr
f
p
delicato
39
dimin.
m.d.
m.s.
dim.
rit.
pp
delicatiss.
a tempo

43
con tenerezza
50
sotto voce
55
leggiero

sotto voce
pp
Ped.
Ped.
Ped.

126

Frédéric Chopin (1810–49)
Nocturne in E-flat Major, Op. 9, No. 2
(1830–31)

Reprinted from *Nocturnes,* rev. by Herrmann Scholtz (Frankfurt, etc., Peters, n.d., pl. no. 9025), p. 8–10.

poco rall.
a tempo
fzp
Ped.
simile
14
cresc.
p
19
f
poco rall.
a tempo
fzp

23
poco rubato
sempre pp
dolciss.
28
con forza
stretto
32
senza
tempo
cresc.

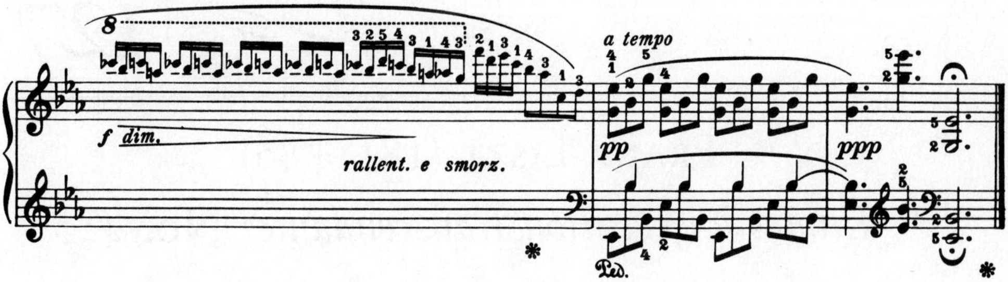
a tempo
f dim.
rallent. e smorz.
pp
ppp

127

Franz Liszt (1811–86)

Etudes d'exécution transcendante: No. 4, *Mazeppa*

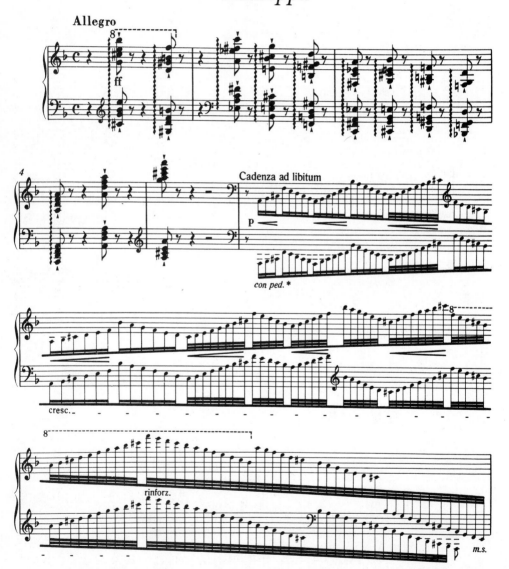

The *Etudes d'exécution transcendante* were first published as *Etudes pour le piano en douze exercises* (Paris, 1827); they were revised as *Grandes Etudes* in 1837. The title "Mazeppa" dates from the 1852 edition. Reprinted by permission of Bärenreiter-Verlag, Kassel, Basel, Tours, London from: *Neue Ausgabe sämtlicher Werke,* Serie I, Vol. I (Kassel, 1970), pp. 15–28.

Allegro [♩ = 112-116]
7
sempre fortissimo e con strepito
m.s.
m.d.
m.s.
Ped.
9
simile
11
Ped. simile
13

15
sf
ten.
18
20
22
8

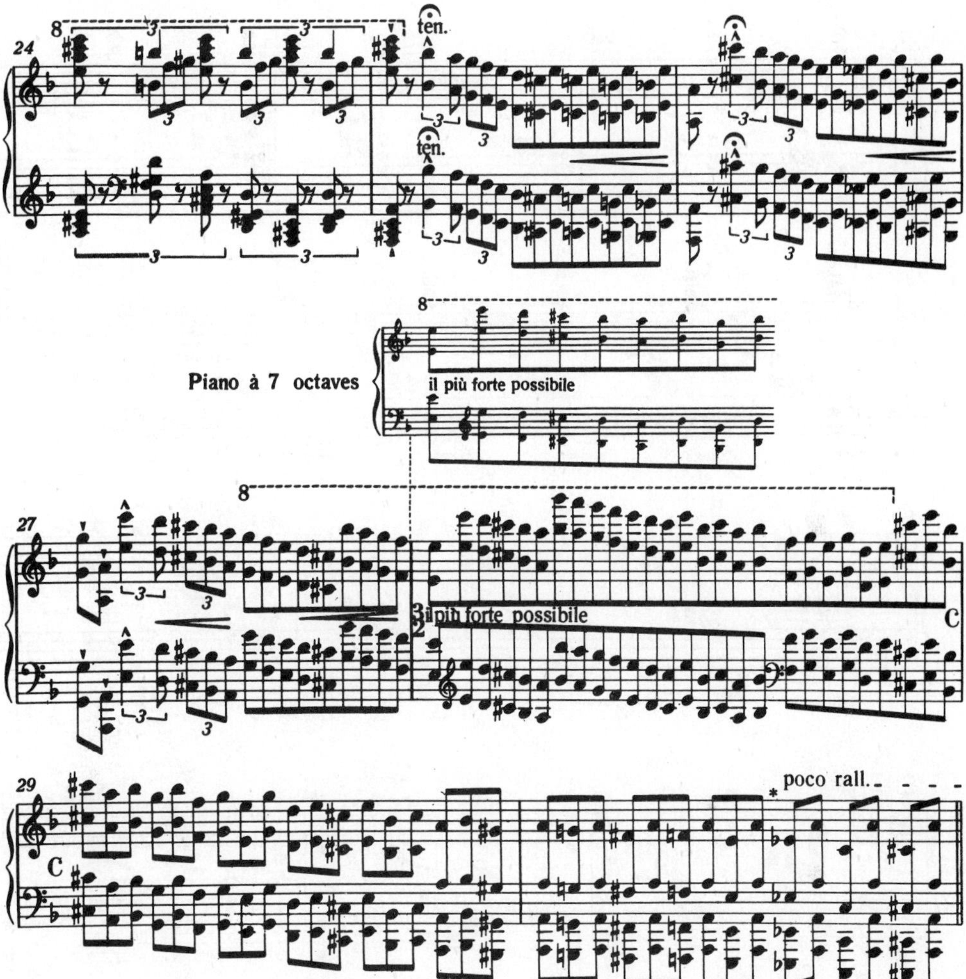
ten.
ten.
Piano à 7 octaves
il più forte possibile
il più forte possibile
C
C
poco rall.
sempre ff
ten.
ten.
simile

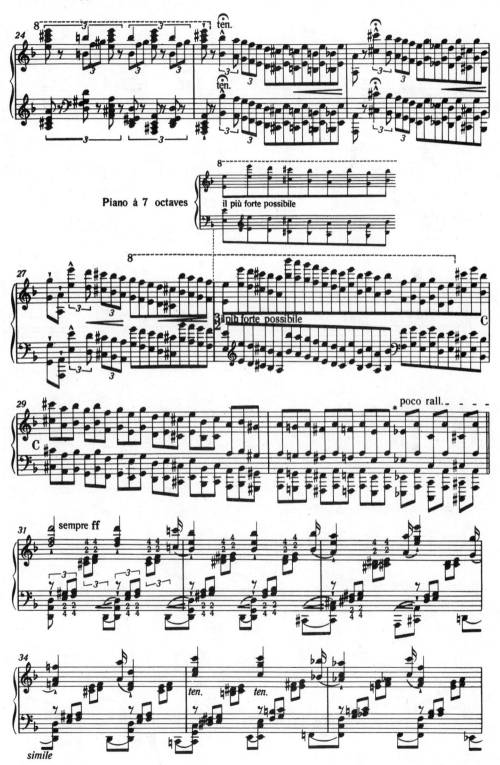

37
ten.
ten.
meno f
40
ten.
cresc.
43
rinf.
ten.*
46
sf
ff
49
sf
sf
52
sf
ten.
sf
ten.

55
57
60
quasi cadenza
rfz
rit.
a tempo
62
p il canto marcato e vibrato assai
con ped.

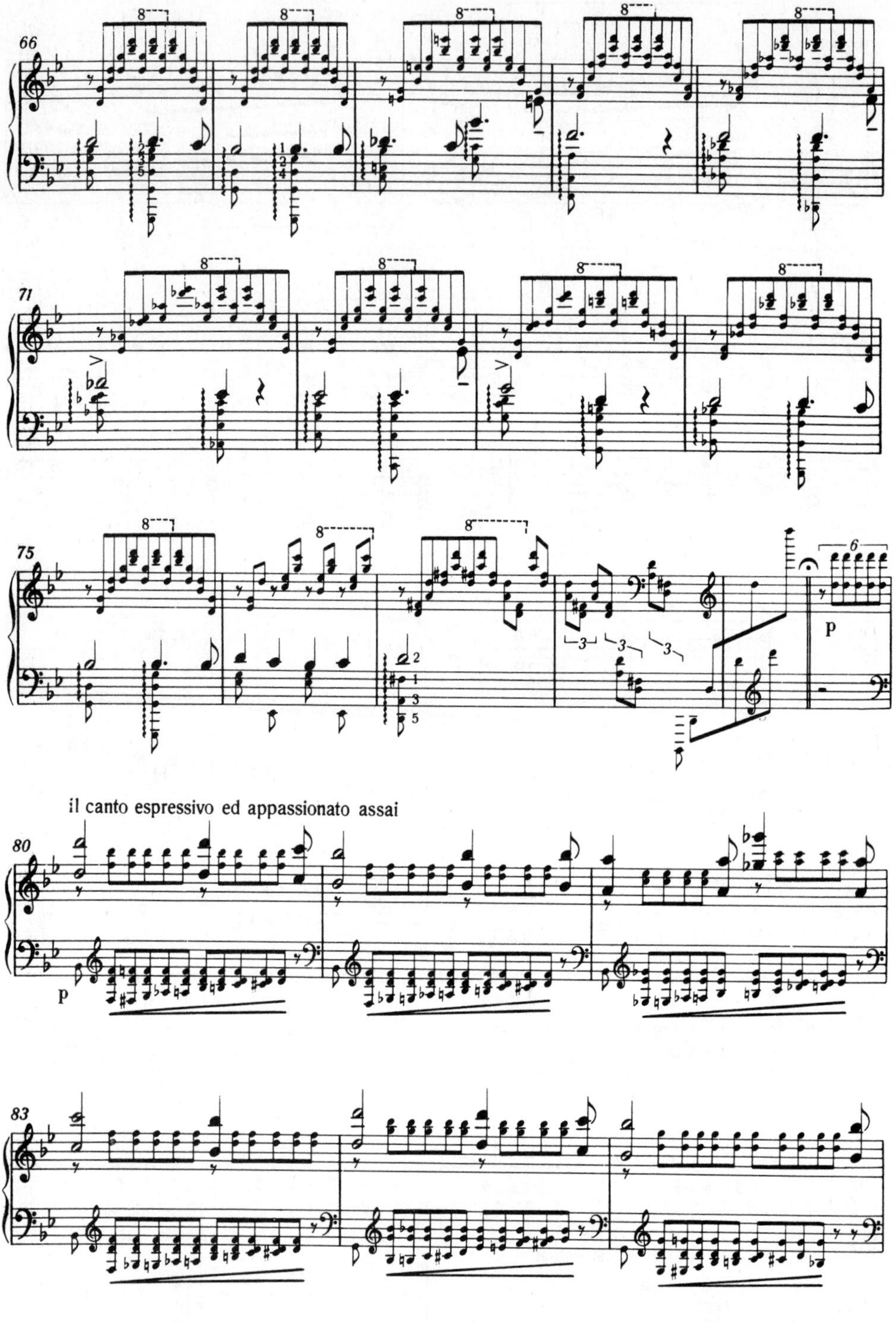
il canto espressivo ed appassionato assai

86
cresc.
89
più cresc.
92
p
appassionato
94
cresc.
Ossia
97
rinforz.

8
99
rinforz.
con ped.
101
104
poco rit.
stringendo
p sub.
cresc.
108
ff
sf
3

8
Piano à 7 octaves
il più forte possibile
quasi cadenza
8
112
3
3
3
3
il più forte possibile
poco rallentando
Animato
leggero
114
mp
118

122
126
130
8
Allegro deciso
134
ff
139
simile

143
mp
crescendo
148
rinforzando assai
152
159
sempre ff
162

165
168
172
sf
sf
ritenuto
Più moderato
177
più rit.
non piano *
p
184
a tempo
rall.
f

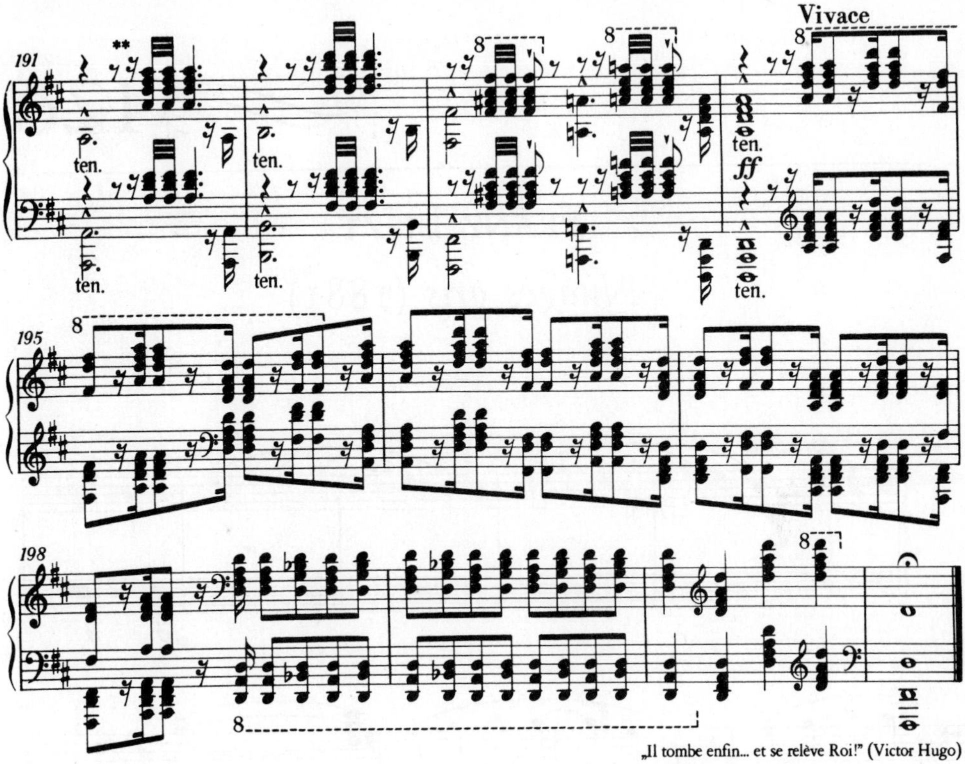

„Il tombe enfin... et se relève Roi!" (Victor Hugo)

128

FRANZ LISZT

Nuages gris (1881)

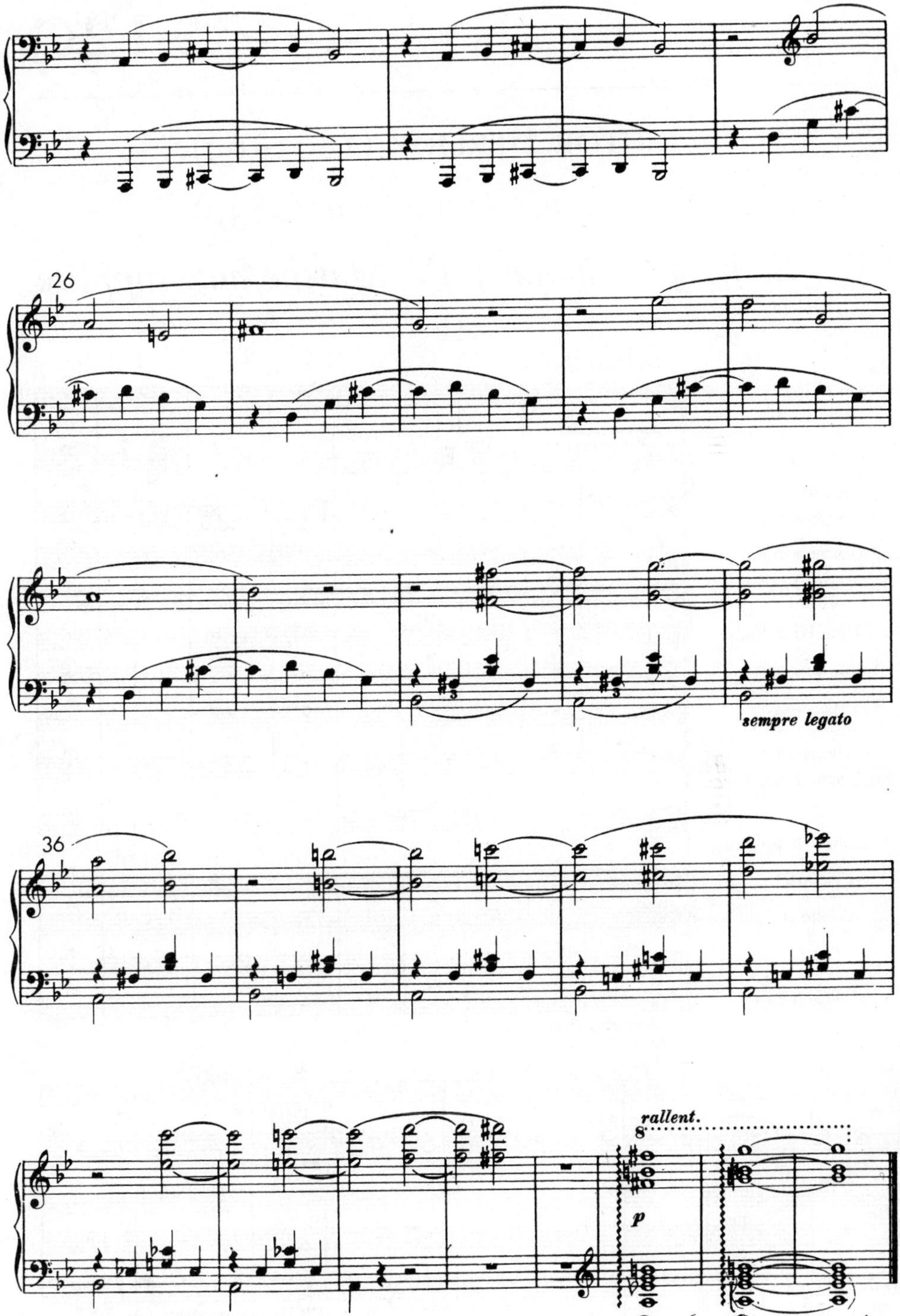
26
sempre legato
36
rallent.
8
p
Ped.
Ped.

129

HECTOR BERLIOZ (1803–69)

Symphonie fantastique (1830)

III. *Scène aux champs;* IV. *Marche aux supplice*

III

19
37
Fl.
I. Solo
Ob.
Le Hautbois rentre à l'orchestre.
The Oboe-player returns to the orchestra.
C.ingl.
Oboe II.
Soli
Viol.
pizz.
unis.
ôtez les sourdines
pizz.
Vcllo.
pizz.
C.B.
37
28
Fl.
cresc. poco a poco
dim.
I. Solo
Clar.
cresc. poco a poco
Solo I.
Corni.(in F)
Viol.
cresc. poco a poco
dim.
arco

37
38
Fl.
Clar.
Cor. I.
Fag.
Viol.
pizz.
div. pizz.
pizz.
cresc.
sf
dim.
arco
leggiero
f

46
38
retenu
a tempo
Fl. I.
Fl. II.
Ob. I.
Ob. II.
Clar. I.
Clar. II.
Cor I. II.
Cor. IV. (in C)
Fag.
unis.
Viol.
arco
pizz.
cresc.
sf
p
f
pp
retenu
a tempo

52
Fl.
Ob.
Clar.
Cor. I. II.
Fag.
Viol.
cresc.
sf
p
f
arco
pizz.

59
Fl.
Ob. I. II.
Clar.
Cor. IV. (in C)
Fag.
unis.
Viol.
cresc.
mf
f
f dim.
arco
39

65
sans presser
Fl.
I.
p
Ob.
Solo I.
pp
Clar.
Solo I.
ppp
Viol.
mf
dim.
pp
ppp
p dim.
sans presser

69
Fl.
pp
Ob.
pp
Clar.
pp
Cor. III. (in E♭)
pp
Fag. (unis.)
mf
sf
Viol.
pizz.
sf
p
pizz.
div.
arco
mf
arco
mf
pizz.
(p)

72
Fl.
Ob.
Clar.
Cor. III.
Fag.
Viol.

77
40
Fl.
Ob.
Clar.
I.
Solo
Cor. I. II. (in F)
Cor. III.
Cor. IV. (in C)
Fag.
Viol.
cresc. molto
arco
pizz.
40

82
Fl.
Ob.
Clar.
Cor. I.II.
Cor. III.
Cor. IV.
Fag.
Viol.
unis.
arco
cresc. poco a poco
cresc. molto
cresc.

87
41
Fl.
Ob.
Cl.
Cor. I. II.
Cor. III.
Cor. IV.
Fag.
unis.
Solo I.
p espressivo
tremolo très serré
very close Tremolo
Viol.
dim. poco a poco
p cresc.
dim.
41

93
Fl.
Ob.
Clar.
Fag.
Viol.
p
f
sf

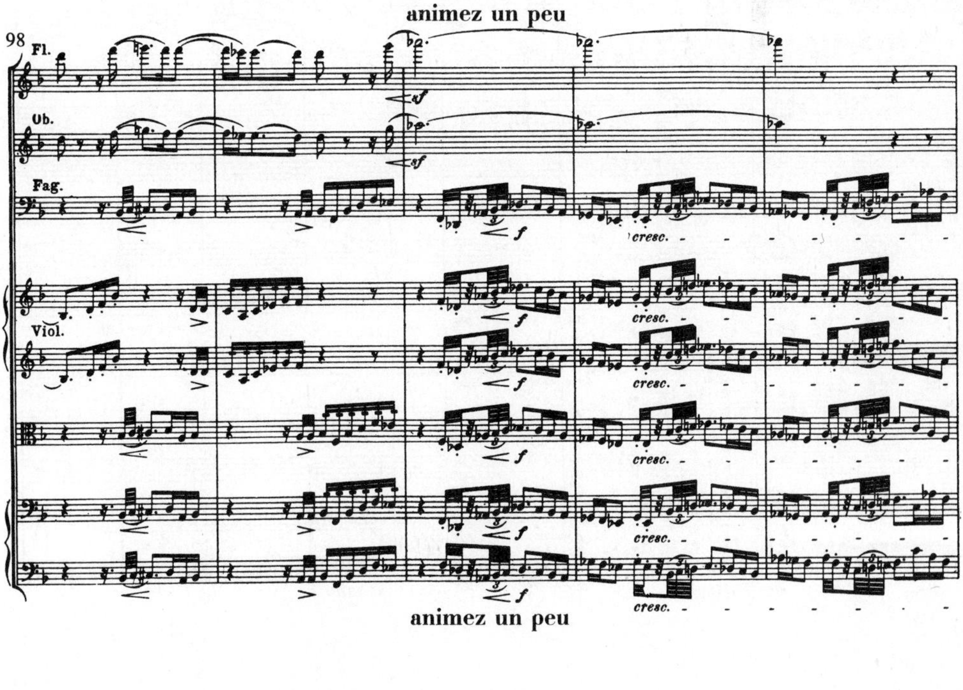
animez un peu
98
Fl.
Ob.
Fag.
Viol.
sf
f
cresc.
animez un peu

103
42 animez un peu
Fl.
Ob.
Clar.
Cor. I.II in F.
Cor. III in Es.
Cor. IV in C.
Fag.
Timp. I.
Baguettes de bois
Wooden drum-sticks
Viol.
cresc.
unis.
a 2.
42 animez un peu

109
rallent.
Tempo I
Fl.
Ob.
Clar.
Cor. I.II.
Cor. III.
Cor. IV.
Fag.
Viol.
dim.
p morendo
pp
pizz.
Soli
rallent.
Tempo I

117
43
Fl.
Solo I
pp
Ob.
Clar.
Solo I.
mf dolce
Cor. IV.
Fag.
Viol.
sempre pizz.
ppp
ancora più
sempre pizz.
ppp
ancora più
43

123
Fl.
Clar.
Echo.
pppp
poco f
cresc.
sf
sf
pppp
tr
ppp
poco f
Viol.
pppp
cresc. un poco
pppp
cresc. un poco
arco
p
poco f
Vcllo. div.
arco
pizz.
p
poco f
C. B.
pizz.
p
poco f

129
44
Fl.
Ob.
I.
Clar.
Cor. I.II.
Cor. III.
Cor. IV.
Fag.
pizz.
Viol.
unis.
arco
cresc.
decresc.
sf
mf
pp
p
44

133
Fl. I.
Ob. I.
Clar. I.
Cor. IV.
Fag. I.
p dolce
p (dolce)
Viol.

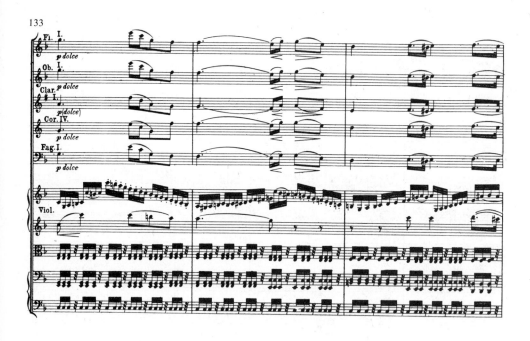

136
Fl.
Ob.
Clar.
Cor. IV.
Fag.
Viol.
presque rien
pppp

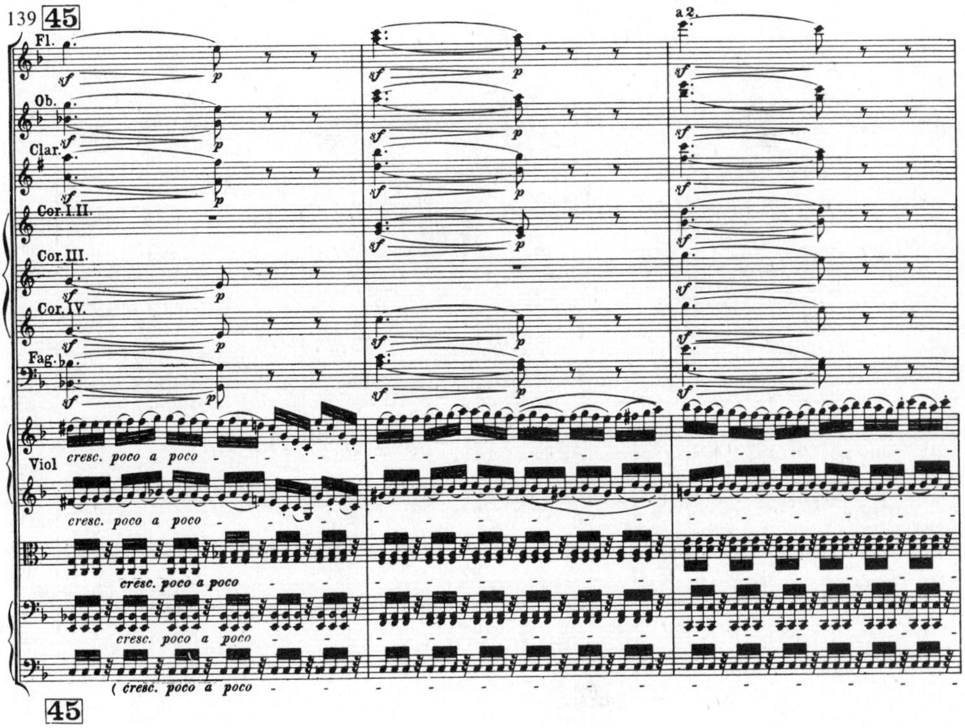
139
45
Fl.
Ob.
Clar.
Cor. I. II.
Cor. III.
Cor. IV.
Fag.
a 2.
sf
p
Viol
cresc. poco a poco
45

142
Fl.
Ob.
Clar.
Cor. I. II.
Cor. III.
Cor. IV.
Fag.
Timp. I.
Viol.
cresc. molto
div.
dim.
ppp
muta in F
unis.
poco f
46
47

148
Fl.
Ob.
Clar.
Cor. I.
Cor. II.
Cor. III. in F (Fa).
Cor. IV.
Viol.
unis.
rall.
a tempo
Solo
p cresc.
47

156
Fl.
Clar.
Fag.
Timp.
Viol.
div.
Solo
I.
p leggiero
Deux Timbaliers, baguettes d'éponge
2 drummers to use sponge-headed drum-sticks
poco f
dim.
pp
pizz.
arco

162
48
Fl.
Ob.
Clar. 2 Solo
Cor. I. II.
Cor. III.
Cor. IV.
Fag.
Viol.
unis. Soli
cresc.
dim.

166
Fl.
Ob.
Clar.
a 2.
Cor.
Fag.
unis.
Viol.
perdendo sempre
pp
Corno inglese.
div.
170
I. Solo
un peu retenu
Cor. I.II.
Cor. III.
Cor. IV.
unis.
pizz.
un peu retenu

175
49
C.ingl. Solo
Timp.I.
Tous les Timbaliers,
baguettes d'éponge
Timp.II.
Timp.III.
All 4 drummers to use
sponge-headed drum-sticks
Timp.IV.
Vcello.
cresc.
sf
dim.
185
C.ingl.
Timp.I.
Timp.II.
Timp.III.
Timp.IV.
poco sf dim.
192
C.ingl.
perdendo
Cor.II.
Solo
Timp.I.
Timp.II.
Timp. III.
Timp. IV.
arco
Viol.

IV

Allegretto non troppo (𝅗𝅥 = 72)
(2) Flutes
(2) Oboes
(2) Clarinets in C
(Natural or with valves)
Horns I and II in B♭ basso
Horns III and IV in E♭
Faites les sons bouchés avec la main sans employer les cylindres.
Soli
II
III.
pp
Produce the stopped tones with the hand without using the valves.
(4) Bassoons
2 Cornets in B♭
2 Trumpets in B♭
Trombones I and II
Trombone III
2 Ophicleides
Timpani I
With sponge-headed drum-sticks
Il faut frapper la première croche de chaque temps avec les deux baguettes et les cinq autres croches avec la baguette de la main droite seulement.
Soli
The first quaver of each half-bar to be played with 2 drum-sticks; the other 5 quavers with the right hand drum-sticks.
Timpani II
With sponge-headed drum-sticks
Snare Drum
Cymbals
Bass Drum
Violin I
Violin II
Viola
Cello
Bass
pizz.
div. in 4.
pp
Allegretto non troppo (𝅗𝅥 = 72)

7
II.
p
I.
p
cresc. poco a poco

15
50
Clar.
Corni
Fag.
unis.
Soli
Ctti
Tr.
Tromb.
Oph. I.
cresc.
Timp.
cresc. molto
cresc.
pizz.
arco
Viol.
unis.
dim.

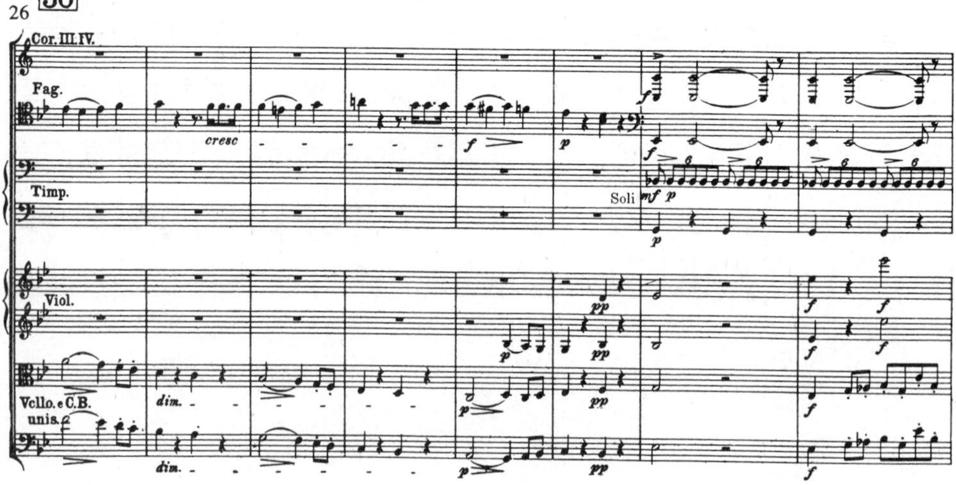
26
50
Cor. III. IV.
Fag.
cresc
Timp.
Soli
Viol.
Vcllo. e C.B.
unis.
dim.

34
Timp.
Viol.
dim.
p

39
51
Fl.
Ob.
Clar.
Corni.
Fag.
Ctti
Tr.
Tromb.
Oph. I.
Timp.
Viol.
ff
mf
p
f
dim.

44
52
Fl.
Ob.
Clar.
Corni.
Fag.
Soli unis.
Timp.
Viol.
pizz.
52
50
Fag.
Viol.
55
Fag.
unis.
Viol.
dim.
pp

60
53
Fl.
Ob.
Clar
a 2.
Corni.
avec les cylindres tous les sons ouverts.
with the valves, all tones open
Fag.
a 2.
Ctti
Tr.
II.
Tromb.
Oph. I.
cresc.
Timp.
cresc.
Cinelli.
Gr.Tamb.
arco
Viol.
arco
arco
Vcllo.
arco
C.B.
arco
53

68
pizz.

75
poco f
p
cresc.
f
arco
pizz.

83
54
I.
Soli
Soli
Soli
Oph. I.
II.
poco f
cresc.
Solo
Solo
Cinelli
Gr. Tamb.
arco
pizz.
cresc.
54

91
a 2.
a 2.

96
mf
cresc.
f
ff

101
55
diminuendo
poco f
Soli
Soli
cresc.
55

106
a 2.
I.
Soli
Soli
unis.
Soli
Soli
pizz.
arco

114
56
mf
a 2.
cresc.
arco
ff
sempre più forte
56

119
a2.
Baguettes de bois
Wooden drum-sticks
cresc.
Baguettes de bois
Wooden drum-sticks

125
57
a 2.
I.
dim.
p
pp
ff
mf
57

136
a 2.
unis.
sul G

144
a 2.
unis.
f
ff
(f)
(ff)

151
58
f
dim.
a 2.
a 4.
(a 2)
2 Oph.
muta in B♮
mf
ff
58

158
a 2.
59
I. Solo
pp dolce assai
ed appassionato
Trois Timbaliers
Three drummers
59

167
rall. poco a tempo
I. II.
a 2.
Fag. III. IV.
a 2.
1. Timpanista.
2. Timpanista.
Soli
3. Timpanista.
Tamburo.
Cinelli.
étouffez le son
damp the tone
Gr. Tamb.
étouffez le son avec la main
damp the tone with the hand
pizz.
arco
rall. poco a tempo

Program note distributed at first performance and published with the score in 1845:

Avertissement
Le Compositeur a eu pour but de développer, dans ce qu'elles ont de musical, différentes situations de la vie d'un artiste. Le plan du drame instrumental, privé du secours de la parole, a besoin d'être exposé d'avance. Le programme suivant doit donc être considéré comme le texte parlé d'un Opéra, servant à amener des morceaux de musique, dont il motive le caractère et l'expression.

Note
The composer's intention has been to develop, insofar as they contain musical possibilities, various situations in the life of an artist. The outline of the instrumental drama, which lacks the help of words, needs to be explained in advance. The following program should thus be considered as the spoken text of an opera, serving to introduce the musical movements, whose character and expression it motivates.

[Précis of First and Second Parts: The author imagines that a young musician has fallen desperately in love with a woman who embodies all that he has imagined in his dreams. She is linked in his mind with a melody, so that the melody and the model become a double *idée fixe,* which reappears in every movement of the symphony. The passage from melancholic reverie to frenzied passion, jealousy, and tenderness is the subject of the first movement. In the second the artist finds himself at a ball, where the beloved image appears and disturbs his peace of mind.]

Troisième partie
Scène aux champs
Se trouvant un soir à la campagne, il entend au loin deux pâtres qui dialoguent un ranz des vaches; ce duo pastoral, le lieu de la scène, le léger bruissement des arbres doucement agités par le vent, quelques motifs d'espérance qu'il a conçus depuis peu, tout concourt à rendre à son coeur un calme inaccoutumé, et à donner à ses idées une couleur plus riante. Il réfléchit sur son isolement; il espère n'être bientôt plus seul . . . . Mais si elle le trompait! . . . Ce mélange d'espoir et de crainte, ces idées de bonheur troublées par quelques noirs pressentiments, forment le sujet de l'ADAGIO. A la fin, l'un des pâtres reprend le ranz de vaches; l'autre ne répond plus . . . Bruit éloigné de tonnerre . . . solitude . . . silence . . . .

Third Part
Scene in the Country
Finding himself one evening in the country, he hears in the distance two shepherds piping a *ranz de vaches* in dialogue. This pastoral duet, the scenery, the quiet rustling of the trees gently brushed by the wind, the hopes he has recently found some reason to entertain—all concur in affording his heart an unaccustomed calm, and in giving a more cheerful color to his ideas. He reflects upon his isolation; he hopes that his loneliness will soon be over.—But what if she were deceiving him!—The mingling of hope and fear, these ideas of happiness disturbed by black presentiments, form the subject of the Adagio. At the end one of the shepherds again takes up the *ranz de vaches*; the other no longer replies.—Distant sound of thunder—loneliness—silence.

Quatrième partie
Marche au supplice

Ayant acquis la certitude que son amour est méconnu, l'artiste s'empoisonne avec de l'opium. La dose du narcotique, trop faible pour lui donner la mort, le plonge dans un sommeil accompagné de plus horribles visions. Il rêve qu'il a tué celle qu'il aimait, qu'il est condamné, conduit au supplice, e qu'il assiste à sa PROPRE EXECUTION. Le cortège s'avance aux sons d'une marche tantôt sombre et farouche, tantôt brillante et solennelle, dans laquelle un bruit sourd de pas graves succède sans transition aux éclats les plus bruyants. A la fin de la marche, les quatre premières mesures de l'IDÉE FIXE reparaissent come un dernière pensée d'amour interrompue par le coup fatal.

Fourth Part
March to the Scaffold

Convinced that his love is unappreciated, the artist poisons himself with opium. The dose of the narcotic, too weak to kill him, plunges him into a sleep accompanied by the most horrible visions. He dreams that he has killed his beloved, that he is condemned and led to the scaffold, and that he is witnessing *his own execution.* The procession moves forward to the sounds of a march that is now sombre and fierce, now brilliant and solemn, in which the muffled noise of heavy steps gives way without transition to the noisiest clamor. At the end of the march the first four measures of the *idée fixe* reappear, like a last thought of love interrupted by the fatal blow.

Translated by EDWARD T. CONE

Felix Mendelssohn (1809–47)
Incidental Music to *A Midsummer's Night's Dream*, Opus 61 (1843): Scherzo.

New York: Dover, 1975, pp. 55–71, reprinted from the Breitkopf & Härtel *Musik zu Sommernachtstraum von Shakespeare* (Leipzig, 1874–77).

cresc.
36
p

tr
p cresc.
cresc.
sf
58
p
pp
pizz.
58

pp
pp
pp
pp
pp
pp
arco
pp
pp

82
p
p
p
p
p
p
p
p
82

cresc.
dim. - - al - pp
p
105
a 2.
p cresc.
arco

cresc.
127
dim.
pizz.
arco

cresc.
f
pp
147
ff
sf
dim.
pizz.
arco
divisi
147

a 2.
cresc.
arco
sf
p
f
168
in C.
tr
ff
sempre ff

dim.
dim.
dim.
dim.
p
dim.
p
pp
pp
pp
pp
dim.
p
dim.
pp
dim.
p
dim.
pp
divisi
p
dim.
pp
pizz.
pp
dim.
pizz.

190
p
p
p
p
p
arco
p
190
pizz.

Vcl.
Basso
pizz.
arco
214
dim.
pizz.
Bassi
in D.
214

p
pp sempre
pp
pp
arco
pp
238
sf
sf
sf
dim.
dim.
pp
Basso
238
Vcl.

p
p
p
pizz.
Bassi
261
a 2.
p
in C.
p
pp
261

cresc.
a 2.
arco
283
283

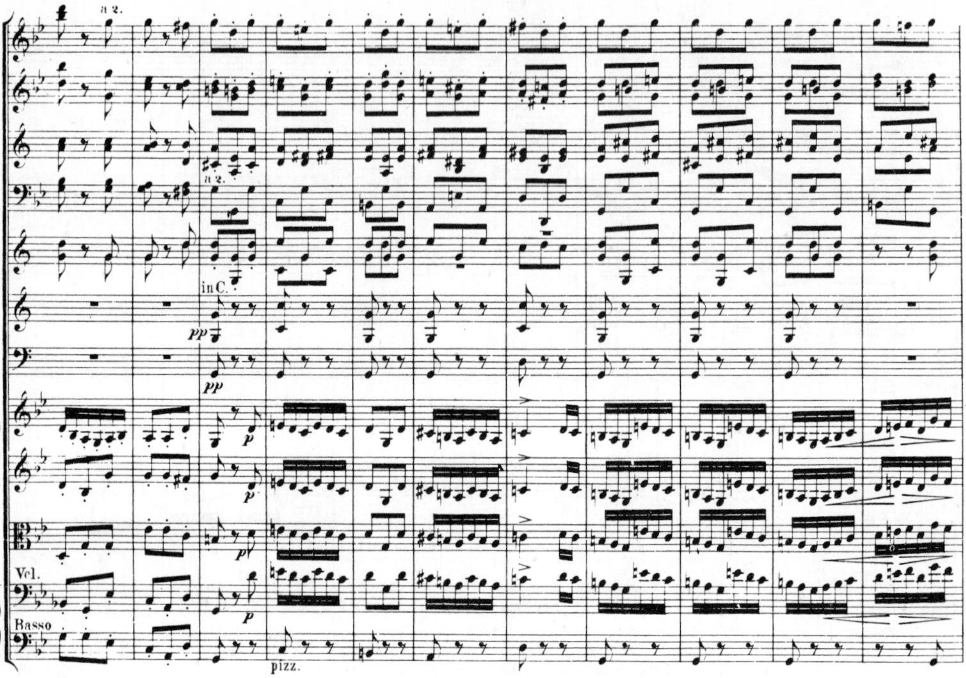
a 2.
a 2.
in C.
pp
pp
p
p
p
Vcl.
p
Basso
pizz.

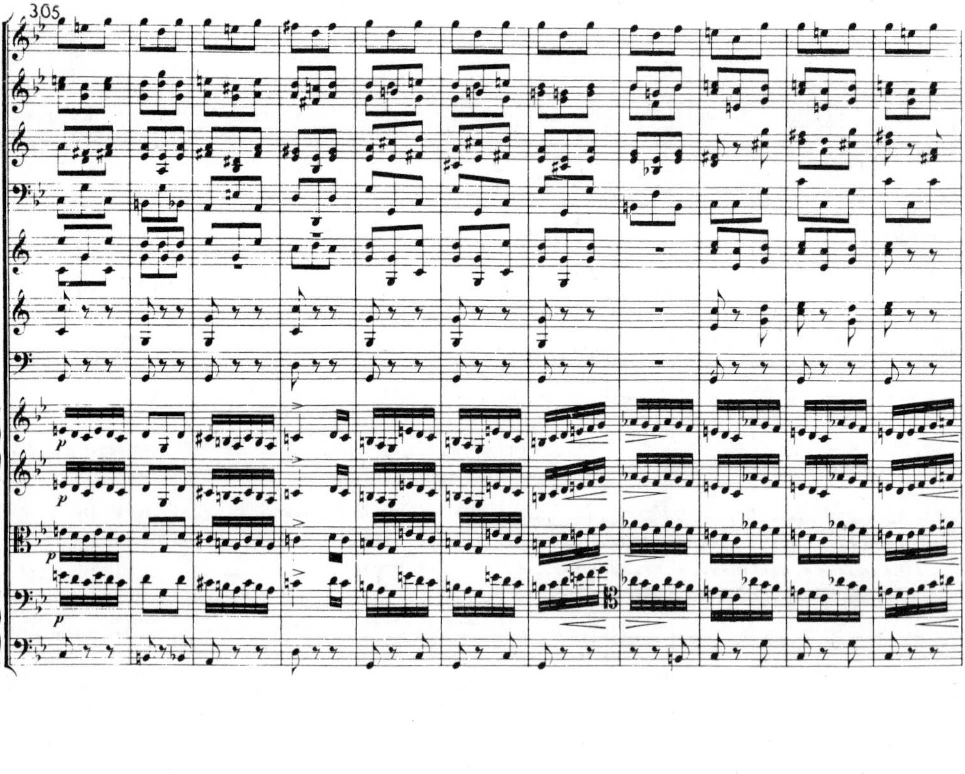
305
p
p
p
p

cresc.
f
p
sf
dim.
327
Bassi
arco

sempre staccato
pp
pizz.
sempre più
349
sempre più pp
sempre stacc.
p

cresc.
dim.
dim.
dim.
dim.
pp
pp
pp
dim.
dim.
dim.
dim.

372
pp
pp
pp
pp
pp
pp
pp
pizz.
pp
pizz.
pp
pizz.
pp
Vorhang auf.
arco
pizz.
pp
372

131

EDWARD MACDOWELL (1861–1908)
Suite for Orchestra, Opus 48 (1897): Dirgelike, mournfully (fourth movement)

First performance, 1896. New York: Associated, n.d., pp. 73–79, reprinted from Breitkopf & Härtel (Leipzig, n.d.).

8
IV senza sord.
G in B♭
pp
Gran cassa con bacchet. d. timpani.
mf
p
f
pizz.
arco
8

15
Fl.
Cl.
A
hinter der Scene
behind the scene
derrière la scène
Cor.
div.
pizz.
arco
15
A
Fl.
poco rall.
B
Ob.
Cl.
Gran cassa con bacchet. d. timpani.
div.
div.
poco rall.
B

31
Fl.
Ob.
Fag.
p
div.
pp
31

Fl.
Ob.
Cl.
C
pp
div.
dolciss.
senza Sord.
C

Fl. 48
Ob.
Cl.
Fag.
Gran cassa con bacch. d. timp.
ppp
p
arco grande
arco grande
arco grande
pp
f
48
Fl.
Cl.
Fag.
Gr. c.
4.
4.
pizz.
pizz.
arco

64 D
senza sord.
senza sord.
hinter der Scene
behind the scene
derrière la scène
a 2.
B in G.
pizz.
arco
64 D

Cor. I.
72
E
arco grande
con Sord.
div.
con Sord.
arco
arco gr.
con Sord.
arco
arco grande
con Sord.
arco
arco
72
E
Cl.
rall.
Fag.
hinter der Scene
behind the scene
derrière la scène
Tr. I.
Timp.
Gran cassa con bacch. d. timp.
dim.
arco grande
div.
arco grande
rall.

132

Johannes Brahms (1833–97)
Piano Quintet in F Minor, Opus 34 (1864): Scherzo

Reprinted from Editions Eulenberg, 1954, pp. 35–47.

pizz.
pp
pizz.
pp
pp
20
arco
ff
arco
ff
ff
arco
ff
ff
fz
30
ff
ff
ff
ff
fz
f
f
ff

40
f
fz
pp
dim.
50
pizz.
arco
p cresc.
ff

60
8
8
70
p
p
pp sempre
pp
p
sempre
molto pp

80
pp
pp
p
p marcato
p marcato
pp
pp sempre
90
pp
pp

cresc.
cresc.
cresc.
cresc.
cresc.
100
ff
ff
ff
ff
ff
ff
ff
ff
ff
ff
ff
ff
ff
ff
ff

110
120
130

140
f
fz
p
f
fz
p cresc.
ff
150
8

160
ff
ff
ff
ff
ff
ff
170
8

8
ff
ff
ff
ff
ff
180
fz
fz
ff

190
fz
fz
fz
fz
Fine
Trio
200
mf
poco f
f

210
f
f
f
pizz.
f
mf non legato
220
230
f
f
arco
mf
mf
3

240
250
dim.

Scherzo da Capo sin al Fine

FRANZ SCHUBERT (1797–1828)

Kennst du das Land (1815)

Compare this setting of Mignon's song from Goethe's *Wilhelm Meister* to Schumann's, p. 338 and Wolf's, p. 343. *Franz Schubert Complete Works* Vol. 14 (New York, Dover, 1965), pp. 155–58, reprinted from the Breitkopf & Härtel critical edition (Leipzig, 1884–97).

Etwas geschwinder.
Da - hin, da - hin! da -
Da - hin, da - hin! da -
p
cresc.
f
23
hin möcht' ich mit dir, o mein Ge - lieb - ter, ziehn; da -
hin möcht' ich mit dir, o mein Beschüt - zer, ziehn; da -
fp
p
hin, da - hin, da - hin! da - hin möcht' ich mit
hin, da - hin, da - hin! da - hin möcht' ich mit
cresc.
ff
p
32
dir, o mein Ge - lieb - ter, ziehn, da - hin, da -
dir, o mein Be - schüt - zer, ziehn, da - hin, da -
cresc.
f
ff
hin, da - hin, da - hin!
hin, da - hin, da - hin!

Wie oben.
Kennst du den Berg und sei-nen Wol-ken-steg? Das Maulthier sucht im Ne-bel
sei-nen Weg; in Höh-len wohnt der Dra-chen al-te
51
Brut; es stürzt der Fels und ü-ber ihn die Fluth,
kennst du ihn wohl?
60
Etwas geschwinder.
Da-hin, da-
cresc.

hin! da - hin geht un - ser Weg! o Va - ter, lass' uns
fp
67
zieh'n! Da - hin, da - hin, da -
p
ff
hin! da - hin geht un - ser Weg! o Va - ter, lass uns
p
cresc.
75
zieh'n! Da - hin, da - hin, da -
f
ff
hin, da - hin!

Kennst du das Land, wo die Zitronen blühn,	Do you know the country where the lemon trees blossom?
Im dunkeln Laub die Gold-Orangen glühn,	Among dark leaves the golden oranges glow.
Ein sanfter Wind vom blauen Himmel weht,	A gentle breeze from blue skies drifts.
Die Myrte still und hoch der Lorbeer steht?	The myrtle is still, and the laurel stands high.
Kennst du es wohl? Dahin, dahin	Do you know it well? There, there
Möcht' ich mit dir, o mein Geliebter, ziehn.	would I go with you, my beloved,
Kennst du das Haus? Auf Säulen ruht sein Dach,	Do you know the house? On pillars rests its roof.
Es glänzt der Saal, es schimmert das Gemach,	The great hall glistens, the room shines,
Und Marmorbilder Stehn und sehn mich an:	and the marble statues stand and look at me, asking:
Was hat man dir, du armes Kind, getan?	"What have they done to you, poor child?"
Kennst du es wohl? Dahin, Dahin	Do you know it well? There, there
Möcht' ich mit dir, o mein Beschützer, ziehn.	would I go with you, oh my protector,
Kennst du den Berg und seinen Wolkensteg?	Do you know the mountain and its path?
Das Maultier sucht im Nebel seinen Weg;	The muletier searches in the clouds for his way;
In Höhlen wohnt der Drachen alte Brut;	In the caves dwells the dragon of the old breed.
Es stürzt der Fels und über ihn die Flut.	The cliff falls, and over it the flood.
Kennst du ihn wohl? Dahin! Dahin	Do you know it well? There, there
Geht unser Weg! o Vater, lass uns ziehn!	leads our way, oh father, let us go!

134

Robert Schumann (1810–56)

Kennst du das Land, Op. 79, No. 29 [Op. 98a, No. 1] (1849)

Compare this setting to Schubert's, p. 333 and Wolf's, p. 343. Reprinted from *Sämtliche Lieder* Vol. II, edited by Max Friedlaender (Frankfurt, 19—), pp. 212–15.

14
fp
cresc.
Myrte still und hoch — der Lor - beer steht? kennst du es
fp
fp
cresc.
Ped.
wohl, kennst du es wohl? Da- hin! da-
f
f
Ped.
21
hin möcht ich mit dir, o mein Ge-lieb-ter, ziehn, da-
dimin.
p
hin, da- hin mit dir, o mein Ge- lieb - ter, ziehn.
dimin.
p
29
p
Kennst du das Haus? Auf Säu-len ruht sein Dach, es
Ped.
Ped.

cresc.
glänzt der Saal, es schim-mert das Gemach, und Marmor-bil-der stehn und
cresc.
Ped. * Ped. *
38
sehn mich an: was hat man dir, du ar- mes
fp
fp
cresc.
Kind, ge- tan? Kennst du es wohl, kennst du es
fp
cresc.
Ped. *
45
f
wohl? Da- hin! da- hin möcht ich mit
f
Ped. *
dimin.
p
dir, o mein Be-schü-tzer, ziehn, da- hin, da-
dimin.
p

51
hin mit dir, o mein Be - schü - tzer, ziehn.
p
Kennst du den Berg und sei-nen Wol-kensteg? Das Maul - tier sucht im Ne-bel sei-nen Weg;
62
cresc.
in Höh - len wohnt — der Dra - chen al - te Brut, es
fp
cresc.
stürzt der Fels und ü - - ber ihn die Flut. Kennst du ihn
70
f
wohl, kennst du ihn wohl? Da - hin, da -

For a translation of the text, see p. 337.

135

Hugo Wolf (1860–1903)

Kennst du das Land (1888)

Compare this setting to Schubert's, p. 333 and Schumann's, p. 338. Reprinted from *Ausgewählte Lieder,* edited by Elena Gerhardt (Frankfurt: Peters, 1932), pp. 134–41. By permission.

15
Wind vom blau-en Him-mel weht, die Myr-te still und hoch
cresc.
der Lor-beer steht,
f
p
Belebt (animated)
leidenschaftlich
(with passion)
f
22
Ruhiger (more calmly)
Belebt (animated)
Kennst du es wohl?
poco rit.
p
molto cresc.
8
più f
poco rit.
Ruhiger (more calmly)
Kennst du es
p

28
wohl?
pp
dim.
Tempo I
leidenschaftlich hingebend (surrendering to passionate emotion)
Da - hin!
da - hin!
p
f
p
34
möcht ich mit dir, o mein Ge - lieb - ter,
fp molto cresc.
f
pp
ziehn.
p

41
Kennst du das Haus? auf Säu - len ruht sein Dach,
espr.
p
pp poco a poco cresc.
es glänzt der Saal, es schim - mert das Ge - mach,
mf
49
und Marmorbilder stehn und sehn mich an:
p
was hat man dir, du ar - mes Kind, ge - tan?
mf
p

57
Belebt (animated)
leidenschaftlich
(with passionate emotion)
pp
f
poco rit.
Ruhiger (more calmly)
Belebt (animated)
Kennst du es wohl?
8
p
molto cresc.
più f
63
Ruhiger (more calmly)
Kennst du es wohl?
poco rit.
p
Tempo I (♩. = ♩)
leidenschaftlich hingebend
(surrendering to passionate emotion)
Da- hin!
pp
dim.
p
f

70
da - hin! möcht ich mit
p
fp molto cresc. f
dir, o mein Be-schü - tzer ziehn.
f
pp
p
77
Kennst du den Berg und sei-nen Wol-kensteg?
espr.
pp
Das Maul-tier sucht im Ne - bel sei-nen Weg; in Höh-len
cresc.
mf
pp

87
wohnt der Dra - - chen al - te Brut; es stürzt der Fels
molto cresc.
und ü - - - ber ihn die Flut.
più f
97
Belebt (animated)
leidenschaftlich
(with passionate emotion)
poco rit.
Ruhiger (more calmly)
Belebt (animated)
Kennst du ihn wohl?
molto cresc.
poco rit.
dim.

105
Ruhiger (more calmly)
Kennst du ihn wohl?
p
pp
dim.
Tempo I
leidenschaftlich hingebend
(surrendering to passionate emotion)
Da - hin!
p
f
111
da - hin!
geht un - ser
p
fp molto cresc.
f
Weg! O Va - ter, laß uns ziehn!
p
f
pp
p

For a translation of the text, see p. 337.

136

Gustav Mahler (1860–1911)

Kindertotenlieder (1902): *Nun will die Sonn' so hell aufgehen*

Reprinted from Edition Eulenburg, n.d., pp. 1–11.

Ob.
Cl. b. (B)
Fg.
Cor. (F)
Arp.
Voce
Vla.
Vcl.
p espress.
klangvoll
mit verhaltener Stimme
hell auf-geh'n,
als sei kein Unglück, kein
con sord.
con sord.
sempre pp
10
Cl. (B)
Cl. b. (B)
Cor. (F)
Arp.
Voce
Vla.
Vcl.
molto espress.
Un-glück die Nacht ge-scheh'n!
sempre pp
15

Ob.
Cl. (B)
Cl. b. (B)
Cor. (F)
Arp.
Camp.
pp subito
p subito
ausdrucks-
20
Fl.
Ob.
Cl. (B)
Fg.
Cor. (F)
Voce
p espress.
a 2
Das Unglück ge-schah nur mir al-lein!
25
30

Ob.
1.
Cl. (B)
a 2
Cl. b. (B)
Cor. (F)
1.
Arp.
sempre marcato
p
Voce
pp
Die Son - ne, die Son-ne, sie schei - net all - ge-
Vl. II
con sord.
pp
Vla.
pp aber ausdrucksvoll
Vcl.
sempre con sord.
pp ohne Ausdruck
35

heftiger
sehr hervor-
Ob.
1.
Cl.
(B)
a 2
espress.
Cl. b.
(B)
Fg.
2.
sehr ausdrucksvoll
Cor.
(F)
p espress.
Arp.
Voce
mein!
Vl. II
Vla.
Vcl.
Cb.
40

Fl.
Ob.
Cl. (B)
Cl. b. (B)
Fg.
Cor. (F)
Camp.
Voce
tretend
45
Du
Arp.
Vl. I
Vcl.
mußt nicht die Nacht in dir ver - schränken, mußt sie ins ew' - ge
senza sord.
pp mit großem Ausdruck
senza sord.
pizz.
50

nicht schleppend
Cl. (B)
Fg.
pp
pp
f pp
Cor. (F)
pp
pp
Arp.
f
Voce
Licht, ins ew' - - - ge Licht ver - sen -
nicht schleppend
Vl. I
sf
Vcl.
p
Cb.
pizz.
(p)
55

Etwas bewegter (Rubato)
Mit leidenschaftlichem Ausdruck
Fl.
Ob.
Cl. (B)
Cl. b. (B)
Fg.
Cor. (F)
Arp.
Voce
ken!
Etwas bewegter (Rubato)
Mit leidenschaftlichem Ausdruck
Vl. I
Vl. II
con sord.
Vla.
arco
Vcl.
Cb.
60

zurückkehrend zum
a 2
1.
1. Solo
2.
Fl.
Ob.
Cl. b.
(B)
Fg.
Cor.
(F)
Arp.
Camp.
Voce
Ein
zurückkehrend zum
Vl. I
Vl. II
Vcl.
Cb.
dim.
65

Ob.
Cl. b. (B)
Fg.
a 2
cresc.
Cor. (F)
p espr.
Voce
Lämp-lein ver-losch- in mei-nem Zelt!
con sord.
Vl. I
70
Tempo I
Cl. b. (B)
Cor. (F)
Arp.
mit Erschütterung
Voce
Heil! Heil sei dem Freu-den-licht der Welt.
Tempo I
molto espr.
Vl. I
con sord.
Vl. II
Vla.
senza sord.
Vcl.
p espr.
arco
Cb.
75

Ob.
Cl. (B)
Cl. b. (B)
Fg.
Cor. (F)
Arp.
Camp.
Voce
dem Freu - den - licht — der Welt!
Vl. I
Vl. II
Vla.
Vcl.
pizz
Cb.
80

Nun will die Sonn' so hell aufgehn,
Als sei kein Unglück die Nacht geschehn!
Das Unglück geschah nur mir allein!
Die Sonne, sie scheinet allegemein!

Du musst nicht die Nacht in dir verschränken,

Musst sie ins ew'ge Licht versenken!
Ein Lämplein verlosch in meinem Zelt!
Heil sei dem Freudenlicht der Welt.

FRIEDRICH RÜCKERT

Now will the sun so brightly rise again,
as if no misfortune occurred during the night.
The misfortune happened to me alone.
The sun shines for everyone.

You must not become tangled up with the night in yourself,
You must be immersed in perennial light.
A little lamp went out in my tent.
Blessed be the joyous light of the world.

137

GIOACCHINO ROSSINI (1792–1868)
Il barbiere di Siviglia (1816): Act I, Scene 5, Cavatina, *Una voce poco fa*

First performance 20 February 1816. Reprinted from the piano-vocal score based on the critical edition of the orchestral score (1969) (Milan, Ricordi n.d.), pp. 102–109. Reprinted by permission.

ROSINA
U - na vo - ce po - co fa qui - nel cor mi - ri - suo - nò; il mio
[p]
18
R.
cor ___ fe - ri - to è già, e ___ Lin - dor ___ fu che il pia - gò. Sì, Lin -
R.
- do - ro ___ mio ___ sa - rà, lo - giu - ra - i, la ___ vin - ce -
sf
pp
25
R.
- rò; sì, Lin - do - ro ___ mio ___ sa - rà, lo giu - -
sf
pp

R.
f
-ra-i, la — vin - ce - rò.
Il Tu-tor ri-cu-se-
sottovoce
[PP]
pp
31
-rà,
io l'in-ge-gno aguz-ze-rò,
al-la fin s'acche-te-
-rà
e con-ten-ta io re-ste-rò. Sì, Lin-do - ro mio sa-
sf
36
-rà,
lo — giu - ra - i,
la — vin - ce - rò; sì, Lin-
pp

R.
-do - ro — mio — sa - rà, lo giu - ra-i, la vin-ce-rò.
sf
pp
sf
43
Moderato
pp dolce
49
ff
tr
tr
p
pp
f
ROSINA
Io so - no — do - ci-le, son — ri - spet -
pp
dolce

58
R.
-to - - sa, so - no ub - bi - dien - te,
61
dol - ce, a - mo - ro - - sa, mi la-scio reg - ge-re, mi la-scio
reg - ge-re, mi fo gui - dar, mi fo gui - dar. Ma se mi
67
f
[p]
toc - ca-no dov'è il mio de - bo-le, sarò u-na vi - pe - ra, sa -
-rò, e cen-to trap - po-le pri-ma di ce - de-re farò gio-

73
R.
car, fa - rò gio - car, e cen-to trap - po-le pri-ma di
R.
ce - de-re fa-rò gio - car, fa - rò gio - car, e cen-to
79
a piacere [a tempo]
R.
trap - po-le pri-ma di ce - de-re, e cen-to trappo- -le fa -
[a tempo]
col canto
R.
-rò, fa - rò gio - car. Io so-no
[P]
leggero

85
R.
do - ci-le, so-no ub-bi - dien-te, mi la-scio
rinf.
f
88
-reg - ge-re, mi fo gui - dar. Ma se mi toc - ca-no dov'è il mio
ff
sf
[p]
de - bo-le, sarò u-na vi - pe - ra, sa - rò, e cen-to
f
95
trap - po-le pri-ma di ce - de-re farò gio-car, fa - rò gio -
-car, e cen-to trap - po-le pri-ma di ce - de-re fa-rò gio-

101
R.
-car, fa - rò gio - car, e - cen-to trap - po-le pri-ma di -
a piacere a tempo
R.
ce - de-re, e cen-to trappo - le fa - rò, fa - rò gio -
a tempo
col canto
107
R.
-car, e cen to trap - po-le fa - rò gio - car, e cen - to
trap-po-le fa - rò gio - car, fa - rò gio - car, fa - rò gio -
113
R.
-car, fa - rò gio - car.

ROSINA

Una voce poco fa	A voice a short while ago
Qui nel cor mi risuonò.	here in my heart resounded.
Il mio cor ferito è già,	My heart is already wounded,
E Lindor fu che il piagò.	and Lindoro is the culprit.
Sì, Lindoro mio sarà,	Yes, Lindoro will be mine
Lo giurai la vincerò	I swore that I would win.
Il tutor ricuserò,	the guardian I shall refuse.
Io l'ingegno aguzzerò.	I shall sharpen my wits.
Alla fin s'accheterà,	In the end he will be appeased,
E contenta io resterò.	and I shall be happy.
Sì, Lindoro mio sarà . . .	Yes, Lindoro will be mine . . .
Io sono docile, son rispettosa,	I am docile, I am respectful,
Sono obbediente, dolce amorosa,	I am obedient, sweetly loving;
Mi lascio reggere, mi fo guidar.	I let myself be governed, to be led.
Ma se mi toccano dov'è il mio debole,	But if they touch my weaker side,
Sarò una vipera, e cento trappole	I can be a viper, and a hundred tricks,
Prima di cedere farò giocar!	I'll play before I give in!

Libretto by CESARE STERBINI
after BEAUMARCHAIS

Vincenzo Bellini (1801–35)

Norma (1831): Act I, Scene 4, Scena e Cavatina, *Casta diva*

First performance 26 December 1831. Reprinted from *Norma* (Milan, Ricordi 1974), pp. 61–84. Reprinted by permission.

NORMA
Ca - - - sta Di - - va, ca - sta Di - va, che i - nar-
19
N
-gen - ti que - - - ste sa - cre, que - ste
N
sa - cre, queste sa - cre an - tiche pian - te, a noi vol - gi il bel sem-
25
sempre cresc. sino al.....
N
-bian - te, a noi vol - gi, a noi vol - gi il bel sem - bian - - - - - -
f
sempre cresc. sino al..........

N
ff
- - - - - - te,il bel sem - bian - te sen - za nu - be e sen - za
dim.
smorz.
ff
30
vel,
OROVESO
Ca - - - sta Di - - -
Soprani
Ca - sta Di - va,che i - nar - gen - ti que - ste sa - cre anti - che
sottovoce
Tenori
Ca - sta Di - va,che i - nar - gen - ti que - ste sa - cre anti - che
Bassi
Ca - - - sta Di - - -
CORO
dolce espressivo e PP sempre

N
sen - - - - - za
O
va, a noi, deh,
pian - te, a noi vol - gi il bel sem - bian - te sen - za nu - be e sen - za
pian - te, a noi vol - gi il bel sem - bian - te sen - za nu - be e sen - za
va, a noi, deh,
34
N
vel, sì,
O
vol - - gi il bel sem - - -
vel. Ca - sta Di - va, che i - nar - gen - ti que - ste sa - cre an - ti - che
vel. Ca - sta Di - va, che i - nar - gen - ti que - ste sa - cre an - ti - che
vol - - - gi il bel sem - - -

N
sen
O
bian te
pian te, a noi vol gi il bel sem
pian te, a noi vol gi il bel sem
bian te
37
N
za
O
sen za
bian te sen za nu be e sen za
bian te sen za nu be e sen za
sen za

N
vel.
O
vel, e sen - za vel.
vel, e sen - - za — vel.
vel, e sen - - za vel.
vel, e sen - za vel.
pp
41
N
Tem - - pra, o Di - va, tem - pra tu de' — co - ri ar -
N
- den - ti, tem - - pra anco - ra, tem - pra an -

47
N
-co - ra, tem - pra ancor lo ze - lo au - da - ce, spar - gi in
O
Di - -
Soprani
Di - -
Tenori
Di - -
Bassi
Di - - -
C O R O
ter - ra, ah, quel - la pa - ce, spar - gi in
-va, spar - - gi in
-va, spar - - gi in
-va, spar - - gi in
-va, spar - - gi in

51
N
O
sempre cresc: al
ter - ra, spar - gi in ter - ra quella pa - - - - - -
ter - - - ra quel - la pa - ce
f
ff
sempre cresc. al
- - - - ce che re - gnar, re - gnar tu fai, tu fai nel
che re - - - gnar tu fai nel
p
pp
dim.
smorz.

55
a piacere
N
ciel, tu fa - - - - - - - i
O
ciel, tu fa - - i
ciel, tu fa - - i
ciel, tu fa - - i
ciel, tu fa - - i
N
nel ciel.
O
nel ciel.
nel ciel.
nel ciel.
nel ciel

61 Allegro
41
(BANDA) f
NORMA
69
All.º assai maestoso
Fi - ne al ri - to; e il sa_cro
All. assai maestoso
ff
42
(ORCHESTRA)
p e marcate
N
bo - sco sia di_sgom_bro dai pro - fa - ni.
ff
76
Quan_do il Nu - me, quando il Nu - me i - ra - to e

N
fo - sco chiegga il san - gue dei Ro - ma - ni, dal dru -
p
82
N
- i - di - co de - lu - bro - la - mia - vo - - ce
f
N
tuo - - ne - rà.
OROVESO
Tuo - ni; e un sol del po - pol
Soprani
Tuo - ni; e un sol del po - pol
Tenori
Tuo - ni; e un sol del po - pol
Bassi
Tuo - ni; e un sol del po - pol
CORO

88
O
em - pio non i - sfug - ga al giu - sto scem - pio; e pri -
em - pio non i - sfug - ga al giu - sto scem - pio; e pri -
em - pio non i - sfug - ga al giu - sto scem - pio; e pri -
em - pio non i - sfug - ga al giu - sto scem - pio; e pri -
f
p cresc.
NORMA
Ca -
O
- mier da noi per - cos - so il Pro - con - so - le ca -
- mier da noi per - cos - so il Pro - con - so - le ca -
- mier da noi per - cos - so il Pro - con - so - le ca -
- mier da noi per - cos - so il Pro - con - so le ca -
ff

94
Poco più lento
N
-drà... punirlo io pos-so... (Ma pu-nir-lo il
O
-drà.
-drà.
-drà.
-drà.
Poco più lento
col canto
ppp
N
cor non sa.)
Opp.
Allegro
Allegro
vibrato
mf
102
ff

NORMA
109
(Ah! bel - lo a me ri - tor - na del
p
fi - do a mor pri - mie - ro: e con - tro il mon - do in -
115
- tie - ro di - fe - sa a te sa - rò. Ah!
f
bel - lo a me ri - tor - na del

120
N
con forza
rag - gio tuo — se - re - no; e vi - ta — nel tuo
Opp.
se - no — e — pa - - - - - -
con abbandono
N
se - no e pa - - - - - - tria e cie - lo a -
pp
Opp.
- vrò, — e
126
N
- vrò, — e cie - - - - - - lo a -

Mosso
N
vrò.)
OROVESO
Sei len - to, sì, sei len - - to, o
Sop.
Sei len - to, sì, sei len - - to, o
Ten.
Sei len - to, sì, sei len - - to, o
Bassi
Sei len - to, sì, sei len - - to, o
CORO
Mosso
p
133
O
gior - no di ven - det - ta; ma i - ra - to il Dio t'af -
gior - no di ven - det - ta; ma i - ra - to il Dio t'af -
gior - no di ven - det - ta; ma i - ra - to il Dio t'af -
gior - no di ven - det - ta; ma i - ra - to il Dio t'af -
f

130
fret - ta che il Te - bro con - dan - nò, ma i -
fret - ta che il Te - bro con - dan - nò, ma i -
fret - ta che il Te - bro con - dan - nò, ma i -
fret - ta che il Te - bro con - dan - nò, ma i -
ff
NORMA
139
Lento stent.
(Ah! Ah!
- ra - to il Dio t'af - fret - ta che il Te - bro con - dan - nò.
- ra - to il Dio t'af - fret - ta che il Te - bro con - dan - nò.
- ra - to il Dio t'af - fret - ta che il Te - bro con - dan - nò.
- ra - to il Dio t'af - fret - ta che il Te - bro con - dan - nò.

I. Tempo
N
bel - lo a me ri - tor - na del fi - do a-mor pri -
45
I. Tempo
p
146
- mie - ro, e con - tro il mon - do in - tie - ro di -
- fe - sa a te sa - - rò. Ah!
f
151
bel - lo a me ri - tor - - na del

N
con forza
rag - gio tuo___ se - re - no; e vi - ta___ nel tuo
Opp.
se - no___ e___ pa - - -
156
con abbandono
N
se - no e pa - - - tria e cie - lo a.
pp
Opp.
_vrò,___ e
N
_vrò,___ e cie - - - - - lo a.

162
Mosso
N
-vrò.)
OROVESO
Ma i - ra - to, sì, il Dio t'af -
Soprani
Ma i - ra - to, sì, il Dio t'af -
Tenori
Ma i - ra - to, sì, il Dio t'af -
Bassi
Ma i - ra - to, sì, il Dio t'af -
CORO
Mosso
f
O
-fret - ta che il Te - bro con - dan -
-fret - ta che il Te - bro con - dan -
-fret - ta che il Te - bro con - dan -
-fret - ta che il Te - bro con - dan -

166
N
(Ah! rie_di an_co_ra qual e_ri al_lo_ra, quan - do, ah,
O
_nò.
_nò.
_nò.
_nò.
pp
N
quan - do il cor ti die - - -
171
N
- - - - - - - - - - - - - di al -
ff

N
-lo - ra, qual e - ri al - lor, ah! riedi an - co - ra qual e - ri al -
O
O gior - no!
Soprani
O gior - no!
Tenori
O gior - no!
Bassi
O gior - no!
CORO
ff
pp
176
-lo - ra, quan - do, ah, quan - do il cor ti die - - - -
- - - - - - - - - - - - di al -
ff

181 Più mosso
N
-lo - ra, qual e - ri al lo - ra, ah, quan do, ah, quan do il cor ti die - di, ah,
O
O gior - no, il Dio t'af - fret - ta
Sop.
O gior - no, il Dio t'af - fret - ta
Ten.
O gior - no, il Dio t'af - fret - ta
Bassi
O gior - no, il Dio t'af - fret - ta
CORO
48 Più mosso
ff
rie - di, ah, rie - - - di a me.)
che il Te - bro con - dan - nò.
che il Te - bro con - dan - nò.
che il Te - bro con - dan - nò.
che il Te - bro con - dan - nò.

Casta Diva, che inargenti
Queste sacre antiche piante,
A noi volgi il bel sembiante;
Senza nube e senza vel!

Tempra, o Diva, tu de' cori ardenti,
Tempra ancora lo zelo audace,
Spargi in terra, ah, quella pace,
Che regnar tu fai nel ciel.

Fine al rito; e il sacro bosco
Sia disgombro dai profani.
Quando il Nume irato e fosco,
Chiegga il sangue dei Romani,
Dal Druidico delubro
La mia voce tuonerà.

Tuoni; e un sol del popol empio

Non isfugga algiusto scempio;
E primier da noi percosso
Il Proconsole cadrà,

Cadrà . . . punirlo io posso . . .
(Ma punirlo il cor non sa.)

(Ah! bello a me ritorna
Del fido amor primiero:
E contro il mondo intiero
Difesa a te sarò.
Ah! bello a me ritorna
Del raggio tuo sereno;
E vita nel tuo seno
E patria e cielo avrò).

Sei lento, si, sei lento,
O giorno di vendetta;
Ma irato il Dio t'affretta
Che il Tebro condannò.

(Ah! bello) . . .

Sei lento . . .

(Ah! riedi ancora
Qual eri allora
Quando, ah, quando il cor
Ti diedi allora).

Libretto by FELICE ROMANI

NORMA
Chaste Goddess, who plates with silver
these sacred ancient plants,
turn your lovely face towards us,
unclouded and unveiled.

Temper, o, Goddess, these ardent hearts,
o temper their bold zeal.
Spread over the earth that peace
that you make reign in heaven.

The rites are finished, and the sacred wood,
be it cleared of intruders.
When the angry and gloomy god
demands the blood of the Romans,
from the Druidic shrine
my voice will resound.

TUTTI
Let it be heard, and let not a single one of the impious race
escape our just massacre,
and the first to feel our blows,
the Proconsul will fall.

NORMA
He will fall . . . punish him I can . . .
(But to punish him my heart does not know how.)

(Ah, return to me, love,
my faithful first love,
and, against the entire world
I shall be your defense.
Ah, return to me, love,
the serene radiance of your gaze;
and living in your bosom
both homeland and heaven I'll possess).

CHORUS
How it drags on, sluggishly,
this day of revenge;
but the angry God hurries you
whom the Tiber condemned.

NORMA
(Ah, return) . . .

CHORUS
How it drags . . .

NORMA
(Ah, return again
to what you were then
when, oh, when my heart
I gave to you).

139

Giacomo Meyerbeer (1791–1864)

Les Huguenots (1835–36): Act II, Scenes 7 and 8

First performance 29 February 1836. The division into scenes, not found in the score, is taken from Scribe's libretto. Reprinted from *Les Huguenots* (Paris: Ph. Maquet & Cie., n.d.), pp. 172–210.

23.
MARGUERITE
Oui, d'un heu_reux hymen pré_pa_ré par mes soins J'ai dé_si_
dolce
31
M.
_ré, Mes_sieurs, que vous fussiez té _ moins.
(La reine présente Raoul aux comtes de Saint-Bris et de Nevers, qui lui tendent la main.)
Sop.
Hon_neur, hon_neur à la plus bel _ le, honneur! Hâ_
Tén.
Hon_neur, hon_neur à la plus bel _ le, honneur! Hâ_
Basses
Hon_neur, hon_neur à la plus bel _ le, honneur! Hâ_

_tons - nous d'ac _ cou_ rir, hâtons - nous d'ac _ cou _ rir; C'est vo _
_tons - nous d'ac _ cou_ rir, hâtons - nous d'ac _ cou_ rir; C'est vo _
_tons - nous d'ac _ cou_ rir, hâtons - nous d'ac _ cou_ rir; C'est vo _
_ler au plai _ sir, c'est vo _ ler au plai _
_ler au plai _ sir, c'est vo _ ler au plai _
_ler au plai _ sir, c'est vo _ ler au plai _
44
_sir, c'est vo _ ler au plai _ sir!
_sir, c'est vo _ ler au plai _ sir!
_sir, c'est vo _ ler au plai _ sir!

Allegro con moto (♩=138)
MARCEL, arrivant tout agité, à Raoul qu'il prend à part.)
(Raoul lui fait signe de se taire)
(Il parle bas à Raoul, mais avec indignation.)
Récit
ff
Ah! qu'est-ce que j'ap_prends!
Vous a_vez recherché la main d'u_
Allegro con moto
mf
Récit
p
52
Mel
RAOUL
MARCEL
_ne Ma_di_a_ni_te! Tais-toi!
Sa mai_son est cel_le du pé_
f
p
RAOUL
MARG.
(à Saint-Bris et à Nevers, après avoir lu des papiers qu'un courrier lui a remis)
_ché. Tais-toi!
Mon frè_re Charles IX, qui connaît vo_tre
f
ff
fp
59
M.
zè_le, Tous les deux à Paris, dès ce soir, vous rap_pel_le, Pour un vas_te projet que j'i_

NEVERS
S.t BRIS
MARG.
_gno _ re. A sa loi Nous nous sou_met_tons. Oui, mais d'a_bord à la
p
65
M.
mien_ne: Grâce à cet hy_men abjurant tou_te bai_ne, Pro_non_cez
And^no con moto (♩=66)
doux
tr
And^no. con moto
donc tous trois, comme aux pieds de l'autel, D'une é_ter_nel_le
73
paix, pro_non_cez le ser_ment, le serment so_len_
Récit (aux gentilshommes protestants et catholiques) Molto moderato
_ nel! Et vous aus_si, mes_sieurs, qu'un seul vœu vous en_chaî_ne! (Tous entourent la reine pour prêter le serment)
Molto moderato
f
Récit

Maestoso (♩. = 54)
79
pp
Marquez chacune de ces 6 notes, mais sans forcer.
(étendant la main)
RAOUL
pp
ff
Par_l'honneur,_ par_le nom que portaient mes an_cê_tres, Nous ju_
NEVERS
pp
ff
St. BRIS
Par_l'honneur,_ par_le nom que portaient mes an_cê_tres, Nous ju_
MARCEL (à part)
pp
ff
Par_Lu_ther,_ par_la foi que je tiens de mes maîtres, Ah! ju_
Ténors
ff
Nous ju_
CHŒUR DES SEIGNEURS
Basses
ff
Nous ju_
ff
12

(étendant la main)
R.
-rons, Par-le roi, par-ce fer- à mon bras con-fi-é,- Nous- ju-
N. S.B.
-rons, Par-le roi, par-ce fer- à mon bras con-fi-é,- Nous- ju-
M.
-rons, Par-la croix, par-ce fer- à mon bras con-fi-é,- Ah!- ju-
-rons, Nous ju-
-rons, Nous- ju-
12
(étendant la main)
R.
-rons, Par-le Dieu- qui con-naît, qui punit tous les traî-tres, Nous- ju-
N. S.B.
-rons, Par-le Dieu- qui con-naît, qui punit tous les traî-tres, Nous- ju-
M.
-rons, Guer-re à mort,- Ro-me, à toi, tes soldats et tes prê-tres, Oui,- ju-
-rons, Nous- ju-
-rons, Nous- ju-
12

95
pp
R.
_rons,__ De_vant vous__ nous_ju_rons__ é_ter_nel _ le a_mi_
N.
S.t B.
_rons,__ De_vant vous__ nous_ju_rons__ é_ter_nel _ le a_mi_
M.
_rons,__ Et_ja_mais__ en_tre nous__ a_mi_tié ni_pi_
rons,
rons,
p
crescendo
_tié! Par_l'honneur et_le nom que_por_
cresc.
_tié! Par l'honneur et le nom que portaient
_tié! Par_l'honneur et_le nom que_por_
_tié! Par_Lu_ther, par_le Dieu que_je
1.rs Ténors
Par_l'honneur et_le nom que_por_
2.ds Ténors
Par l'honneur et le nom que portaient
Basses
Par_l'honneur et_le nom que_por_
p ma marcato
pp
crescendo

102
peu - - - - à - - peu jusqu'au - - -
R.
_taient mes _ a_ïeux, Par _ le Dieu qui _ pu_
N.
_ mes aïeux, Par le Dieu qui punit
S.t B.
_taient mes _ a_ïeux, Par _ le Dieu qui _ pu_
M.
sers, par _ la croix, Par _ ce fer à _ mon
_taient mes _ a_ïeux, Par _ le Dieu qui _ pu_
_ mes aïeux, Par le Dieu qui punit
_taient mes _ a_ïeux, Par _ le Dieu qui _ pu_
peu - - - - à - - - peu jusqu'au - - - -
ff
R.
_nit tous _ les traî _ tres, Nous _ ju_rons de _ vant
N.
_ tous les traî - - - - tres, Nous _ ju_rons de _ vant
S.t B.
_nit tous _ les traî _ tres, Nous _ ju_rons de _ vant
M.
bras con _ fi _ é, Ah! _ ju_rons, et ja_
_nit tous _ les traî _ tres, Nous _ ju_rons de _ vant
_ tous les traî - - - tres, Nous _ ju_rons de _ vant
_nit tous _ les traî _ tres, Nous _ ju_rons de _ vant

108
détaché et marqué
R.
vous éternelle a_mitié, devant vous nous jurons é_ternelle ami _ tié !
ff
N.
vous éternelle a_mitié, devant vous nous jurons é_ternelle ami _ tié !
ff
St. B.
vous éternelle a_mitié, devant vous nous jurons é_ternelle ami _ tié !
ff
M.
mais entre nous a_mitié ni pi _ tié, non, jamais ami_tié ni pi _ tié !
1rs et 2ds Ténors
ff Unisson
vous éternelle a_mitié, devant vous nous jurons é_ternelle ami _ tié !
CHOEUR
Basses
ff
vous éternelle a_mitié, devant vous nous jurons é_ternelle ami _ tié !
ff détachez et marquez chaque note
rallentando
più rallent.
pp
Andante (♩.=42) très doux et lié
R.
fp
Pro _ vi _ den _ ce, mè _ re ten _ dre, Sur _ la ter _ re fais _ des_
N.
fp
Pro _ vi _ den _ ce, mè _ re ten _ dre, Sur _ la ter _ re fais des_
St. B.
fp
Pro _ vi _ den _ ce, mè _ re ten _ dre, Sur _ la ter _ re fais des_
M.
fp
Pro _ vi _ den _ ce, mère ten _ _ dre, Sur mon maî _ tre, mon
Andante

116
R.
N.
S.B.
M.
fp
p
pp
crescendo
cresc.
_cen _ dre La_con_cor _ de, pour_nous ren _ dre Tous_des frè _ res, tous_a_
_cen _ dre__ La con_cor _ de, pour nous ren _ dre Tous des frè _ res, tous a_
_cen _ dre__ La_con_cor_ de, pour_nous ren_ dre Tous des frè _ res, tous a_
maî _ tre fais des_cen _ dre Ta lu_miè_re, pour le rendre__ A ses frè_res, à tes
_mis, tous des frè _ res, tous des frè _ res, tous des
_mis, tous des frè _ res, tous des frè _ res, tous des
_mis, tous des frè _ res, tous des frè _ res, tous des
fils! Jus _ te ciel! jus _ te ciel!

rallentando
123
R.
frè - res, tous a - mis, oui, tous des frè - res, tous a -
N.
frè - res, tous a - mis, oui, tous des frè - res, tous a -
St B.
frè - res, tous a - mis, oui, tous des frè - res, tous a -
cresc.
M.
Fais descen - dre ta lu - miè - re, Pour le ren - dre à tes
a tempo
MARGUERITE
Que le ciel daigne en - tendre et bénir à jamais ces ser - ments, ces ser -
LE PAGE
UNE DAME D'HONNEUR
Ciel, daigne en -
R.
- mis! Nous le ju -
N.
- mis! Nous le ju -
St B.
- mis! Ah!
M.
fils! Guer - re,
Soprani
CHŒUR
Dieu, bé - nis
Ténors et Basses
Nous le ju -
a tempo
Ped.
Ped.

129
M.
ments !
P. D. d'H.
ten dre,
R.
rons, oui,
N.
rons, oui,
S^t B.
Nous jurons devant vous a_mitié pour tou_jours !
M.
guerre à mort et ja_mais a_mi_tié ni pi tié !
sez
rons !
fp
rallentando
M.
Ah ! dai gue en
P. D. d'H.
bé nis ces ser
R.
p
de vant vous ju
N.
p
de vant vous ju
(avec vigueur)
S^t B.
p
Oui, oui, nous ju rons à ja
M.
p
Oui, oui, nous ju rons à ja
p
rallentando

cadenza a piacere
molto cresc.
134
M.
_ten _ _ dre ces ser _ ments !
P. D. d'H.
_ments, ces ser _ ments !
R.
_rons a _ mi _ tié !
N.
_ rons a _ mi _ tié !
(St. BRIS sort)
St. B.
_mais a _ mi _ tié !
M.
_ mais guerre à mort !
CHŒUR
ces ser _ ments !
Ah ! nous ju _ rons !
ff
fp
pp
(Timbales)
pp
142
ff
Ped.

Récitatif
MARGUERITE
Et mainte_nant je dois offrir à vo_tre vu_e Votre charman_te pré_ten-
Récitatif
f fp
147
M.
(St BRIS reparaît, conduisant Valentine vers Raoul)
_du_e, Qui ren_dra vos serments fa_ci_les à te_nir!
p
f
RAOUL All°. moderato (𝅗𝅥=84)
(d'une voix étouffée)
p
Ah! grand Dieu! qu'ai-je vu?
MARGUERITE
Qu'avez-
All°. moderato
pp staccatissimo
pp
157
M.
p RAOUL (pouvant à peine parler)
vous? Quoi!.. c'est el_le! el_le... que m'of_fraient en ce

163
MARGUERITE
RAOUL
R.
jour... Et l'hy_men et l'a_mour! Trahi_son! Perfi_
ff
VALENTINE, MARGUERITE et URBAIN
(long silence)
Ciel!
_di _ e! Moi, son é_poux? jamais! ja_mais!
NEVERS
Ciel!
St. BRIS
Ciel!
Soprani
Ciel!
Ténors
Ciel!
Basses
Ciel!
CHŒUR
(long silence)
p
Ped.

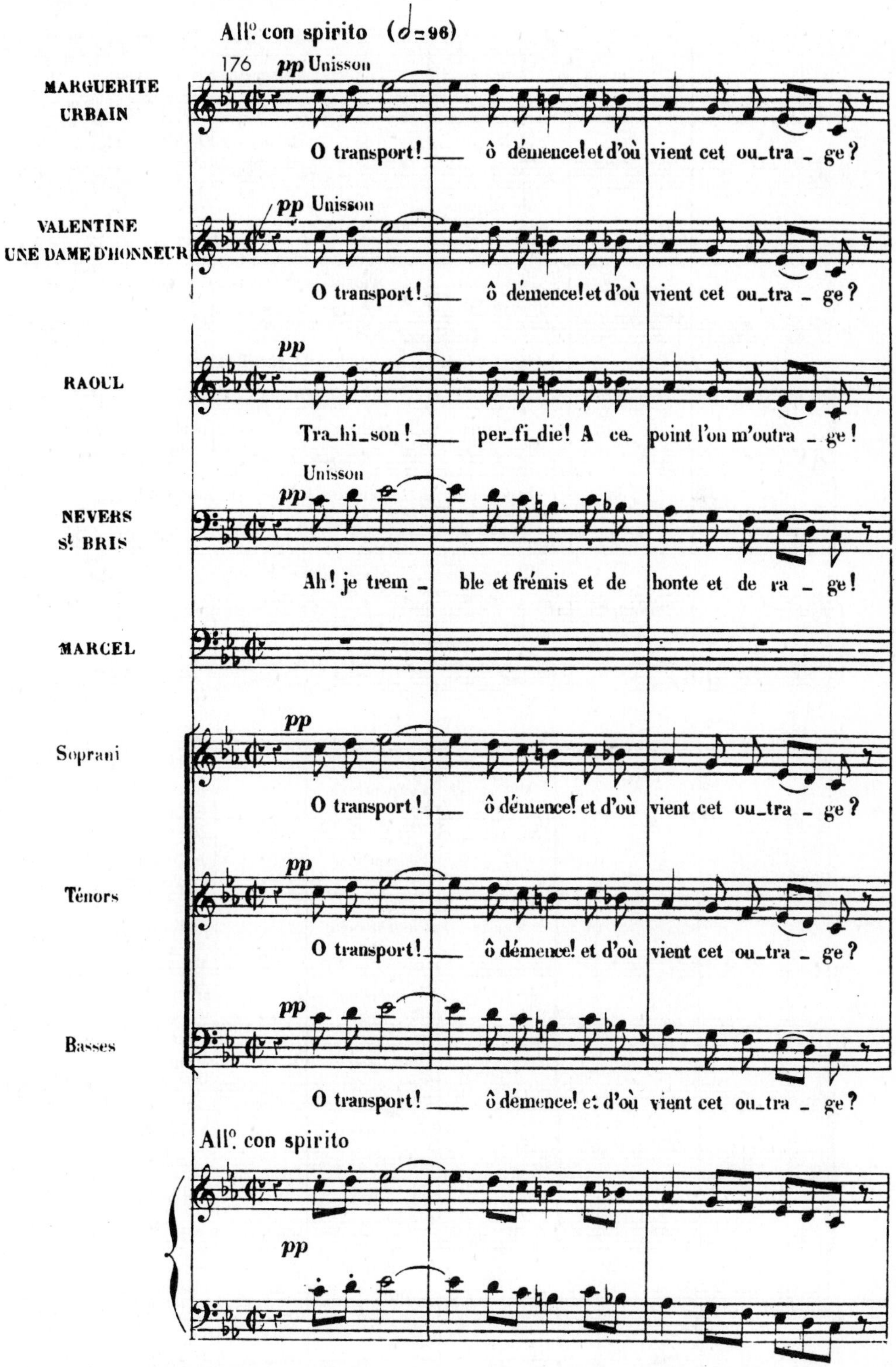
All.° con spirito (𝅗𝅥=96)
176
pp Unisson
MARGUERITE
URBAIN
O transport! ô démence! et d'où vient cet ou_tra _ ge?
pp Unisson
VALENTINE
UNE DAME D'HONNEUR
O transport! ô démence! et d'où vient cet ou_tra _ ge?
pp
RAOUL
Tra_hi_son! per_fi_die! A ce point l'on m'outra _ ge!
Unisson
pp
NEVERS
S.t BRIS
Ah! je trem _ ble et frémis et de honte et de ra _ ge!
MARCEL
pp
Soprani
O transport! ô démence! et d'où vient cet ou_tra _ ge?
pp
Ténors
O transport! ô démence! et d'où vient cet ou_tra _ ge?
pp
Basses
O transport! ô démence! et d'où vient cet ou_tra _ ge?
All.° con spirito
pp

M. U.
A bri_ser de tels nœuds quel dé_ li _ re l'en_ga _ ge?
V. D. d'H.
A bri_ser de tels nœuds quel dé_ li _ re l'en_ga _ ge?
R.
Je re_pous _ se à jamais un hon_ teux ma_ri_a _ ge!
N. S.t B.
C'est à moi d'im_mo_ler l'en_ne_ mi qui m'outra _ ge!
M.
Oui, mon cœur ap_plau_dit, cher Ra_ oul, ton cou_ra _ ge!
Et pourquoi rompre ainsi le ser_ ment qui l'en_ga _ ge?
Et pourquoi rompre ainsi le ser_ ment qui l'en_ga _ ge?
Et pourquoi rompre ainsi le ser_ ment qui l'en_ga _ ge?
pp
184
D'un penchant in_connu
D'un penchant in_connu
Plus d'hymen, je l'ai dit;
C'est son sang qu'il me faut
Che_va_lier et chrétien,
Cet af_front veut du sang;
Cet af_front veut du sang;
Cet af_front veut du sang;
p

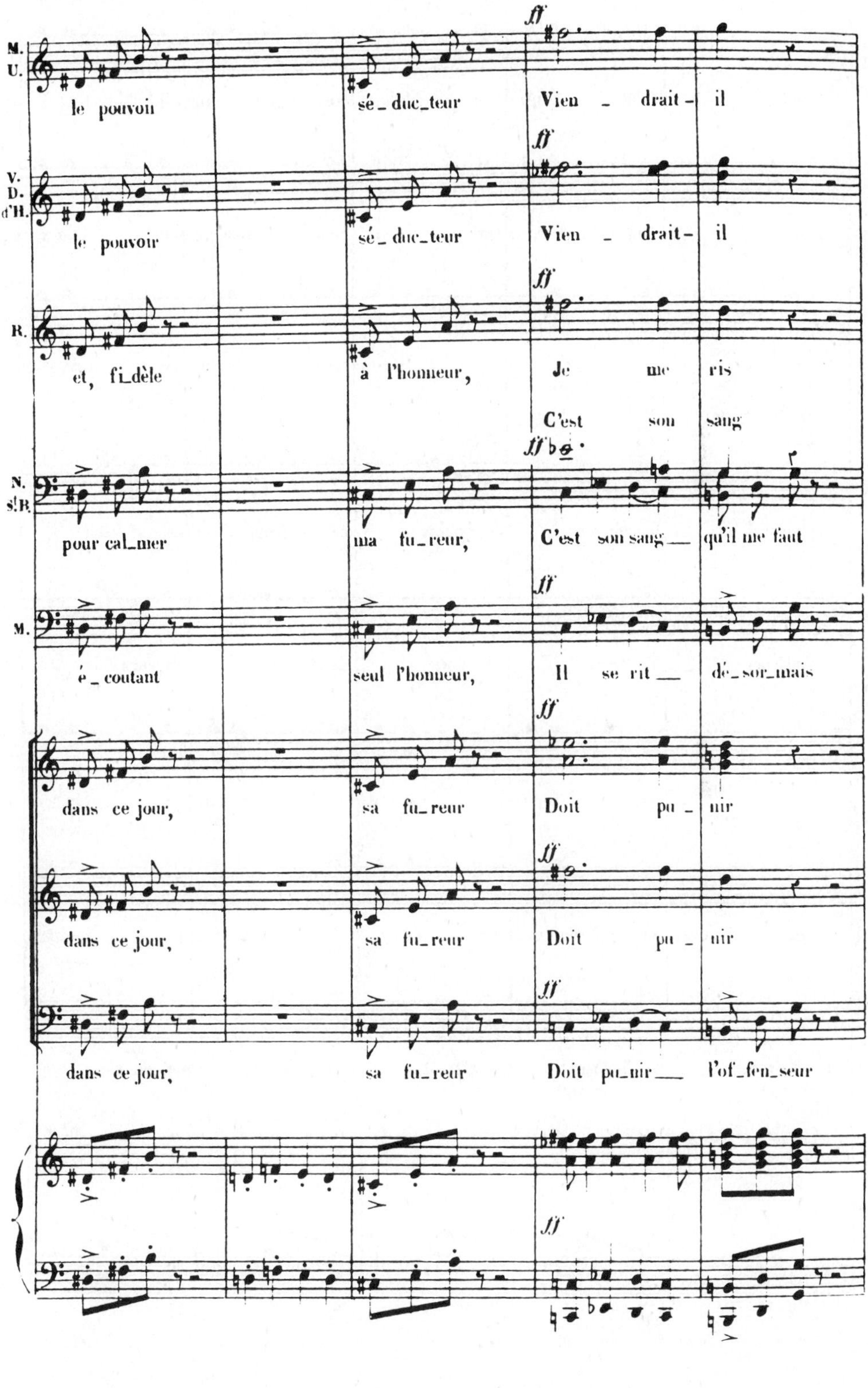
M. U.
le pouvoir sé_duc_teur Vien - drait - il
ff
V. D. d'H.
le pouvoir sé_duc_teur Vien - drait - il
ff
R.
et, fi_dèle à l'honneur, Je me ris
C'est son sang
ff
N. St B.
pour cal_mer ma fu_reur, C'est son sang qu'il me faut
ff
M.
é_coutant seul l'honneur, Il se rit dé_sor_mais
ff
dans ce jour, sa fu_reur Doit pu - nir
ff
dans ce jour, sa fu_reur Doit pu - nir
ff
dans ce jour, sa fu_reur Doit pu_nir l'of_fen_seur
ff

197
M.
U.
tout à coup s'empa_ rer de son cœur, viendrait_il tout à
V.
D.
d'H.
tout à coup s'empa_ rer de son cœur, viendrait_il tout à
R.
dé _ sor_ mais deleurs cris de fu_ reur, Je me ris dé_sor_
qu'il me faut
N.
S!B.
pour cal_mer_ ma fu_reur, Pour punir cet af_front, cet af_front
M.
de leurs cris de fu_reur, Il se rit dé_sormais de leurs cris,
ce cru_ el, doit pu_ nir ce cru_ el et ven_ ger son hon_
ce cru_ el, doit pu_ nir ce cru_ el et ven_ ger son hon_
et ven_ger son honneur! Cet affront veut du sang, veut du sang,

M.
U.
coup s'em_pa_rer, s'em_pa_rer
de son cœur?
V.
D.
d'Il.
coup s'em_pa_rer, s'em_pa_rer
de son cœur?
R.
_mais de leurs cris, de leurs cris
de fu_reur!
N.
St B.
oui, pour ven_ger, pour ven_ger
mon honneur!
M.
oui, il se rit de leurs cris
de fu_reur!
_neur, doit pu_nir et ven_ger
son honneur!
_neur, doit pu_nir et ven_ger
son honneur!
il doit pu_nir et ven_ger
son honneur!
207
dim.
p

VALENTINE (avec une expression douloureuse)
Et comment ai-je donc mé-ri-
214
V.
-té tant d'ou-tra-ge? Dans mon cœur é-per-
RAOUL
O dou-leur! tris-te
NEVERS et S! BRIS.
Unisson
Fré-missant
V.
-du s'est gla-cé mon cou-ra-ge!
R.
sort! A ce point l'on m'ou-tra-ge!
N. S! B.
et tremblant, Plein de hon-te et de ra-ge,

MAUR. et URBAIN Unis. cresc.
D'un pen_chant in - con_nu le pou_
VAL. et DAME cresc.
D'un pen_chant in - con_nu le pou_
R.
Plus d'hymen, plus d'hymen,
N. St B. cresc.
C'est son sang qu'il me faut pour calmer
MARCEL cresc.
Oui, mon cœur ap - plaudit au coura - ge
Sop. 4 CORYPHÉES cresc.
Cet af_front veut du sang; dans ce
Tén.
CHŒUR
Bses 4 CORYPHÉES cresc.
Cet affront veut du sang; dans ce jour,
f
223
M. U. ff mf
_voir sé_duc_teur Vien - drait - il tout à
V. D. ff mf
_voir sé_duc_teur Vien - drait - il tout à
R. ff
je l'ai dit! Je me ris
N. St B. ff
ma fu_reur, pour pu_nir
M. ff
de Ra_oul; il re_pousse
jour, sa fu_reur
ff 4 CORYPHÉES
(Tous) O trans_port! Doit pu_nir l'of - fen_
ff 4 CORYPHÉES
Sa fu_reur Doit pu_nir
ff (Tous)
sa fu_reur
ff

M. U.
coup s'em - pa rer de son cœur? O transport! ô dé
V. D.
coup s'em - pa rer de son cœur? O transport! ô dé
R.
dé - sormais de leur fu - reur! Tra - hi son! Per-fi-die! à ce
N. St. B.
son affront, son af - front! Ah! je trem-ble, je tremble et fré
M.
à jamais cet hy - men! Oui, mon cœur applaudit, applau
et venger so hon - neur!
2 CORYPH.
-seur (Tous) O fu - reur! O fu-reur! et d'où
2 CORYPH.
l'of - fenseur. (Tous) O fu - reur! O fu-reur! et d'où
2 CORYPH.
(Tous) O fu - reur! O fu-reur, démence! et d'où
230
-mence! et d'où vient - cet ou - tra - ge? D'un
-mence! et d'où vient - cet ou - tra - ge? D'un
point, à ce point - l'on m'ou - tra - ge? Plus
-mis - et de honte - et de ra - ge! C'est
-dit - à son no - ble cou - ra - ge! Che
vient, et d'où vient - cet ou - tra - ge? (Tous) Cet
vient, et d'où vient - cet ou - tra - ge? (Tous) Cet
vient, et d'où vient - cet ou - tra - ge? (Tous) Cet
stacc.

M. U.
penchant in - con_nu le pouvoir sé - ducteur Vien - drait-il tout à
V. D.
penchant in - con_nu le pouvoir sé - ducteur Vien - drait-il tout à
R.
d'hymeu, je l'ai dit, et, fi_dèle à l'honneur, Je me ris, je me
N. S.B.
à moi d'im - mo_ler l'en - ne_mi! C'est son sang qu'il me faut, Pour pu_
M.
va_lier et chrétien, é - coutant seul l'honneur, Il se rit de leur
CHOEUR
af_front veut du sang; dans ce jour sa fu_reur Doit pu_nir, doit pu_
238
coup s'empa_rer de son cœur, s'em - pa - rer de son cœur?
ris désormais de leur vai - ne fu - reur!
nir son affront et ven - ger mon hon - neur!
(a part dans une effusion de joie)
vai_ne fureur! Sei -
nir l'offenseur et ven_ger et ven_ger son hon_neur!

MARGUERITE
Un semblable re_fus...
RAOUL
N'est que trop légi_ti_me!
M.
_gneur, rem_part_ et seul_sou_tien du
ff
marquez bien
p
f
f
248
MARGUERITE
Dites-m'en la rai_
M.
fai _ ble qui _ t'a _ do _ _ re!
p
Mte
_son.
O trans_
RAOUL
(avec force)
Je ne le puis sans cri_me; mais cet hymen, jamais!
p

257
M.
R.
-port! ô dé-men-ce! et pour-quoi cet ou-tra-ge? A bri-ser de tels nœuds quel dé-li-re l'en-ga-ge?
O douleur! tris-te sort! A ce point l'on m'ou-tra-ge!
St. BRIS.
Fré-missant et tremblant et de hon-te et de ra-ge,
p
263
NEVERS et St. BRIS (à Raoul)
Unisson
Sor-tons! Qu'il tombe sous nos
St.B.

RAOUL
D'un tel hon_neur mon cœur est plus ja_loux!
MARGUERITE
Arrê_tez!..
N. S.t B.
coups!
CHŒUR
Cet af _ front veut du sang!
Cet af _ front veut du sang!
Cet af _ front veut du sang!
f
mezza voce
270
(faisant signe a un officier de désarmer Raoul)
M.
Devant moi quelle in_sul _ te nou_vel _ le!.. Vous, Ra_
M.
_oul, votre é _ pée!
(à St Bris)
Et vous, oubliez-vous Qu'à l'ins_
cresc.

276
RAOUL
MARG.
tant près de lui votre roi vous rappel - le?
Je les suivrai!
Non pas; près de
M.
moi dans ces lieux Vous res - tez!
Temé
St BRIS.
Le lâche est trop heureux Que cette main roy - ale ait un tel privi -
f
284
M.
- rai - re!
RAOUL (d'une voix suffoquée, à St Bris)
p
C'est vous qu'elle pro - tè - ge en désar - mant mon
p
St B.
- lège!
C'est en vain
qu'on prétend
enchaîner
dim.
dolce
p

MARG. et URB. Unisson
M.
cresc.
ff
Témé_rai _ re! Tous les deux ___ redou_tez ___ ma co_lè _ re! O trans
VALENTINE
VAL. et DAME ff Unisson
p
cresc.
Mais comment ai-je donc méri_té cet affront! O trans_
R.
p
cresc.
ff
bras, ___ Et bientôt je serai près de vous, près de vous! C'est en
S.t B.
NEVERS et S.t BRIS
C'est en
p
cresc.
ff
mon coura_ge; Je saurai retrouver l'ennemi, l'offenseur!
MARCEL
cresc.
Oui! ___ mon cœur, ___ mon
ff
C'est en
CHŒUR
ff
C'est en
cresc.
ff

294
M. V.
-port! ô dé mence! et pourquoi cet ou tra ge? A bri ser de tels
Unisson
V. D.
-port! ô dé mence! et pourquoi cet ou tra ge? A bri ser de tels
Unisson
R.
vain qu'on prétend enchaîner mon cou ra ge; Je sau rai retrou
vain qu'on prétend enchaîner mon cou ra ge; Je sau rai retrou
N. S.t B.
O dé men ce! D'où
M.
cœur ap plau dit Ra oul de
vain qu'on prétend enchaîner son cou ra ge; Il sau ra retrou
Unisson
vain qu'on prétend enchaîner son cou ra ge; Il sau ra retrou
ff
O dé men ce! D'où

M. U.
nœuds — quel dé - li - re - l'en - ga - ge? qui l'en - ga - - - -
V. D.
nœuds — quel dé - li - re - l'en - ga - ge? qui l'en - ga - - - -
R.
- ver — l'enne - mi — qui m'ou - tra - ge, qui m'outra - - -
- ver — l'enne - mi qui m'ou - tra - ge!
Unisson
N. St B.
vient cet ou - tra - ge? Ah! par - tons, é -
M.
son no - ble cou - ra - ge! Ah! par - tons, é -
CORYPHÉE
- ver — l'enne - mi — qui l'ou - tra - ge! Ah! partons, —
- ver — l'enne - mi — qui l'ou - tra - ge! Ah! par - - -
vient cet ou - tra - ge? Ah! partons, par - tons, é -

304
U.
ge? O triste sort! O triste sort! D'un penchant incon_
V. D.
ge? O triste sort! O triste sort! Il faut perdre à la
R.
ge! Allons, par_tons, é_loignons-nous! C'est en vain qu'on pré_
N. St B.
_loi _ gnons - nous! Allons, par_tons, é_loignons-nous! C'est en vain qu'on pré_
M.
_loi _ gnons - nous! Allons, par_tons, é_loignons-nous! C'est en vain qu'on pré_
par _ tons! Rien ne pour_ra sauver Ra_oul! Par_
tons! Rien ne pour_ra sauver Ra_oul! Par_
_loi _ gnons - nous! Rien ne pour_ra sauver Ra_oul! Par_
U.
_nu _ le pouvoir _ sé_duc _ teur
V. D.
fois _ son a_mour _ et l'hon_ neur!
R.
_tend _ enchaî_ner _ mon cou_ ra
N. St B.
_tend _ enchaî_ner _ mon cou_ ra
M.
_tend _ enchaî_ner _ son cou_ ra
tons! Par tons! Al_lons, partons, é_loi_gnons-
tons! Par tons! Al_lons, partons, é_loi_gnons-
tons! Par tons! Al_lons, partons, é_ loi_gnons-

311
M. U.
Viendrait-il tout à coup s'em_pa_rer de son cœur?
V. D.
Viendrait-il tout à coup s'em_pa_rer de son cœur?
R.
-ge; Je sau_rai re_trou_ver l'en_ne_mi qui m'ou_tra
N. St B.
-ge; Je sau_rai re_trou_ver l'en_ne_mi qui m'ou_tra
M.
-ge; Il sau_ra re_trou_ver l'en_ne_mi qui l'ou_tra
nous! Il sau_ra re_trou_ver l'en_ne_mi qui l'ou_tra
nous! Il sau_ra re_trou_ver l'en_ne_mi qui l'ou_tra
nous! Il sau_ra re_trou_ver l'en_ne_mi qui l'ou_tra
Hé
Hé
-ge!
Oui,plus tard je sau_rai, par ma seu_le va_leur,Repousser son of_
Ah! partons! C'est à moi,
ge!
(à Valentine)
Viens, partons! C'est à moi, dans ma jus_te fu_reur, A punir un per_
ge!
Ah! partons! Il sau_ra dans sa jus_te fu_reur, Retrouver un per_
ge! Cet affront veut du sang, et sa jus_te fu_reur Doit punir un per_
ge! Cet affront veut du sang, et sa jus_te fu_reur Doit punir un per_
ge! Cet affront veut du sang, et sa jus_te fu_reur Doit punir un per_
ff

Ph.M.& Cie 9209

318
_las! hé _ _ las!
V. D.
_las! hé _ _ las!
R.
_fense et ven_ger mon hon_neur! Oui, plus tard je sau_rai, par ma seu_le va_
Oui, par_tons!
N. St B.
_fide et ven_ger mon hon_neur! Viens, par_tons! C'est à moi, dans ma jus_te fu_
M.
_fide et ven_ger son hon_neur!
_fide et ven_ger son hon_neur! Cet af_front veut du sang, et sa jus_te fu_
_fide et ven_ger son hon_neur! Cet af_front veut du sang, et sa jus_te fu_
_fide et ven_ger son hon_neur! Cet af_front veut du sang, et sa jus_te fu_
8
M. U.
hé _ _ las! hé _ _ las!
V. D.
hé _ _ las! hé _ _ las!
R.
_leur, Repousser son of_fense et ven_ger mon hon_neur!
_reur, A pu_nir un per_fide et ven_ger mon hon_neur! (à part, avec joie)
ff Tu
_reur Doit pu_nir un per_fide et ven_ger son hon_neur!
_reur Doit pu_nir un per_fide et ven_ger son hon_neur!
_reur Doit pu_nir un per_fide et ven_ger son hon_neur!
8

324
M. U.
V. D.
R.
N. S.B.
M.
Al_lez, partez, é_loignez-
Allons, partons, é_loignous-
Allons, partons, é_loignons-
Allons, partous, é_lo.gnons-
nous dé - fends en - cor, mon
Allons, partons, é_loignons-
Allons, partons, é_loignons-
Allons, partons é_loignons-
vous!
nous!
nous!
nous!
Dieu! Tu nous dé - fends en - -
nous!
nous!
nous!

330
M. U.
Allez, partez, é_loignez- vous!
O transport! ô dé_
V. D.
Allons, partons, é_loignons- nous!
Et comment ai - je
R.
Allons, partons, é_loignons- nous!
C'est en vain qu'on vou
N. B.
Allons, partons, é_loignons- nous!
C'est en vain qu'on vou_
M.
_cor, mon Dieu!
C'est en vain qu'on vou_
Allons, partons, é_loignons - nous!
C'est en vain qu'on vou_
Allons, partons, é_loignons- nous!
C'est en vain qu'on vou_
Allons, partons, é_loignons - nous!
C'est en vain qu'on vou_
M. U.
_mence! et d'où vient _ cet ou _ tra_ge?
A briser de tels
V. D.
donc _ mé_ri_te cet ou _ tra_ge?
Dans mon cœur é_per_
R.
_drait _ en_chaîner _ mon cou _ ra _ ge!
Je saurai retrou
N. B.
_drait _ en_chaîner _ mon cou _ ra _ ge!
Je saurai retrou
M.
_drait _ en_chaîner _ son cou _ ra _ ge!
Il saura retrou
_drait _ en_chaîner _ son cou _ ra _ ge!
Il saura retrou
_drait en_chaîner _ son cou _ ra _ ge!
Il saura retrou
_drait _ en_chaîner _ son cou _ ra _ ge!
Il saura retrou

338
M. U.
V. D.
R.
N. S.t B.
M.
nœuds tout à coup qui l'en_ga_ge? D'un penchant in_con_nu le pouvoir sé_duc_
_du _ s'est glacé _ mon cou_ra_ge! Il faut perdre à la fois son amour et l'hon_
_ver _ l'en_nemi _ qui m'ou_tra_ge! Cet af_front veut du sang; dans ce jour, ma fu_
_ver _ l'en_nemi _ qui m'ou_tra_ge! Cet af_front veut du sang; dans ce jour, ma fu_
_ver _ l'en_nemi _ qui l'ou_tra_ge! Cet af_front veut du sang; dans ce jour, sa fu_
_ver _ l'en_nemi _ qui l'ou_tra_ge! Cet af_front veut du sang; dans ce jour, sa fu_
_ver l'en_nemi _ qui l'ou_tra_ge! Cet af_front veut du sang; dans ce jour, sa fu_
_ver _ l'en_nemi _ qui l'ou_tra_ge! Cet af_front veut du sang; dans ce jour, sa fu_
_teur Viendrait-il, viendrait-il tout à coup s'empa_rer, s'em _ pa_
_neur, Et pour moi dé_sor_mais, dé_sormais plus d'es_poir, plus
_reur Doit pu_nir, doit pu_nir l'of_fenseur et ven_ger, ven _
_reur Doit pu_nir, doit pu_nir l'of_fenseur et ven_ger, ven _
_reur Doit pu_nir, doit pu_nir l'of_fenseur et ven_ger, ven _
_reur Doit pu_nir, doit pu_nir l'of_fenseur et ven_ger, ven _
_reur Doit pu_nir, doit pu_nir l'of_fenseur et ven_ger, ven _
_reur Doit pu_nir, doit pu_nir l'of_fenseur et ven_ger, ven _
ff

345
M.
G.
_rer de son cœur?
V
D
de bon _ heur!
R.
_ger mon hon_neur!
N.
St B.
_ger mon hon_neur!
M.
_ger son hon_neur!
_ger son hon_neur!
(St Bris et Nevers entraînent Valentine à moitie évanouie, et sortent en défiant Raoul, qui veut les suivre et que retiennent le soldats de la reine.)
_ger son hon_neur!
_ger son hon_neur!
f

(The gentlemen of the court, led by St.–Bris and Nevers, enter during the ritornello The Catholics are arranged on one side, the Protestants on the other).

MARGUERITE

Oui, d'un heureux hymen préparé par mes soins	Yes, of a happy marriage arranged with my blessing
J'ai désiré, Messieurs, que vous fussiez témoins.	I wished, Sirs, that you be the witnesses.

(The queen presents Raoul to the Counts of St.–Bris and Nevers, who extend their hands to him).

CHORUS

Honneur, honneur à la plus belle!	Honor, honor to her who is most beautiful!
Hâtons – nous d'accourir;	Let us hasten to approach.
C'est voler au plaisir!	Let us hurry to pleasure.

MARCEL

(arriving, all excited, taking Raoul aside)

Ah' qu'est – ce que j'apprends!	Ah, what do I hear?

(Raoul makes a sign to him to keep quiet).

(Marcel speaks softly to Raoul, but with indignation).

Vous avez recherché la main d'une Madianite!	You sought the hand of a Madianite?

RAOUL

Tais–toi!	Be quiet!

MARCEL

Sa maison est celle du péché.	Her house is a den of sin.

RAOUL

Tais–toi!	Be quiet!

MARGUERITE

(to St.–Bris and to Nevers, after having read some papers that a courier has delivered)

Mon frère Charles IX, qui connait votre zèle.	My brother, Charles IX, who knows your ardor,
Tous les deux, à Paris, dès ce soir vous rappelle,	summons you both to Paris for this evening,
Pour un vaste projet que j'ignore.	for a great plan that I know nothing about.

NEVERS, ST.–BRIS

A sa loi	To his commands
Nous nous soumettons.	we submit.

MARGUERITE

Oui, mais d'abord à la mienne:	Yes, but first of all to mine.
Grâce à cet hymen, abjurant toute haine,	Thanks to this marriage that renounces all hate,
Prononcez donc tous trois, comme aux pieds de l'autel,	pronounce, all three, as if at the foot of the altar,
D'une éternelle paix, prononcez le serment solennel!	of eternal peace, pronounce a solemn oath.

(*to the Protestant gentlemen and to the Catholics*)

Et vous aussi, messieurs, qu'un seul voeu vous enchaîne!	And you, too, gentlemen, may a single vow bind you together.

(*All surround the Queen to swear the oath*).

RAOUL, ST.–BRIS, NEVERS

Par l'honneur, par le nom que portaient mes ancêtres,	By our honor, by the name that our ancestors bore,
Nous jurons,	we swear;
Par le roi, par ce fer à mon bras confié,	by the King, by this sword on my arm,
Ah! jurons.	ah, let us swear.

ALL

Nous jurons!	We swear.

RAOUL, ST.–BRIS, NEVERS

Devant vous nous jurons éternelle amitié.	In your presence we swear eternal friendship.

MARCEL
(*aside*)

Par Luther, par la foi que je tiens de mes maîtres,	By Luther, by the faith that I have from my masters,
Ah! jurons,	Ah, we swear,
Par la croix, par ce fer à mon bras confié,	by the cross, by this sword on my arm,

ALL

Ah! jurons,	Ah, we swear.
Guerre à mort, Rome, à toi tes soldats et tes prêtres,	War to death, Rome, to you, your soldiers and your priests,
Oui, jurons!	yes, let us swear.
Et jamais entre nous amitié, ni pitié!	And let there never be between us friendship nor mercy!

ALL, EXCEPT MARCEL

Par l'honneur, par le nom que portaient mes ancêtres,	By our honor, by the name my ancestors bore,
Par le Dieu qui punit tous les traîtres,	by the god who punishes all the traitors,
Nous jurons devant vous, éternelle amitié!	we swear in your presence eternal friendship.

RAOUL, NEVERS, ST.–BRIS

Providence, mère tendre,	Providence, tender mother
Sur la terre fais descendre	make descend to the earth
La concorde, pour nous rendre,	harmony, to make us
Tous des frères, tous amis.	all brothers, all friends.

MARCEL

Providence, mère tendre	Providence, tender mother,
Sur mon maître, fais descendre	on my Lord, make descend
Ta lumière, pour le rendre	your light, to return him
A ses frères, à tes fils!	to his brothers, to your sons!
Juste ciel!	Just heavens!

MARGUERITE

Que le ciel daigne entendre et bénir, à jamais ces serments.	May heaven deign to hear and bless these oaths.

RÉCITATIF

Et maintenant je dois offrir à votre vue
Votre charmante prétendue,
Qui rendra vos serments faciles à tenir!

And now I must offer to your sight
your charming fiancée,
who will make your oath easy to keep.

(*St.–Bris reappears, leading Valentine toward Raoul*).

RAOUL
(*with muffled voice*)

Ah! grand Dieu! qu'ai–je vu?

Ah! Great God! What do I see?

MARGUERITE

Qu'avez–vous?

What's wrong with you?

RAOUL
(*barely able to speak*)

Quoi! . . . c'est elle!
Que m'offraient en ce jour . . .

What! . . . It is she! She
whom they offer to me today.

MARGUERITE

Et l'hymen et l'amour!

Marriage and love, together!

RAOUL

Trahison! Perfidie!
Moi, son époux? jamais! jamais!

Treason! Treachery!
I, her spouse? Never! Never!

ALL

Ciel!

Heavens!

MARQUERITE, URBAIN, VALENTINE, A LADY OF HONOR

O transport! ô démence! et d'où vient cet outrage?
A briser de tels noeuds quel délire l'engage?

O rapture! O madness! Whence comes this outrage?
To break these knots, what delirium inspires him?

RAOUL

A ce point l'on m'outrage!
Je repousse à jamais un honteux mariage!

At this point I am outraged!
I reject forever this shameful marriage!

NEVERS, ST.–BRIS

Ah! je tremble et frémis et de honte et de rage!
C'est à moi d'immoler l'ennemi qui m'outrage!

Ah I shake and shiver from shame and anger.
It is up to me to sacrifice the enemy who insults me!

MARCEL

Oui, mon coeur applaudit, cher Raoul, ton courage!

Yes, my heart applauds, dear Raoul, your courage!

CHORUS

Et pourqoui rompre ainsi le serment qui l'engage?

And why break thus the oath that he swore?

MARGUERITE, URBAIN, VALENTINE, A LADY OF HONOR

D'un penchant inconnu le pouvoir seduc-teur
Viendrait–il tout à coup s'emparer de son coeur?

Has an unknown impulse, its seductive power,
all of a sudden taken possession of his heart?

RAOUL

Plus d'hymen, je l'ai dit; et, fidèle à l'honneur,	No marriage, as I said. Loyal to my honor,
Je me ris désormais de leurs cris de fureur!	I laugh now at their cries of fury.

NEVERS, ST.–BRIS

C'est son sang qu'il me faut pour calmer ma fureur,	It is his blood that I need to calm my fury.
Pour punir cet affront, pour venger mon honneur!	To punish this affront, to avenge my honor!

MARCEL

Chevalier et chrétien, écoutant seul l'honneur,	Knight and Christian, listening only to his conscience,
Il se rit désormais de leurs cris de fureur!	he laughs now at their cries of fury.

CHORUS

Cet affront veut du sang; dans ce jour, sa fureur	This affront calls for blood. On this day his fury
Doit punir l'offenseur et venger son honneur!	must punish the offender and avenge his honor.

VALENTINE
(*with pained expression*)

Et comment ai-je donc mérité tant d'outrage?	How did I deserve such an insult?
Dans mon coeur éperdu s'est glacé mon courage!	In my desolate heart has frozen my courage.

RAOUL

O douleur! triste sort!	O misery! Sad destiny!
A ce point l'on m'outrage!	To such a point they insult me!

NEVERS AND ST.–BRIS

Frémissant et tremblant,	Shuddering and trembling,
Plein de honte et de rage, . . .	full of shame and anger, . . .

MARCEL
(*aside, in an outpouring of joy*)

Seigneur, rempart et seul soutien du faible qui t'adore!	Lord, rampart and only support of the feeble who adore you!

MARGUERITE

Un semblable refus . . .	Such a refusal . . .

RAOUL

N'est que trop légitime!	Is only right!

MARGUERITE

Dites-m'en la raison.	Give me a reason

RAOUL

Je ne le puis sans crime,	I cannot without incriminating myself;
mais cet hymen, jamais!	but this marriage, never!

MARGUERITE

O transport! ô démence! et pourquoi cet outrage?	O rapture, o madness! And why this outrage?
A briser de tels noeuds quel délire l'engage?	To undo these knots what delirium inspires him?

NEVERS AND ST.–BRIS

(*to Raoul*)

Sortons! Qu'il tombe sous nos coups!	Let's go. Let him fall beneath our blows.

RAOUL

D'un tel honneur mon coeur est plus jaloux!	Of such an honor my heart is too eager.

MARGUERITE

Arrêtez! Devant moi quelle insulte nouvelle!	Halt! In my presence, what new insult?

(*signaling an officer to disarm Raoul*)

Vous, Raoul, votre épée!	You, Raoul, your sword.

(*to St.–Bris*)

Et vous, oubliez-vous	And you, do you forget
Qu'à l'instant près de lui votre roi vous rappelle?	that at this moment your king summons you to his side?

RAOUL

Je les suivrai!	I shall follow them.

MARGUERITE

Non pas; près de moi dans ces lieux	No. Near me in this place
Vous restez!	You will remain.

ST.–BRIS

Le lâche est trop heureux	The coward is too happy
Que cette main royale ait un tel privilège!	that this royal hand have such a privilege.
C'est en vain qu'on pretend enchaîner mon courage;	It's in vain that they claim they can enchain my courage.

RAOUL

(*in a muffled voice, to St.–Bris*)

C'est vous qu'elle protège en désarmant mon bras,	It is you she protects in disarming my hand,
Et bientôt je serai près de vous!	and soon I shall be close to you.

MARGUERITE

Téméraires! Tous les deux redoutez ma colère!	Fools! Both of you better dread my anger.

NEVERS AND ST. BRIS

Je saurai retrouver l'ennemi, l'offenseur!	I shall know how to find the enemy, the offender.

MARCEL

Oui! mon coeur applaudit Raoul de son noble courage!	Yes, my heart applauds Raoul for his noble courage.

CHORUS

C'est en vain qu'on prétend enchaîner son courage;	It's in vain that they claim they can enchain his courage.
Il saura retrouver l'ennemi qui l'outrage!	He will know how to find the enemy that offends.
Ah! partons, éloignons—nous!	Ah. let's go, let's get away.
Allons, partons, éloignons—nous!	Let's go, let's leave, let's get away.
Rien ne pourra sauver Raoul!	Nothing can save Raoul.

MARCEL

(*aside, joyfully*)

Tu nous défends encor, mon Dieu!	You defend us still, my God!

(*St.–Bris and Nevers drag Valentine, half fainting, and exit, defying Raoul, who wants to follow but it restrained by the Queen's soldiers*).

Libretto by EUGÈNE SCRIBE

140

Carl Maria von Weber (1786–1826)

Der Freischütz (1817–21)

a) Overture

First performance 18 June 1821. Reprinted by permission from *Der Freischütz* (Leipzig: C. F. Peters, n.d.), pp.3–18; 114–43

Clar.
Fag.
Corni.
Corni.
Timp.
Viol.I.
Viol.II.
Viola.
Vcello.
Basso.
Muta in Es.
SOLO.
Muta A in G.
pizz.
pp
mf
31
Molto vivace.
cresc.
decresc.
ff
arco
Ob.
p marcato
Corni in C.

Clar.
50
Fag.
cresc.
poco
a
poco
50
a 2.
Fl.
Ob.
Clar.
Fag.
a 2.
Corni.
Trombe.
Timp.
Tromboni.
Viol.
Viola.
Vcello.
Basso.

69
a 2.
ff
Vcello e Basso.
69

86
a 2.
a 2.
Corni.
Tromboni.
86
SOLO.
Clar.
con molta passione
Corni.
Trombone.
tenuto

Ob.
110
Clar.
Fag.
Corni in Es.
Viol.
Viola.
Vcello.
Basso.
pizz.
pizz.
pizz.
pizz.
pizz.
110
Clar.
Fag.
arco
dolce
arco
arco
arco
dolce
arco
dolce
129
Clar.

SOLO.
Fl.
Clar.
Fag. SOLO.
dolce
Corni in Es.
Viol.
Viola.
Vcello e Basso.
145
Fl.
Ob.
Clar.
Fag.
Corni.
mf
cresc.
f
145
a 2.
ff stacc.
a 2.

159
Fl.
Ob.
Clar.
Fag.
Corni.
Trombe.
Timp.
Tromboni.
Viol.
Viola
Vcello e Basso.
159
ff

178
a 2.
Corni.
Tromboni.
178
Ob.
SOLO.
p dol.
p dolce
cresc.
cresc.
p dolce
p dolce
p dolce
p dolce

SOLO.
dolce
Fl.
Ob.
Fag.
pp
Tromboni.
Viol.
Viola.
Vcello.
Basso.
196
Fl. 205
Ob.
Clar.
pp marcato
Fag.
f
ff
Corni.
cresc.
Timp.
Tromboni.
p
pp
cresc.
205

Ob.
Clar.
Fag.
Corni in C.
Viol.
Viola.
Vcello.
Basso.
mf
229
Fl.
a 2.
Ob.
Clar.
Fag.
Corni.
Trombe.
Timp.
Tromboni.
Viol.
Viola.
Vcello e Basso.
string.
f
ff
229

a 2.
ff
248
p
cresc.
f
SOLO.
in G.
p dolce
fp
pizz.
arco

Clar.
Fag.
Viol.
Viola.
Vcello.
pizz.
SOLO. arco
Basso.
pizz.
arco
277
Fl.
Ob.
Clar.
Fag.
in G.
Corni.
in C.
Trombe.
Timp.
Tromboni.
a 2.
Viol.
Viola.
Vcello. arco
Basso. arco

a 2.
298
ff

316

ff
ff
ff
331

b) Act II, Finale, Wolf's Glen Scene

14
U - hui! U - hui!
U - hu - i! U - hui!
U - hu - i! U -
fiel auf's Kraut,
Spinnweb ist mit Blut bethaut!
Eh noch wieder Abendgraut.

24
hu-i!
U - hu-i! U - hu-i!
hu-i!
U - hu-i! U - hu-i!
ist sie todt, die zar-te Braut!
Eh' noch wieder sinkt die Nacht, ist das Opfer dar - ge-

35
ff
muta in Es
pp
ten.
U - hu - i! U - hu - i! U - hu - i!
Die Uhr schlägt ganz
in der Ferne 12.
U - hu - i! U - hu - i! U - hu - i!
(Caspar reisst heftig den Hirschfänger heraus und stösst ihn mitten in den Todtenschädel.)
Caspar erhebt den Hirschfänger mit dem Todtenkopfe, dreht sich dreimal herum u. ruft:
Samiel! Samiel! erschein'!
bracht.

43
Ob.
a 2.
pp
Clar.
Fag.
Corni 3.4. in C.
Timp.
Tromboni.
ff
Agitato.
Bei des Zaub'rers Hirngebein!
Samiel! Samiel! erschein'! (er stellt beides wieder in die Mitte des Kreises.)
Samiel: (tritt aus einem Felsen.) Was rufst du?
Caspar (wirft sich nieder.)
pizz.
arco
Agitato.
53
Fl.
Corni.
p
(kriechend.)
Du weisst, dass mei - ne
Vcello. pizz.
pizz.

58
Fl.
Clar.
Corni.
Timp.
Frist
schier ab-gelaufen ist.
Samiel. Morgen!
arco
Ver-läng - re sie noch einmal mir;
pizz.
64
Fag.
a 2.
ich brin - ge neue O - pfer dir.
Mein Jagd - gesell, er naht,
Samiel. Nein!
arco
pizz.
Samiel. Welche?
arco
pizz.
arco

70
f
er der noch nie dein dunkles Reich be-trat.
Samiel. Was sein Begehr?
Frei - - kugeln
pizz.
arco
pizz.
Fl. 75
Ob.
a 2.
pp
Clar.
Corni in Es.
f
Corni in C.
Timp.
pp
Tromboni.
sind's, auf die er Hoff - nung baut.
Samiel. Sechse treffen! Siebenäffen!
Die siebente sei dein: aus
pizz.
arco
arco

82
Fag.
sei - nem Rohr
lenk' sie nach seiner Braut!
Dies wird ihn der Verzweiflung weih'n,
pizz.
arco
cresc.
88
Ob.
Timp.
ihn und den Va-ter.
Samiel. Noch hab'ich keinen Theil an ihr!

93
Fl.
pp
Clar.
Corni in C.
Genügter dir al-lein?
Samiel. Das findet sich!
arco
pizz.
Doch schenkst du Frist,
und wieder auf drei
99
Fl.
Ob.
Clar.
Fag.
Corni in Es.
Corni in C.
Jahr,
bring' ich ihn dir zur Beute dar?!
Samiel. Es
pizz.
arco
f
ff

105
Fag.
Corni in C. SOLI.
Timp.
Tromboni.
Allegro.
sei! Bei den Pforten der Hölle! morgen Er oder Du!
Verschwindet unter dumpfem Donner.
Caspar richtet sich langsam und erschöpft auf und
Allegro.

Fl. 112
Ob.
Clar.
Fag.
Corni in C.
cresc.
trocknet sich den Schweiss von der Stirn. Der Hirschfänger mit dem Todtenkopf ist verschwunden; an dessen Stelle kommt ein kleiner Heerd mit glimmen-

121
ff
tr
string.
f
den Kohlen, dabei einige Reissbunde, aus der Erde.
Caspar (sie erblickend) Trefflich bedient! Thut einen Zug aus der Jagdflasche. Gesegn'es Samiel!
Trinkt.
128
Fl.
Er hat mir warm gemacht!
Aber wo bleibt Max?
Sollte er wortbrüchig werden?
Samiel, hilf!
Caspar geht, nicht
p
135
Fl.
Clar.
pp
ohne Beängstigung, im Kreise hin und her. Die Kohlen drohen zu verlöschen; er kniet zu ihnen nieder, legt Reiss auf und bläst an. Die Eule und andere

141
Fl.
Clar.
Fag.
Corni 1.2. in Es.
pp
cresc. poco a poco
Vögel heben dabei die Flügel, als wollten sie anfachen.
Das Feuer raucht und knistert.
Max wird
151
Fag.
Corni in Es.
Corni in C.
Recit.
Max.
Ha!
Recit.
auf einer Felsenspitze, dem Wasserfall gegenüber, sichtbar und beugt sich in die Schlucht herab.
Furchtbar gähnt der düst're Abgrund! Welch' ein
162
Andante.
Grau'n, das Auge wähnt in einen Höllenpfuhl zu schau'n!
Wie dort sich Wetterwolken bal - len; der
Andante.

168
Fl.
Fag.
a 2.
Mond verliert von seinem Schein; ge - spenst' - ge Ne - belbil - der wal - len, be-
172
Recit.
lebt ist das Ge - stein, und hier
Recit.
husch, husch! fliegt Nachtgevögel auf im
177
Fag. a tempo
ten.
Busch! Rothgraue, narb'ge Zweige strecken nach mir die Riesen - faust! Nein, ob das Herz auch
a tempo

186
Ob.
Clar.
Fag.
Corni in C.
Recit.
Vivace.
a 2.
string.
ff
f
graust
ich muss!
ich trotze allen Schrecken!
Er klettert einige Schritte herab.
Recit.
Vivace.
192
Fl.
Ob.
Clar.
Fag.
Corni in Es.
Corni in C.
pp
Caspar. Dank Samiel! die Frist ist gewonnen!

198
Max. (nach dem Adlerflügel starrend.)
zu Max. Kommst du endlich, Kamerad!?Ist das auch recht, mich so allein zu lassen? Siehst du nicht, wie mir's sauer wird? (Er hat das Feuer mit dem Adlerflügel angefacht und erhebt diesen im Gespräch gegen Max.)
Ich schoss den Ad - ler aus ho - her Luft; ich
Vcello.
Corni in C.
Recit.
Vivace.
Recit.
(Er klettert einige Schritte, bleibt dann wieder stehen und blickt starr nach
kann nicht rückwärts, mein Schicksal ruft!
Recit.
Vivace.
209
Fl.
a 2.
Recit.
Ob.
Clar.
Fag.
Trombone Basso.
dem gegenüberstehenden Felsen.)
Recit.
(Der Geist seiner Mutter erscheint im Felsen.)
Weh' mir!
Ich kann nicht hin - ab!
Caspar. So komm doch! Die Zeit eilt.
Haasenherz! klimmst ja
Recit.

215
Fl.
Ob.
Clar.
Fag.
a tempo poco ritenuto
Er deutet nach dem Felsen; man erblickt eine weisse verschleierte Gestalt, die die Hand erhebt.
Sieh dort hin, sieh.
Was dort sich weist, ist
sonst wie eine Gemse!
a tempo poco ritenuto
222
Fag.
Vivace.
Recit.
ritard.
meiner Mutter Geist. So lag sie im Sarg; so ruht sie im Grab.
Sie fleht mit warnendem
Vcello.
Bassi.
Vivace.
Recit.
230
Blick, sie winkt mir zu-rück!
Caspar. (für sich.) Hilf Samiel!
(laut.) Alberne Fratzen! Ha! Ha! Ha!
Sieh noch einmal hin, damit du die Folgen deiner feigen Thorheit erkennst!

236
Agitato assai.
Fl.
p a 2.
cresc.
Fag.
Die verschleierte Gestalt ist verschwunden, man erblickt Agathens Gestalt. Sie gleicht völlig einer Wahnsinnigen, und scheint in dem Begriff, sich in den Wasserfall hinab zu stürzen.
Basso.
Agitato assai.
240
sempre
Max.
A - ga - the! Sie springt in den
244
Fl.
Ob. cresc.
Clar.
Fag.
Fluss! Hin - ab! hin - ab! ich muss! A -

248
Fl.
Ob.
Clar.
Fag.
Corni in Es.
Corni in C.
ga - the!
Sie springt in den Fluss!
A - ga - the!
252
a 2.
bis.
Max klimmt vollends herab; der Mond fängt an sich zu verfinstern.
hinab!
ich muss! hinab, ich muss! hinab, ich muss!
Die Gestalt verschwindet.
Caspar. (höhnisch für sich.)
C.B.
Vcello.
Anmerkung. Die folgenden beiden bis kommen in Anwendung im Fall Max nicht genug Zeit haben sollte.

258
pp
Max. (heftig zu Caspar.)
Hier bin ich, was hab' ich zu thun?
Ich denke wohl auch, dass du musst.

Caspar.
(Wirft ihm die Jagdflasche zu, die Max weglegt.) Zuerst trink' einmal! Die Nachtluft ist kühl und feucht — Willst du selbst giessen?

Max.
Nein! das ist wider die Abrede!

Caspar.
Nicht? So bleib' ausser dem Kreise, sonst kostet's dein Leben!

Max.
Was hab' ich zu thun, Hexenmeister?

Caspar.
Fasse Muth! Was du auch hören und sehen magst, verhalte dich ruhig. (Mit eigenem heimlichen Grauen.) Käme vielleicht ein Unbekannter, uns zu helfen, was kümmert's dich? Kommt was Anderes, was thut's? So etwas sieht ein Gescheidter nicht.

Max.
O wie wird das enden!

Caspar.
Umsonst ist der Tod! Nicht ohne Widerstand schenken verborgene Naturen den Sterblichen ihre Schätze. Nur wenn du mich selbst zittern siehst, dann komm' mir zu Hülfe und rufe, was ich rufen werde, sonst sind wir Beide verloren.

Max.
(Macht eine Bewegung des Einwurfs.)

Caspar.
Still! die Augenblicke sind kostbar!
(Der Mond ist bis auf einen schmalen Streifen verfinstert.)

Caspar.
(nimmt die Giesskelle) Merk' auf, was ich hinein werfen werde, damit du die Kunst lernst.
(Er nimmt die Ingredienzien aus der Jagdtasche und wirft sie nach und nach hinein.)

261
Fl. SOLO.
tenuto
Timp.
Andante. Melodram.
pp
Caspar. Für erst das Blei! Etwas Glas von zerbrochnen Kirchenfenstern; das findet sich. Etwas Quecksilber. Drei Kugeln, die schon einmal getroffen.
Das rechte Auge eines Wiedehopfs, das linke eines Luchses! Probatum est!
Und nun den Kugelsegen!
(in drei Pausen sich gegen die Erde neigend.)
pizz.
arco
Andante.

267
Schütze, der im Dunkeln wacht, Samiel! Samiel! Hab'
acht, steh' mir bei in dieser
Nacht bis der Zauber ist voll
- bracht. Salbe mir so Kraut als

271
Clar.
Corni in C.
Timp.
Allegro moderato.
SOLO.
pp
pizz.
Blei, segn'es Sieben, Neun und Drei, dass die Kugel tüchtig sei!
Samiel! Samiel! her - bei!
Vcello.
Die Masse in der Giess-
277
Allegro moderato.
kelle fängt an zu gähren und zu zischen, und giebt einen grünlich weissen Schein.
Eine Wolke läuft über den Mondstreif, dass die ganze Gegend nur noch von dem Heerdfeuer, den Augen der Eule und dem faulen Holze des Baumes beleuchtet ist.
Caspar giesst, lässt die Kugel aus der Form fallen und ruft:
Fl.
Eins!
Das Echo wiederholt Eins!
287
Fl.
Ob.
Clar.
Waldvögel kommen herunter, setzen sich um das Feuer, hüpfen und flattern.

291
Fl.
Ob.
Clar.
Fag.
Tromb. B.
Poco più moto.
Caspar giesst und zählt: Zwei! Echo. Zwei!
Bassi
Ein schwarzer Eber raschelt durch's Gebüsch und jagt wild vorüber.
f
ff
298
Clar.
Fag.
Tromb. B.
Caspar scheint zu stuzen und zählt:
ff
305
Clar.
a 2.
Fag.
Corni in C.
Tromb. B.
Timp.
p
pp
fp
cresc.
Drei! Echo. Drei!
Ein Sturm erhebt sich, beugt und bricht Wipfel der Bäume,

310
Ob.
p cresc.
Clar.
Fag.
Corni in Es.
p cresc.
Corni in C.
jagt Funken vom Feuer u.s.w.
314
Fl.
unis.
318
a 2.
Caspar zählt

322
ängstlich:
Vier! Echo Vier!
Man hört Rasseln, Peitschengeknall und Pferdegetrappel.
327
a 2
Vier feurige Funkenwerfende Räder rollen über die Bühne.
331
Caspar immer ängstlicher, zählt:
Fünf! Echo. Fünf!

336
Fag.
Corno in B. sempre tutto fortissimo possibile
Corno in F. sempre tutto fortissimo possibile
Corni in E. sempre tutto fortissimo possibile
ff
ff Tromboni
ff
Hundegebell und Wiehern in der Luft.
Nebelgestalten von Jägern zu Fuss und zu Ross, Hirsche und Hunde ziehen in der
Chor. (Tenori e Bassi) unsichtbar.
ff
Durch
347
Timp.
ff
Höhe vorüber.
Berg und Thal, durch Schlund und Schacht, durch Thau und Wolken, Sturm und Nacht, durch Thau und Wolken, Sturm und Nacht!

358
Tromb. B.
Durch Höh-le, Sumpf und Er-den-kluft, durch Feu-er, Erde, See und Luft! Jo-ho, wau wau, jo-ho, wau wau, jo-
367
Presto.
Fl. picc.
Fl.
Ob.
Clar.
ten.
muta in F.
a 2.
Trombe in C.
Timp. in C. A.
Tromboni.
ho! ho! ho! ho! ho! ho! ho!
Caspar.
Wehe, das wilde Heer!
Sechs! Wehe! Echo. Sechs! Wehe!
Der ganze Himmel wird schwarze Nacht.
Presto.

376

Corni in F.
Corni in E.
Die Gewitter treffen furchtbar zusammen. Flammen schlagen aus der Erde. Irrlichter zeigen sich auf den Bergen u.s.w.

a 2.
ff

394

404

ff
Samiel!
Er wird zu Boden geworfen.
hilf!
Max gleichfalls vom Sturm hin und her geschleudert, schreit
Sieben!
Samiel!
Samiel. Hier bin ich!
Max stürzt zu Boden.

416

ff
fp
pp
Es schlägt Eins.
Max richtet sich convulsivisch auf.
Der Vorhang fällt.
Ende des zweiten Actes.

(A frightful glen with a waterfall. A pallid full moon. A storm is brewing. In the foreground a withered tree shattered by lightning seems to glow. In other trees, owls, ravens, and other wild birds. Caspar, without a hat or coat, but with hunting pouch and knife, is laying out a circle of black fieldstones, in the center of which lies a skull. A few steps away a hacked-off eagle wing, a ladle, and bullet moulds.)

CHORUS OF INVISIBLE SPIRITS

Milch des Mondes fiel auf's Kraut
Uhui! Uhui!
Spinnweb' ist mit Blut bethaut!
Eh' noch wieder Abend graut,
Uhui! Uhui!
Ist sie todt, die zarte Braut!
Eh' noch wieder sinkt die Nacht,
Ist das Opfer dargebracht!

The milk of the moon fell on the herbs.
Uhui! Uhui!
Spider webs dabbed with blood.
Before another evening darkens,
Uhui! Uhui!
will she die, the lovely bride.
Before another night falls,
will the sacrifice be offered.

(A clock in the distance strikes twelve. The circle of stones is completed.)

CASPAR

Samiel! Samiel! erschein!
Bei des Zaub'rers Hirngebein!
Samiel! Samiel! erschein!

Samiel, Samiel, appear!
By the wizard's skull-bone,
Samiel, Samiel, appear!

SAMIEL *(steps out of a rock)*

Was rufst du mich?

Why do you call me?

CASPAR *(throws himself at Samiel's feet)*

Du weisst, dass meine Frist
Schier abgelaufen ist.

You know that my days of grace
are coming to an end.

SAMIEL

Morgen!

Tomorrow!

CASPAR

Verläng're sie noch einmal mir!

Will you extend them once more?

SAMIEL

No!

No!

CASPAR

Ich bringe neue Opfer dir.

I bring you new sacrifices.

SAMIEL

Welche?

Which ones?

CASPAR

Mein Jagdgesell, er naht, er, Der noch nie dein dunkles Reich betrat.	My hunting companion—he approaches —who has never before set foot in your dark kingdom.

SAMIEL

Was sein Begehr?	What does he want?

CASPAR

Freikugeln sind's, auf die er Hoffnung baut.	Magic bullets, in which he puts his hope.

SAMIEL

Sechse treffen, sieben äffen!	Six strike, seven deceive!

CASPAR

Die siebente sei dein! Aus seinem Rohr lenk' sie nach seiner Braut! Dies wird ihn der Verzweiflung weih'n, Ihn, und den Vater.	The seventh is yours! From his own gun it will aim at his bride. That will drive him to despair, both he and his father.

SAMIEL

Noch hab' ich keinen Teil an ihr.	I side with neither party.

CASPAR *(afraid)*

Genügt er dir allein?	Will he be sufficient for you?

SAMIEL

Das findet sich!	Perhaps.

CASPAR

Doch schenkst du Frist, Und wieder auf drei Jahr, Bring ich ihn dir zu Beute dar!	If you will grant me grace for another three years, I will bring him to you as prey.

SAMIEL

Es sei! Bei den Pforten der Hölle! Morgen, Er oder Du!	So be it. By the gates of hell, Tomorrow: he or you!

(He disappears amidst thunder. Also the skull and knife disappear. In their place a small stove with glowing coals is seen.)

CASPAR

Trefflich, bedient!	Splendidly served.

(He takes a drink from his canteen.)

Gesegn' es Samiel!	Thank you, Samiel.
Er hat mir warm gemacht! Aber wo bleibt denn Max?	It warms my heart. But what is keeping Max?
Sollte er wortbrüchig werden?	Would he break his word?
Samiel hilf!	Help, Samiel!

(He puts more wood on the coals and blows at it. Owls and other birds flap their wings, as if they wanted to fan the fire. The fire smokes and crackles.)

MAX *(appears on top of a rock, opposite the waterfall; he looks down into the glen)*

Ha! Furchtbar gähnt der düst're Abgrund!	Ah, how frightful is this gloomy abyss!
Welch' ein Grau'n! Das Auge wähnt	How dreadful! The eyes fancy
In einen Höllenpfuhl zu schau'n!	seeing a pool of hell.
Wie dort sie Wetterwolken ballen,	Behold the storm clouds forming.
Der Mond verliert von seinem Schein,	The moonlight is dimming.
Gespenst'ge Nebelbilder wallen,	Ghostly, misty apparitions float in.
Belebt ist das Gestein, und hier	The stones appear alive.
Husch! husch! fliegt Nachtvögel	Hush, hush, the nightbird flies
Auf in Busch! Rotgraue, narb'ge Zweige	into the bush. Scarred red-grey
Strecken nach mir die Riesenfaust!	boughs shake their giant claws at me.
Nein! Ob da Herz auch graust . . .	No. Whether the heart feels horror
Ich *muss* . . . ich trotze allen Schrecken	or not . . . I *must* . . . despite all the terrors.

CASPAR (aside)

Dank, Samiel! die Frist is gewonnen.	Thanks, Samiel, the grace period is granted.

(to Max)

Kommst du endlich, Kamerad? Ist das	You have finally arrived, friend?
euch recht, mich so allein zu lassen	Was it right to make me wait so long?
Siehst du nicht, wie mir's sauer wird?	Can't you see how painful it has been?

(He fans the fire with the eagle's wing.)

MAX *(staring at the wing)*

Ich schoss den Adler aus hoher Luft,	I shot the eagle at a higher altitude.
Ich kann nicht rückwärts, mein Schicksal ruft!	I cannot ask my fate to march in reverse

(He climbs a few steps, then stands still, gazing fixedly at the opposite rock.)

Weh mir!	Help me!

CASPAR

So komm doch, die Zeit eilt!	Come on, time flies.

MAX

Ich kann nicht hinab!	I can't go ahead.

CASPAR

Hasenherz! Klimmst ja sonst wie eine Gemse!	Coward! You always climbed like a mountain goat.

MAX

Sie dorthin, sieh!	See there, see!

(He points to the moonlit rock. A white and worn-out female form becomes evident, raising her hands.)

Was dort sich weist, is meiner Mutter Geist So lag sie im Sarg, so ruht sie im Grab. Sie fleht mit warnendem Blick, Sie winkt mir zurück!	What you see there is my mother's ghost. She lies in the coffin, resting in the grave. She implores with a cautioning glimpse. She nods to me to return.

CASPAR *(to himself)*

Hilf, Samiel!	Help, Samiel!

(aloud)

Alberne Fratzen! Ha ha ha ha! Sieh noch einmal hin, damit du die Folgen deiner feigen Thorheit erkennst!	Silly fools! Ha ha ha ha! Look once more, and recognize your faint-hearted folly.

(The vision disappears. Agathe's form now is apparent, her hair disheveled and adorned with leaves and straw. She acts like a madwoman about to throw herself into the abyss.)

MAX

Agathe! Sie springt in den Fluss! Hinab! Hinab! Ich muss! Agathe! Hinab ich muss! Hinab! Ich muss!	Agathe. She is jumping into the river. Go to her. Go to her. I must! Agathe, I must go down. I must!

(The moon darkens. The apparition evaporates. Max climbs down.)

CASPAR *(jeering, to himself)*

Ich denke wohl auch, du musst!	I think likewise, you must.

MAX *(forcefully to Caspar)*

Hier bin ich! Was hab ich zu thun?	Here I am. What do I have to do?

CASPAR *(hands him the canteen, which Max puts aside)*

Zuerst trink einmal! Die Nachtluft ist kühl und feucht. Willst du selbst giessen?	First drink. The night air is and damp. Do you want to cast the bullets yourself?

MAX

Nein! das ist wider die Abrede.	No, that was not the agreement.

CASPAR

Fasse Mut! Was du auch hören und sehen magst, verhalte dich ruhig. Käme vielleicht ein Unbekannter, uns zu helfen, was kümmert's dich? Kommt was andres, was thut's? So etwas sieht ein Gescheidter gar nicht!	Courage! Whatever you hear or see, stay calm. Should a stranger come to help us, don't let it bother you. Whatever happens, fear not. If you are wise, you will pay no attention.

MAX

O, wie wird das enden!	How will this ever end?

CASPAR

Umsonst ist der Tod! Nicht ohne Widerstand schenken verborgene Naturen den Sterblichen ihre Schätze. Nur du mich selbst zittern siehst, dann komm mir zu Hülfe und rufe, was ich rufen werde, sonst sind wir beide verloren.	Death is in vain. Not without resistance will the invisible powers give up their treasures. But when you see me falter, then come to my aid and repeat the call that I make; otherwise we shall both be lost.

(Max stirs to raise an objection.)

Still! Die Augenblicke sind kostbar! — Be quiet. The moments are precious.

(The moon is barely visible. Caspar seizes the crucible.)

Merk' auf, was ich hineinwerfen werde, damit du die Kunst lernst. — Now mark me, that you may learn the art.

(He takes the ingredients from his pouch and throws them in one by one.)

Hier erst das Blei. Ewas gestossenes
Glas von zerbrochenen Kirchenfenstern,
das findet sich. Etwas Quecksilber.
Drei Kugeln, die schon einmal
getroffen. Das rechte Auge eines
Wiedehopfs, das linke eines Luchses –
Probatum est! Und nun den Kugelsegen!

First, then, the lead. Then this
piece of glass from a broken church
window, some mercury,
three balls that have already hit the
mark. The right eye of a
lapwing, and the left of a lynx.
Probatum est! Now to bless the balls.

MELODRAMA

CASPAR *(pausing three times, bowing to the earth)*

Schütze, der im Dunkel wacht,
Samiel! Samiel! Hab' *acht!*
Steh mir bei in dieser *Nacht,*
Bis der Zauber is voll*bracht!*
Salbe mir so Kraut als *Blei,*
Segn' es sieben, neun und *drei,*
Dass die Kugel tüchtig *sei!*
Samiel! Samiel! Her*bei!*

Hunter, who watches in the darkness,
Samiel! Samiel! Pay attention!
Stay with me through this night
until the magic is achieved.
Anoint for me the herbs and lead.
Bless the seven, nine and three,
so that the bullet will be fit.
Samiel! Samiel! Come to me!

(The material in the crucible begins to hiss and bubble, sending forth a greenish flame. A cloud passes over the moon, obscuring the light.)

(casts the first bullet, which drops in the pan)

EINS! — ONE

(The echo repeats: EINS! *Nighbirds crowd around the fire.)*

ZWEI! — TWO

(The echo repeats: ZWEI! *A black boar passes) (startled, he counts)*

DREI — THREE

(Echo: DREI! *A storm starts to rage)*
(continues to count anxiously)

VIER! — FOUR

(Echo: VIER! *Cracking of whips and the sound of galloping horses is heard)*
(more and more alarmed)

FÜNF! — FIVE

(Echo: FÜNF! *Dogs barking and horses neighing are heard: the devil's hunt.)*

Wehe! Das wilde Heer! — Woe is me! The wild chase!

CHORUS

Durch Berg und Thal,
Durch Schlucht und Schacht,
Durch Thau und Wolken,
Sturm und Nacht!
Durch Höhle, Sumpf und Erdenkluft,
Durch Feuer, Erde, See und Luft,
Jo ho! Wau wau! jo ho! Wau wau!
Ho ho ho ho ho ho ho ho!

Through hill and dale,
through glen and mire,
through dew and cloud,
storm and night!
Through marsh, swamp, and chasm,
through fire, earth, sea, and air,
Yo ho! Wow wow! Jo ho! Wow wow!
Ho ho ho ho ho ho ho ho!

CASPAR

SECHS! SIX!

(Echo: SECHS! *Deepest darkness. The storm lashes with terrific force.)*

Samiel! Samiel! Samiel! Hilf! Samiel! Samiel! Samiel! Help!

SAMIEL *(appears)*

Hier bin ich! Here I am.

(Caspar is hurled to the ground)

MAX

(nearly losing his balance from the impact of the storm; he jumps out of the magic circle and grips a dead branch, shouting)

Samiel! Samiel!

(The storm suddenly dies down. Instead of the dead tree, the black hunter appears before Max, grabbing his hand.)

SAMIEL

Hier bin ich! Here I am.

(Max makes the sign of the cross as he is thrown to the ground. The clock strikes one. Dead silence. Samiel has disappeared. Caspar remains motionless, face to the ground. Max rises convulsively.)

141

Richard Wagner (1813–83)

Tristan und Isolde (1856–59): Act I, Scene 5 (excerpt)

Composed 1857–59; first performance 10 June 1865. Reprinted from *Tristan und Isolde,* edited by Felix Mottl (Frankfurt: Peters, 1914), pp. 85–102. Reprinted by permission.

Tristan (wild auffahrend)
T.
Los den An - ker! Das Steu - er dem
Strom! Den Win - den Se - gel und
Mast!
(er entreißt ihr die Trinkschale)
Wohl kenn' ich
Ir - lands Kö - ni - gin und ih - rer Kün - ste Wun - der -
kraft:
den Bal - sam nützt' ich, den sie
Str.
Pos.
Hob.
dim.
Holzbl.
cresc.

21
T.
bot: den Be - cher nehm' ich nun, daß ganz ich
cresc.
Holzbl. u. Hörn.
ff
Str.
f dim.
heut' ge - ne - se.
ff Str.
29
Und ach - te auch des Süh - ne-eids, den ich zum Dank dir
Holzbl.
Hr.
f
mf
p
cresc.
sa - ge!
Viol. Fl.
Trp.
ff
Str.
ff
Str.
(gedehnt)
37
Tri - stans Eh - re höch - ste Treu! Tri - stans
Kl. Hr.
marcato
meno f
Hörn.
Fag.
p
Hob. Hr.
marc.
p
Str.

B. Den Blick auf den Becher gerichtet.
p zögernd
(rasch)
(langsam)
più p
T.
E - lend kühnster Trotz! Trug des Herzens! Traum der Ah - nung!
Kl.
Viol. u. Vcll.
Str.
Fag.
più p
cresc.
50
(gesteigert)
(etwas breit)
Ew'ger Trau - er einz'ger Trost: Ver - gessens güt'ger Trank,
Hob.
Trp.
Str.
Holzbl.
Hörn.
Pos.
Pk
Isolde
I.
Be - trug auch hier. Mein die
(lebhafter)
(er setzt an und trinkt)
dich trink' ich son - der Wank!
Sehr lebhaft
Hob.
Holzbl.
Pos.
Str.
Holzbl. Hörn.
61
(sie entwindet ihm den Becher)
Hälf - te! Ver - rä - ter!
Hr.
più f
l. H.

B. Bewegung des Zutrinkens.
(Sie trinkt)
I.
Ich trink' sie dir!
Hob.
Hr.
molto espress.
V. Orch.
ff
Pk.
68 Langsam
dim.
Holzbl.
Hob.
pp
Vell.
B. Isolde wirft die Schale nicht fort, dieselbe entsinkt vielmehr ihrer allmäh-
(Dann wirft sie die Schale fort.)
lich sich öffnenden Hand.
Beide, von Schauer erfaßt, blicken sich mit höchster Aufregung, doch mit
Br.
Fag.
Baßkl.
79 starrer Haltung, unverwandt in die Augen, in deren Ausdruck der Todestrotz bald der Liebesglut weicht.)
Kl.
p
Holzbl.
(Zittern ergreift sie.
Etwas bewegt
cresc.
Kb.
Sie fassen sich krampfhaft an das Herz, —
Hob. Kl. Viol. u. Br.
f
ff

und führen die Hand wieder an die Stirn. —
Dann suchen sie
91 rallent.
Langsam
Hob.
Egl. H.
Bkl.
Fag.
Viol.
Harfe
sehr ausdrucksvoll
Br. u. Vcll.
sich wieder mit dem Blick, —
senken ihn verwirrt, —
Fl.
Holzbl.
Kl.
Egl. H.
und heften ihn wieder mit steigender Sehnsucht auf einander.)
100
Hob. u. Kl.
Holzbl. u. Hörn.
più f
Isolde (mit bebender Stimme)
Tri - stan!
Tristan (überströmend)
I - sol - de!
(an seine Brust sinkend)
Treu - lo - ser Hol - der!
cresc.
108 (Er umfaßt sie mit Glut.)
Tristan
Se - ligste Frau!
(Sie verbleiben in stummer Umarmung.)
Lebhaft mit Steigerung
Viol. u. Hr.
Str.

(Brangäne, die mit abgewandtem Gesicht, voll Verwirrung und Schauder sich über den Bord gelehnt hatte, wendet sich jetzt dem Anblick des in
Tenor II
Alle Männer (außen)
Baß I
Baß II
ff
Heil! König
Heil! König
Heil! König Marke Heil!
Hob.
Str.
Holzbl. sempre più f
Hörn.
116 Liebesumarmung versunkenen Paares zu und stürzt händeringend voll Verzweiflung in den Vordergrund.)
Brangäne
B.
Wehe!
Tenor I
Heil! König Marke Heil!
Marke Heil!
Marke Heil!
Heil! König Marke Heil!
Tromp. auf dem Theater, wie vom Lande her.
Viol.
Weh! Unabwendbar ew'ge

123
B.
Not für kur - zen Tod!
Tör' - - ger
Treu - - e trug - - vol - les Werk blüht
Pk.
129
nun jam - - - mernd em - por!
B. Sehr leidenschaft-
(Tristan und Isolde fahren aus der Umarmung auf.)
Br. u. Vcll.
più f
ff
l.H.
Pos.
p dolce
Bkl. u. Hr.
Fag.
lich drängend.
Tristan (verwirrt)
T.
Was träum - te mir von Tri - stans Eh - -
cresc.

138
I.
T.
Isolde
Was träum - te
- re?
Hob.
Hörn. Pos.
ff
Kb. Tuba
Str.
p dolce
Vcll. u. Harfe
Hr.
Viol. u. Fl. in Okt.
cresc.
mir von I - sol - - des Schmach?
Tristan
Du mir ver-
Holzbl.
Hörn. Pos.
ff
Str.
146
Du mich ver - sto - ßen?
Tö - ri - gen
lo - ren?
Trü - gen - den Zau - bers tü - cki - sche
p
Pk.
Str.
fp
Holzbl.
fp
Str.
fp

I.
Zür - nens eit - les Dräu'n! Tri -
T.
List! I - sol -
cresc.
Harfe
ff V. Orch.
152
I.
- stan! Trau - te-ster
T.
- de! Sü - ße - ste Maid!
Str. Holzbl. u. Hörn.
ff V. Orch.
p f p f cresc.
I.
Mann! Wie sich die Her - zen wo - gend er - he - ben, wie al - le
T.
Wie sich die Her - zen wo - gend er - he - ben, wie al - le
Str.
p f p f p cresc.

158
I.
Sin - ne won - nig er - be - - - ben! Seh - - - nen-der
T.
Sin - ne won - nig er - be - - - ben! Seh - - - nen-der
Str. Holzbl.
Hr.
Harfe
Pk.
I.
Min - - - ne schwel - - len-des Blü - - - hen,
T.
Min - - - ne schwel - - len-des Blü - - - hen,
cresc.
164
I.
schmach - - ten-der Lie - - be se - - - - li-ges
T.
schmach - - ten-der Lie - - be se - - - - li-ges
Hr. Hob. in Okt.
Str.
Pos.

I.
T.
Glü - hen! Jach in der Brust jauch - zende
Glü - hen! Jach in der Brust jauch - zende Lust!
Fl.
Str.
m. Fl.
f
più f
Hr. u. Hob.
Str.
Pos.
170
Lust! Tri - stan! Tri - stan! Wel -
I - sol - de! I - sol - de! I - sol -
Viol. u. Hob.
Fl. Kl.
f
cresc.
ff
Str.
- ten entronnen, du mir gewonnen,
- de, I - sol - de, mir ge-
Fl. u. Hob.
p
Harfe
Viol.
Vell. u. Hr.

178
I.
Tri - stan!
Du mir ge - won - nen, du mir
T.
won - nen! I - sol - de!
Du mir
Fl.
Hob.
Viol.
Str.
Hr.
Fag.
dolce
cresc.
ein - zig bewußt, höch - ste
ein - zig bewußt, höch - ste
Str. Hob. u. Hörn.
più f
(Die Vorhänge werden weit auseinandergerissen; das ganze Schiff ist mit Rittern und Schiffsvolk bedeckt, die jubelnd über Bord winken, dem
186
Lie - bes -
Lie - bes -
dim.
Hob. Kl. Egl. H.
Holzbl.
Hörn.
Str.
Hörn.
f
p
cresc.
stacc.
Fag.

Ufer zu, das man, mit einer hohen Felsenburg gekrönt, nahe erblickt.)
I.
lust!
Brangäne (zu den Frauen, die auf ihren Wink aus dem Schiffsraum heraufsteigen).
(Zwischen Tristan und Isolde stürzend)
B.
Schnell den Man-tel, den Kö-nigsschmuck!
(Tristan und Isolde bleiben, in ihren gegenseitigen Anblick verloren, ohne Wahrnehmung des um sie Vorgehenden.)
T.
lust!
Pos.
molto cresc.
Brangäne
192
(Sie legt Isolden, die es nicht gewahrt, den Königsmantel an.)
B.
Un - sel' - ge! Auf! Hört, wo wir sind!
Etwas zurückhaltend
Str.
sempre stacc.
sehr kräftig
Alle Männer (auf dem Schiff)
Tenöre
Heil! Heil! Heil! Kö-nig Mar-ke Heil!
Bässe
Heil! Heil! Heil! Kö-nig Mar-ke Heil!
Etwas breiter im Zeitmaß
Holzbl. Hörn.
più f
ff
Str.
Trp. Pos.
Tuba

199
Kö - nig Mar - ke Heil!
Heil!
Heil
Kö - nig Mar - ke Heil!
Heil!
Heil
3 Trp. u. Pos. auf dem Theater, wie vom Lande her.
ff
ff
marcato
Bässe, Fag.
Kurwenal (lebhaft herantretend)
K.
Heil, Tri - stan!
dem Kö - - - - - - nig!
dem Kö - - - - - - nig!
Pos. Okt. tiefer
V. Orch.
f
Str.
205
Glück - li-cher Held!
Mit
Heil Kö - nig Mar - ke!
Heil Kö - nig Mar - ke!
Viol. u. Fl.
f
più f
V. Orch.
ff

B. Vorwärts im Tempo
K.
rei - chem Hof - ge- sin - de, dort auf Na - chen naht Herr Mar - ke.
Viol. u. Kl.
Hob.
p Str.
poco cresc.

212
K.
Hei! wie die Fahrt ihn freut, daß er die Braut sich
Viol.
p Fag. Hr.
cresc.

Tristan (in Verwirrung aufblickend)
T.
Wer naht?
K.
freit!
Der Kö -
accelerando
Hob.
Str. Fl. Hob.
Hr.
Vell.
Hörn. u. Fag.
Fag.

219
B. Zurückhaltend
B. Hauptzeitmaß
T.
Wel - cher Kö - nig?
(Kurwenal deutet über Bord.)
K.
- - nig!
Tenöre.
Heil! Kö-nig Mar-ke Heil!
Alle Männer (die Hüte schwenkend)
Bässe
Heil! Kö-nig Mar-ke Heil!
Trp. auf dem Theater
ff V. Orch.
Trp.
Pk.
Pos. Tuba
(Tristan starrt wie sinnlos nach dem Lande, bis Isolde seinen Namen ruft)
Kö - nig Mar - ke Heil!
Kö - nig Mar - ke Heil!
Str.
più f
ff
Hob. Trp.

224
B. Dieses kleine Gespräch sehr deutlich
B. Brangäne etwas beiseite ziehend
Isolde (in Verwirrung)
Was ist, Bran - gä - ne? Wel - cher Ruf!
Brangäne
I - sol - de!
Wieder etwas bewegter
Viol.
p Str. legato
cresc.
Str.
Fag.
Fag. Tuba
Her-rin! Fassung nur heut'!
Wo bin ich? Leb'ich? Ha! Welcher
Hr.
230
(Isolde starrt entsetzt auf Tristan)
Trank? (verzweiflungsvoll)
Der Lie - bestrank!
Hob.
Str.
Hörn.
più f
V. Orch.
Pos.

I.
Tri - stan!
Muß ich le - - ben?
T.
Tristan
I - sol - - de!
Hob. Kl.
Viol.
Str.
Holzbl. u. Hörn.
238
(sie stürzt ohnmächtig an seine Brust)
Brangäne (zu den Frauen)
B. Brangäne trennt sofort die beiden.
B. Isolde in den Armen ihrer Frauen
B.
Helft der Herrin!
T.
più f
T.
Won - ne vol - ler Tü - cke! O trug - ge - weih - - tes
Holzbl.
Hörn.
Hob. Kl.
Trp.
Pos.
Hörn.
Tuba
Fag.

248
Tristan
(Leute sind über Bord gestiegen, andere haben eine Brücke ausgelegt, und die Haltung aller deutet auf die soeben bevorstehende Ankunft der Erwarteten.)
T.
Glü - cke!
Tenöre
Alle Männer
(Ausbruch allgemeinen Jauchzens.)
Bässe
Korn - wall
Heil!
Trp.u.Pos.a.d.Th.
(in Okt.)
Str.u.Fl.
V.
Orch.
più f
Trp.
Hörn.
Vcll.
Kb.u.Fag.
Pos.u.Tub.
Pos.
(Der Vorhang fällt schnell)
256
Trp.u. Pos.in Okt.

SAILORS
(*outside*)

Auf das Tau!
Anker ab!

Haul the line.
Drop the anchor.

TRISTAN
(*starting wildly*)

Los den Anker!
Das Steuer dem Strom!
Den Winden Segel und Mast!

Drop the anchor.
Stern to the current.
Sail and mast to the wind.

(*He takes the cup from Isolde*)

Wohl kenn' ich Irlands
Königin,
Und ihrer Künste
Wunderkraft:
Den Balsam nützt' ich,
Den sie bot:
Den Becher nehm' ich nun,
Dass ganz ich heut' genese.
Und achte auch
Des Sünne eid's,
Den ich zum Dank dir sage.
Tristans Ehre,
Höchste Treu!
Tristans Elend,
Kühnster Trotz!
Trug des Herzens!
Traum der Ahnung:
Ew'ger Trauer
Einz'ger Trost:
Vergessens güt'ger Trank,
Dich trink' ich sonder Wank.

Well know I Ireland's
Queen,
and her art's
magic.
The balsam I used
that she brought.
The goblet I now take
so that I might altogether today recover.
And heed also
the oath of atonement,
which I thankfully made to you.
Tristan's honor,
highest truth.
Tristan's anguish,
brave defiance.
Betrayel of the heart,
Dream of presentiment,
eternal sorrow,
unique solace,
forgetting's kindly draught,
I drink without wavering.

(*He sits and drinks*)

ISOLDE

Betrug auch hier?
Mein die Hälfte!

Betrayed even in this?
The half is mine!

(*She wrests the cup from his hand,*)

Verräter! Ich trink' sie dir!

Traitor, I drink to you!

(*She drinks, and then throws away the cup. Both, seized with shuddering, gaze at each other with deepest agitation, still with stiff demeanor, as the expression of defiance of death fades into a glow of passion. Trembling grips them. They convulsively clutch their hearts and pass their hands over their brows. Then they seek each other with their eyes, sink into confusion, and once more turn with renewed longing toward each other*).

ISOLDE
(*with wavering voice*)

Tristan!

Tristan!

TRISTAN
(*overwhelmed*)

Isolde!

Isolde!

ISOLDE

(*sinking on his chest*)

Treuloser Holder!	Treacherous lover!

TRISTAN

Seligste Frau!	Divine woman!

(*He embraces her with ardor. They remain in silent embrace*).

ALL THE MEN

(*outside*)

Heil! Heil! König Marke! König Marke, Heil!	Hail! Hail! King Mark! King Mark, hail!

BRANGÄNE

(*who, with averted face, full of confusion and horror, had leaned over the side, turns to see the pair sunk into a love embrace, and hurls herself, wringing her hands, into the foreground*).

Wehe! Weh! Unabwendbar Ew'ge Not Für kurzen Tod! Tör'ger Treue Trugvolles Werk Blüht nun jammernd empor!	Woe's me! Woe's me! Inevitable, endless distress, instead of quick death! Misleading truth, deceitful work now blossoms pitifully upward.

(*They break from their embrace*).

TRISTAN

(*bewildered*)

Was träumte mir Von Tristans Ehre?	What did I dream of Tristan's honor?

ISOLDE

Was träumte mir Von Isoldes Schmach?	What did I dream of Isolde's disgrace?

TRISTAN

Du mii verloren?	Are you lost to me?

ISOLDE

Du mich verstossen?	Have you repulsed me?

TRISTAN

Trügenden Zaubers Tückische List!	False magic's nasty trick!

ISOLDE

Törigen Zürnes Eitles Dräu'n!	Foolish wrath's vain menace!

TRISTAN

Isolde! Süsseste Maid!	Isolde, sweetest maiden!

ISOLDE

Tristan! Trautester Mann!	Tristan; most beloved man!

BOTH

Wie sich die Herzen wogend erheben,	How, heaving, our hearts are uplifted!
Wie alle Sinne wonnig erbeben!	How all our senses blissfully quiver!.
Sehnender Minne	Longing, passion,
Schwellendes Blühen,	swelling, blooms,
Schmachtender Liebe	languishing love,
Seliges Glühen!	blessed glow!
Jach in der Brust	Precipitate in the breast
Jauchzende Lust!	exulting desire!
Isolde! Tristan!	Isolde! Tristan!
Tristan! Isolde!	Tristan!. Isolde!
Welten entronnen	Escaped from the world,
Du mir gewonnen!	you have won me.
Du mir einzig bewusst,	You, my only thought,
Höchste Liebeslust!	highest love's desire!

(*The curtains are now drawn wide apart. The entire ship is filled with knights and sailors, who joyfully signal the shore from aboard. Nearby is seen a cliff crowned by a castle. Tristan and Isolde remain lost in mutual contemplation, unaware of what is taking place*).

BRANGÄNE

(*to the women, who at her bidding ascend from below*)

Schnell den Mantel,	Quick, the cloak,
Den Königsschmuck!	the royal robe.

(*rushing between Tristan and Isolde*)

Unsel'ge! Auf!	Up, unfortunate pair! Up!
Hört, wo wir sind.	See where we are!

(*She puts the royal cloak on Isolde, who does not notice anything*).

ALL THE MEN:

Heil! Heil!	Hail, hail!
König Marke!	King Mark!
König Marke, Heil!	King Mark, hail!

KURWENAL

(*advancing cheerfully*)

Heil Tristan!	Hail, Tristan!
Glücklicher Held!	Fortunate hero!
Mit reichem Hofgesinde	With splendid courtiers
Dort auf Nachen	there in the skiff
Naht Herr Marke.	Mark approaches.
Heil! wie die Fahrt ihn freut,	Ah, how the ride delights him,
Dass er die Braut sich freit!	for soon he will be wooing the bride.

TRISTAN

(*looking up, bewildered*)

Wer naht?	Who comes?

KURWENAL

Der König!	The King.

TRISTAN

Welcher König?	Which King?

(*Kurwenal points over the side. Tristan stares stupefied at the shore*).

ALL THE MEN
(*waving their hats*)

Heil! König Marke!	Hail, King Mark!

ISOLDE
(*confused*)

Marke! Was will er? Was ist, Brangäne! Welcher Ruf?	Mark! What does he want? What is that, Brangäne? What is the shouting?

BRANGÄNE

Isolde! Herrin! Fassung nur heut!	Isolde! Mistress, get hold of yourself.

ISOLDE

Wo bin ich? Leb' ich? Ha! Welcher Trank?	Where am I? Am I alive? Oh, what drink was it?

BRANGÄNE
(*despairingly*)

Der Liebestrank!	The love potion.

ISOLDE
(*stares, frightened, at Tristan*)

Tristan!	Tristan!

TRISTAN

Isolde!	Isolde!

ISOLDE
(*She falls, fainting, upon his chest*).

Muss ich leben?	Must I live?

BRANGÄNE
(*to the women*)

Helft der Herrin!	Help your mistress!

TRISTAN

O Wonne voller Tücke! O Truggeweihtes Glücke!	O rapture full of cunning! O fraudulently won good fortune!

ALL THE MEN
(*in a general acclamation*)

Heil dem König Kornwall, Heil!	Hail the King! Hail, Cornwall!

(*People have climbed over the ship's side, others have extended a bridge, and the atmosphere is one of expectation of the arrival of those that have been awaited, as the curtain falls*).

Giuseppe Verdi (1813–1901)

Il trovatore: Part 4, Scene 1, No. 12: Scene, Aria, and Miserere

First performance 19 January 1853. Reprinted from *Il trovatore*, edited by Mario Parenti (Milan: Ricordi, 1944), pp. 184–201. Reprinted by permission.

I. Tempo
(Ruiz si allontana)
19
L
prenda. Salvarlo io potrò, forse.
Timor di
I. Tempo
pp
(i suoi occhi figgonsi ad una gemma che fregia
me?.. Sicu-ra, presta è la mia di-fe-sa!
pp
27
la sua destra)
In quest'oscura notte ravvolta, presso a te son i-o, e tu nol sai!.. Gemente
ppp
au-ra, che intorno spiri, deh, pi-e-to-sa, deh, pie-
dolce
34
to-sa gli ar-re-cai miei so-spi-ri!
ppp

pp con espressione
tr
L
2 ADAGIO (♩ = 50)
D'a_mor sull'a_ _li ro_se_ _e
pp
41
van_ne, sospir.... do_len_ _te, del.... prigionie_ro
mi_ _se_ro con_ _for_ta l'e_gramen_te... com'au_ra di spe_
dolc
3
pp
47
ran _za a_leg_gia in quel_la stan_ _za, lo
de_sta al_le me_ _mo_ _rie, ai so_gni, ai so_gni
dolce secondando il canto

53
dolce
L
del - l'a - mor!...... ma, deh! non dir - gli im - prov - vi - do, le pe - ne, le
p
Oppure
deh! non dir - - gli im -
pe - ne, le pene del mio cor, deh! non dir - - gli im -
p
cres.
con forza
dolce
- prov - vi - do le pe - - ne del mio
- provvido le pe - ne del mio cor, le pe - - - -
tr
58
p
- ne, le pe - - - - - - - - ne del

61
ANDte ASSAI SOSTENUTO (♩ = 54)
cor.
Ten. Imi divisi
a mezza voce
Mi_se_re_re d'un'al_ma già vi_ci_na al_la par-
Ten. 2di divisi
Mi_se_re_re d'un'al_ma già vi_ci_na al_la par-
CORO INTERNO
Bar. e Bassi
Mi_se_re_re d'un'al_ma già vi_ci_na al_la par-
4
ANDte ASSAI SOSTENUTO (♩ = 54)
La Campana dei morti
p
mf
pp
-tenza che non ha ri_tor_no; mi_se_re_re di lei, bontà di_vi_na; pre_da non
-tenza che non ha ri_tor_no; mi_se_re_re di lei, bontà di_vi_na; pre_da non
-tenza che non ha ri_tor_no; mi_se_re_re di lei, bontà di_vi_na; pre_da non

LEO.
69
finire pp
Quel suon, quelle
sia dell' in - fernal sog - gior - no.
sia dell' in - fernal sog - gior - no.
sia dell' in - fernal sog - gior - no.
finire pp
5
ppp
L
pre - ci, so - len - ni, fu - ne - ste, empi - ron que -
74
I.
- st'a - e - re di cu - po ter - ror! Contende l'am -

L
-ba - scia, che tut-ta m'in-ve-ste, al labbro il respi-ro, i pal-pi-ti al
78
L
cor, il re - spi - ro, i pal - pi - ti al
L
cor!
MAN. (dalla torre)
Ah!............ che la mor-te o-gno - ra è................ tar-da nel ve-
6
Arpa

83
M
-nir a chi de-si-a, a chi de-si-a mo-rir!.. Addi - -
ppp
LEO.
Oh ciel! Sento mancarmi...
M
-o, addio, Leonora, addi - o!
CORO
Ten. 1!
Mi - se-re-re d'un'al-ma già vi-
Ten. 2!
Mi - se-re-re d'un'al-ma già vi-
Bar. e Bassi
Mi - se-re-re d'un'al-ma già vi-
Orch.
89
-ci-na al-la par-ten-za che non ha ri-tor-no; mi-se-re-re di lei, bontà di-
pp
-ci-na al-la par-ten-za che non ha ri-tor-no; mi-se-re-re di lei, bontà di-
-ci-na al-la par-ten-za che non ha ri-tor-no; mi-se-re-re di lei, bontà di-
Campana

LEO.
finire pp
Sull'or - ri-da
- vi-na; preda non sia dell'in-fernal sog-gior - no.
- vi-na; preda non sia dell'in-fernal sog-gior - no.
- vi-na; preda non sia dell'in-fernal sog-gior - no.
finire pp 7
Orch.
97
L
tor - re ahi! par che la mor - te con a - li di
Mi - se-re-re! mi - se - re-re!
Mi - se-re-re! mi - se - re-re!
Mi - se-re-re! mi - se - re-re!

L
te - nebre librando si va... Ah for - se di -
mi - se - re - re! mi - se - re - re!
mi - se - re - re! mi - se - re - re!
mi - se - re - re! mi - se - re - re!

101
L
- schiu - se gli fian queste por - te sol quando ca - da - ver già fred - do sa -
mi - se - re - re!
mi - se - re - re!
mi - se - re - re!

L
dimin.
-rà,quan - do ca - da - ver fred - do sa -
mi - se - re -
mi - se - re -
mi - se - re -
dimin.
105
L
-rà.
MAN.
Scon - to col san - gue mi - o l'a - mor che po - si in
-re!
-re!
-re!
8
Arpa

M
pp
te!... Non ti scor_dar, non ti scordar di me, Leono _ ra ad_
LEO.
110
Di te,..... di te.... scor_dar_mi! di
M
_dio, Leonora addi _ o, addi _ o! Sconto col san _ gue
CORO
Mi _ se_re_re!
Mi _ se_re_re!
Mi _ se_re_re!
9
Orch.ed Arpa
ppp
p

L
te,...di te...scordarmi!
di te scordarmi! di te scordarmi!
M
mi - o l'amor che po - si in te!
Non ti scordar, non ti scordar di
mi - sere - re! mi - sere - re!
mi - sere - re! mi sere - re!
mi - sere - re! mi sere - re!
114
Sento mancar - mi...
Di te, di te scordarmi! di
me, ad - dio, Leono - ra, addi - o.
Sconto col san - gue
mi - se - re - re! mi - se - re - re!
mi - se - re - - re! mi - se - re - re!
mi - se - re - - re! mi - se - re - re!

L
te, di te scordarmi! di te scordarmi! di te scordarmi!...
M
mi - o l'amor che po - si in te! Non ti scordar, non ti scordar di
mi - se-re-re! mi - se-re - re!
mi - se-re-re! mi - se-re - re!
mi - se-re-re! mi - se-re - re!
118
L
Sento mancar - mi... Di te scordarmi! di te, di te scordarmi! di
M
me, ad - dio, Leono - ra, addi - o! Leo - no - ra ad -
mi - se - re - re! mi - se-re - re! mi - se -
mi - se - re - re! mi - se-re - re! mi - se -
mi - se - re - re! mi - se-re - re! mi - se -

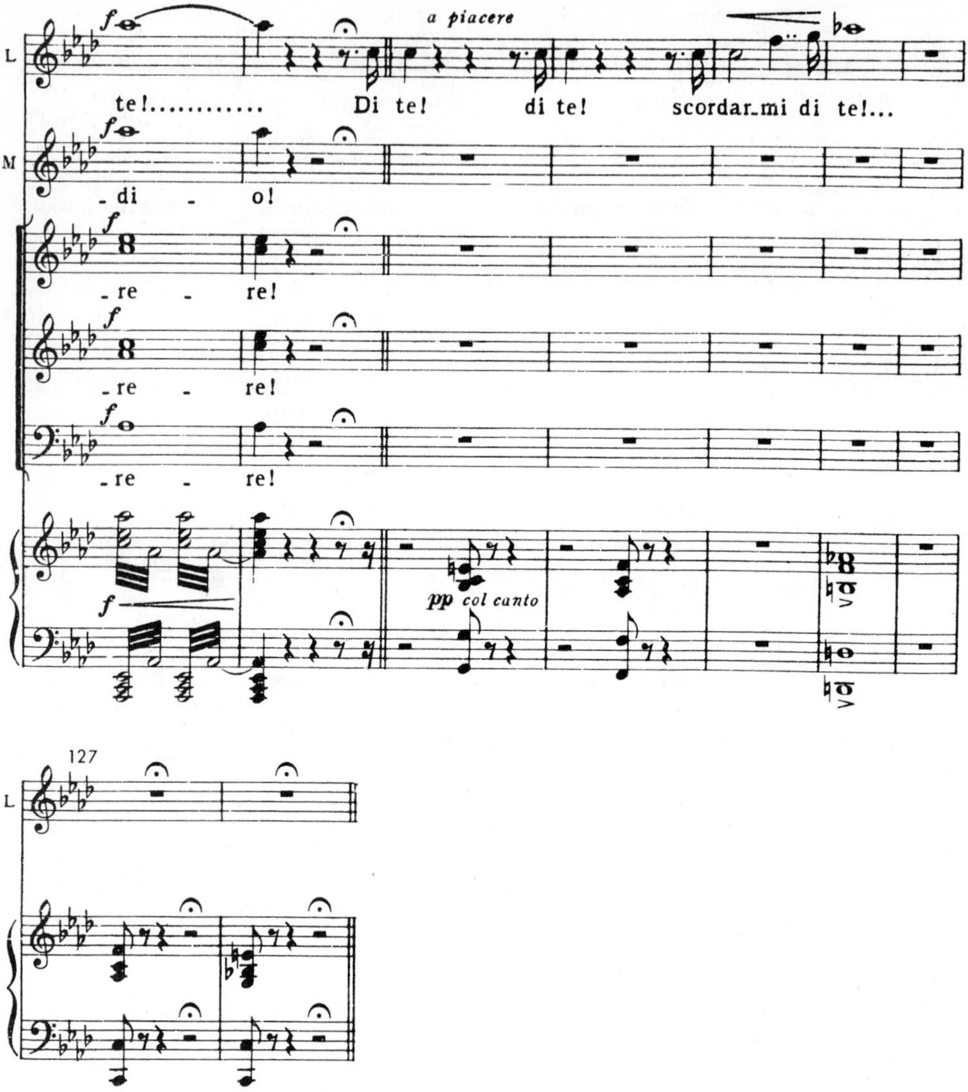

(*A wing in the palace of Aliaferia. At one end a window barred with iron. A very dark night.*
Two persons advance, wrapped in cloaks. They are Ruiz and Leonora).

RUIZ
(*softly*)

Siam giunti: Ecco la torre, ove di Stato Gemono i prigionieri! . . . Ah! l'infelice Ivi fu tratto!	We have arrived: here is the tower, where the State's prisoners moan . . . Ah, unhappy fate, it was here he was brought!

LEONORA

Vance.	Go.
Lasciami, nè timor di me ti prenda.	Leave me alone, and don't worry about me.
Salvarlo io potrò forse.	Perhaps I'll be able to save him.

(*Ruiz goes off*).

Timor di me? . . . Sicura,	Fear for me? . . . Surely,
Presta è la mia difesa!	quick is my defense.

(*Her eyes fasten on a jewel that ornaments her right hand*).

In quest'oscura notte ravvolta,	Enveloped in this dark night,
Presso a te son io, e tu nol sai!	I am near to you, but you do not know it.
Gemente	Moaning
Aura, che intorno spiri,	breeze that spirals around us,
Deh, pietosa gli arreca i miei sospiri!	o, for pity's sake, yield to my sighs!
D'amor sull'ali rosee	On the rose-colored wings of love,
Vanne, sospir dolente,	go, sad sigh,
Del prigioniero misero	the wretched prisoner's
Conforta l'egra mente . . .	sick soul to comfort . . .
Com'aura di speranza	Like a breeze of hope
Aleggia in quella stanza:	flap to that dungeon,
La desta alle memorie,	there to stir those memories,
Ai sogni dell'amor!	arouse dreams of love.
Ma, deh! non dirgli, improvvido,	But, please, tell him not, thoughtlessly,
Le pene del mio cor!	of the troubles of my heart.

LEONORA, MANRICO, & CHORUS

Miserere, d'un alma già vicina	Have mercy for a soul already near
Alla partenza che non ha ritorno.	to the departure that has no return.
Miserere di lei, bontà divina,	Have mercy on him, Divine Goodness,
Preda non sia dell'infernal soggiorno.	that his soul not be victim of infernal sojourn.

LEONORA

Quel suon, quelle preci,	That sound, those prayers,
Solenni, funeste,	solemn, dismal,
Empiron quell'aere	that tune—they are replete
Di cupo terror!	with somber horror.
Contende l'ambascia,	Relieve the agony
Che tutta m'investe,	that overwhelms me,
Al labbro il respiro,	that robs my lips of breath,
I palpiti al cor!	that makes my heart palpitate.

MANRICO

Ah che la morte ognora	Ah, how death is ever
È tarda nel venir,	slow to arrive
A chi desia morir!	to him who desires to die!
Addio, Leonora, addio!	Farewell, Leonora, farewell!

LEONORA

Oh ciel! Sento mancarmi!	O heavens! I feel faint.

CHORUS

Miserere, etc.	Have mercy, etc.

LEONORA

Sull'orrida torre, ahi! par che la morte
Con ali di tenebre librando si va!
Ah! forse dischiuse gli fian queste porte
Sol quando cadaver già freddo sarà!

Over that horrible tower, alas, it appears that death
with its dark wings hovers.
Ah, perhaps the doors swing open to death
only when a cadaver is already cold.

MANRICO

Sconto col sangue mio
L'amor che posi in te!
Non ti scordar di me!
Leonora, addio!

I expiate with my blood
the love that I vowed to you.
Forget me not.
Leonora, farewell.

LEONORA

Di te, di te scordarmi!

I shall not forget you.

Libretto by SALVATORE CAMMARANO

ANTON BRUCKNER (1824–96)
Motet: *Virga Jesse*

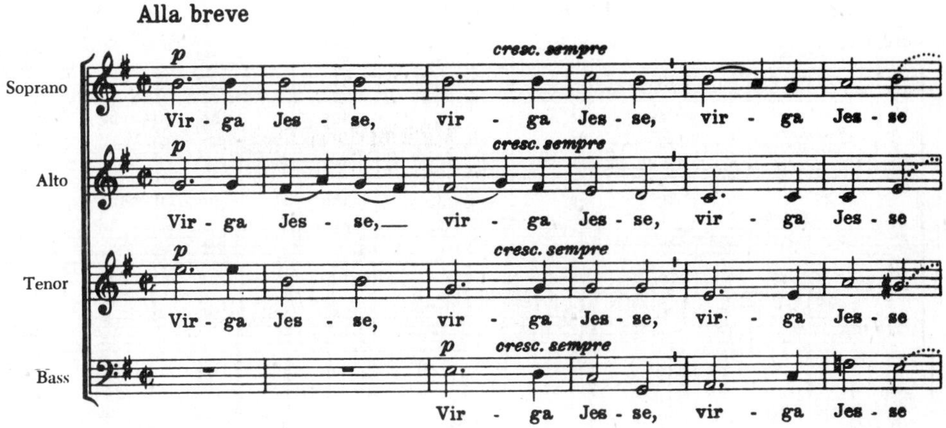

Composed 1885. Reprinted from *Virga Jesse* (New York: Peters, 1961). Reprinted by permission.

14
ff
G.P.
Jes - se, vir - ga Jes - se flo - - - - ru - it:
ff
Jes - se, vir - ga Jes - se flo - - - - ru - it:
ff
Jes - se, vir - ga Jes - se flo - - - - ru - it:
ff
Jes - se, vir - ga Jes - se flo - - - - ru - it:
21
ff sempre
Vir - - go De - - - - um et ho - mi - nem ge -
ff sempre
Vir - - go De - - - - um et ho - mi - nem ge -
ff sempre
Vir - - go De - - - - um et ho - mi - nem ge -
ff sempre
Vir - - go De - - - - um et ho - mi - nem ge -
28
- nu - - it, vir - go De - um et ho - mi - nem ge - -
- nu - - it, vir - go De - um et ho - mi - nem ge - -
- nu - - it, vir - go De - um et ho - mi - nem ge - -
- nu - - it, vir - go De - um et ho - mi - nem ge - -
33
G. P.
pp
cresc.
mf
- nu - it: pa - cem De - us red - di - dit, pa - cem
pp
cresc.
mf
- nu - it: pa - cem, pa - cem, pa - cem De - us red - di - dit,
pp
cresc.
mf
- nu - it: pa - cem De - us red - di - dit, pa - cem, pa - cem
p
mf
- nu - it: pa - cem De - us red - di - dit,

40
cresc.
ff
De - us red - di - dit, pa - - - - - cem,
cresc.
f
pa - cem, pa - cem De - us red - di - dit, pa - cem,
cresc.
cresc.
ff
De - us red - di - dit, pa - cem, pa - - - - - cem,
f
cresc.
pa - cem De - us red - di - dit,
45
cresc.
fff
pa - - - - - - - - cem De - us red - - - di -
ff
cresc.
fff
pa - - - - - - - - cem De - us red - - - di -
cresc.
fff
pa - - - - - - - - cem De - us red - - - di -
ff
cresc.
fff
pa - - - - - - - - cem De - us red - - - di -
51
pp
dit, in se, in se, in se re - con -
pp
dit, in se, in se, in se re - con -
pp
dit, in se, in se, in se re - con -
pp
dit, in se, in se, in se re - con -
59
mf cresc.
dim.
ff
ci - - li - ans i - ma sum - - mis. Al - le - lu - -
mf cresc.
dim.
ff
ci - - li - ans i - ma sum - - mis. Al - le -
mf cresc.
dim.
ci - - li - ans i - ma sum - - mis.
mf cresc.
dim.
ci - - li - ans i - ma sum - - mis.

64
-ja, al-le-lu- -ja, al-le - lu - ja,
lu- -ja, al-le-lu- -ja, al-le - lu - ja,
Al-le-lu- -ja, al-le-lu- -ja, al-le - lu - ja,
Al-le-lu- -ja, al-le - lu - ja, al-le-
69
al-le-lu-ja, al-le-lu- -ja.
al-le-lu-ja, al-le-lu- -ja. Al-le-
al-le-lu-ja, al-le-lu- -ja.
lu- -ja, al-le-lu- -ja. Al-le-lu-
76
Al-le-lu- -ja, al-le - lu-
lu - ja, al-le-lu- -ja, al-le - lu-
Al-le-lu- -ja, al-le-lu - ja, al-le - lu-
-ja, al-le - lu- -ja, al-le - lu-
81
-ja, al-le-lu-ja, al-le-lu-ja,
-ja, al-le-lu-ja, al-le-lu-ja,
-ja, al-le-lu-ja, al-le-lu-ja, al-le - lu-ja, al-le-
-ja, al- -le- -lu-
pp
p
mf
ff
fff
dim.

Virga Jesse floruit
Virgo Deum et hominem genuit:
pacem Deus reddidit,
in se reconcilians ima summis.

Alleluja.

The rod of Jesse blossomed:
a virgin brought forth God and man;
peace God restored,
in himself reconciling the lowest with the highest.

Alleluia.

144

Claude Debussy (1862–1918)

Trois Nocturnes (1893–4): *Nuages*

See p. 714. Musorgsky *Okonchen praedny,* for the source of the figure in the clarinets and bassoons. Reprinted from *Nocturnes* (New York: Kalmus, n.d.), pp. 2–18.

Fl. 5
pp
COR ANG.
expressif
3
p
CL.
pp
1er et 2e Bons
pp
pp
CORS
pp
TIMB.
tr
ppp
pppp
1
pp
Div. en 6
pp
pp

11
TIMB.
1ers VONS
à 3
pp
2ds VONS
à 2
ALTOS
pizz.
16
COR ANG.
très expressif
(un peu en dehors)
velles
Div.

22

27
COR ANG.
CORS
p
pp
f

32

37
HAUTB.
à 2
CL.
BONS
p
cre - - scen - - do
à 4

42
HAUTB
COR ANG
CL
BONS
1°
CORS
3°
f
pp
pizz.
Div.

46
COR ANG.
1er COR
sourdines
p
pizz.
pizz.
arco
pizz.
arco
pp

50
COR ANG.
1er et 2e Bons
1er COR
p
pp
più p
HAUTB.
COR ANG
p expressif
ALTO SOLO
sans sourdines
p expressif
ppp

59
HAUTB.
CL.
ALTO SOLO
pp
più p

64 Un peu animé
1er FL.
1r
très expressif
CL.
pp
1er et 2e BONS
pp
pp
HARPE
(Sol ♭, Réb, La ♭, Mi ♭, Si ♭)
Un peu animé
pp
pp
pp
pp
pp
pp
pp
pp
pp

1re Fl.
69
Cl.
1o sourdines
pp
Cors
3o sourdines
Harpe
1 Von SOLO (sans sourdines)
p très expressif et très soutenu
Alto SOLO
très expressif et très soutenu
velle SOLO
sans sourdines
très expressif et très soutenu
pizz.
arco

1re Fl.
74
p
CL.
1er et 2e Bons
pp
1o
CORS
3o
HARPE
Von SOLO
ALTO SOLO
Velle SOLO
ppp

1er FL. 79
1° tempo
più p molto dim.
COR ANG.
CL.
1er et 2e BONS
CORS
HARPE
sur la touche
sur la touche
sur la touche
sur la touche

HAUTB.
85
1o
più p pp
COR ANG.
p molto dim.
CL.
CORS
3o
TIMB.
tr
ppp
pp
à 4 sur la touche

91
COR ANG
Plus lent
pp
1er et 2e Bons
1o
pp
TIMB.
tr
ppp
pp
à 8
à 4
ppp
1re FL. 97
Encore plus lent
SOLO
CORS
Sourdines
pp
ppp
TIMB.
tr
pizz.
pp
ppp

145

Maurice Ravel (1875–1937)

Le Tombeau de Couperin (1917): Menuet

10
Htb
Cl.
Bons
Cors
Harpe
Réb
Réb
pp
Div. arco
Unis.
Div.
17
Fl.
Htb
Cor A.
Cl.
Bons
Cors
Trp.
Harpe
1o
mp
Sourd.
arco
Unis. pizz.
Div. arco
pizz.
sur Sol
p

22
Fl.
1º Solo
p expressif
Htb
Cl.
Bons
Cors
2º
1º
Harpe
22
Div.
Unis.
pizz.
sur Ré
28
Fl.
Solo
Htb
Cl.
Bons
Cors
1a
2a
28
Div.
pp
Unis.
Div.
arco
pizz. Sourdines la 2e fois (1ers seulement)
Velles Div.
pizz.
sur Ré
1.2.
6 C.B. Div.
3.4. 5.6.

Fl.
Cl.
Bons
Harpe
35
1o
pp
Lab Sib
Utb Réb
Velles
1. 2.
C:B.
3. 4.
5. 6.
sur Sol
45
Cors
Trp
1o Sourd.
pizz.
ppp
Div.
2.

50
Htb
Cl.
Bons
Div.
arco
cresc.
Otez les Sourdines
Velles
Tutti. Unis.
C.-B.
mf
55
Fl.
Cor A.
à 2
poco dim.
1° Ôtez la Sourdine
Cors
Ôtez la Sourdine
Trp.
Harpe
Div.

61
Fl
Htb
Cor A.
Cl.
Bons
Cors
Trp.
1º Sourd.
Sourd.
Unis.
velles
Div.
pizz.
1.2.
Div.
3.4.
5.6.
3 C.B.
pp
f
67
Harpe
Ré
Velles
C.B

75
1°
Fl.
Htb
Solo
pp
Cors
Sourd.
Harpe
Div. pizz.
ppp
Sourd.
Div.
Unis.
Velles
C.B.
79
Cl.
Bons
2°
Ôtez la Sourdine
Lab
arco
Otez les Sourd.
Tutti
sur Ré
pizz.
p

85
Fl
Htb
Cl.
Bons
Cors
Trp.
Harpe
1º
pp
mp
Fa♮
Div.
Unis.
pizz.
arco
91
Fl.
Htb
Cor A.
2de Prenez la Pte Fl.
p

1° Solo
98
Fl
p expressif
Htb
Solo
pp
Cl.
p
Bons
1°
p
Cors
2°
p
Trp.
p
98
Div.
pp
pp
pp
pizz.
p
sur Ré
103
Htb
Cor A.
Solo
pp expressif
p poco cresc.
Cors
pp
poco cresc.
103
Unis.
Div.
Unis.
poco cresc.
arco
poco cresc.
pp
poco cresc.

109
1°
Fl.
Htb
Cor A.
Cl.
à 2
Bons
Cors
Harpe
Unis.
Div.
sur Ré
sur Sol
Div
115
Fa♭
Ut♭
gliss.
Unis.
sur Ré

121
Molto rall.
Pte Fl.
Gde Fl.
Htb
Cor A.
Cl.
Bons
Cors
Trp.
Harpe
pp
1o
8
121
Molto rall.
pizz.
Unis.
Sourd.
Unis.
pizz.
arco
perdendosi

146

Richard Strauss (1864–1949)
Don Quixote: Opus 35 (1896–97): Themes, and Variations 1 and 2

a) Don Quixote's theme

Reprinted from *Don Quixote, Symphonic Poem* (New York: Edition Peters, n.d.), pp. 37–59. By permission.

127
Englh.
1.2. Pos.
3. Pos.
Btb.
Bck.
1. Vl. Solo.
Vlc. Solo.
Vlc. die übrig.
Kb. vierfach.
pp
grazioso
ausdrucksvoll
grazioso
130
Englh.
1.2. Pos.
3. Pos.
Btb.
1. Vl. Solo.
Vlc. Solo.
2. 3. Vlc. die übrig. 4. 5. Pult
Kb. (alle)

b) Sancho Panza's theme

143
kl. Fl.
2. Kl. (B)
1.2.3. Fag.
Br. Solo.
2.
mf
pp
3

146
kl. Fl.
B.-Kl. (B)
1.2.3. Fag.
Tentb. (B)
Br. Solo.
mf
lebhaft
f
3

150
1.2. Kl. (B)
B.-Kl. (B)
2. Vl.
Br. Solo.
Br.
pizz.
p
espr.
3

c) Variation I

164
B.-Kl.(B)
1.2. Fag.
1. H. (F)
1. Pos.
Bck.
Vlc. Solo.
167
1 gr. Fl.
1. Ob.
Englh.
Bkl. (B)
1.2. Fag.
1. H.(F)
1. Vl.
Br. Solo.
Solo.
Vlc.
die übrig.
ausdrucksvoll
ausdrucksvoll
ausdrucksvoll
mit Dämpfer
grazioso
alle
4. Pult.

170
1.gr. Fl.
1. Ob.
Englh.
Bkl.(B)
p
1.2.H.(F)
pp
3.4.H.(F)
pp
Hfe.
p
1. Vl.
Br.Solo.
p
Vlc.Solo
p
Vlc.
pp
pizz.
Kb.
p

173
1.gr.Fl.
1.Ob.
Englh.
B:Kl.(B.)
cresc.
1.2.H.(F)
3.4.H.(F)
p
Tentb.(B.)
mf
dim.
Hfe.
cresc.
1.Vl.
Br.Solo.
cresc.
f
Solo
Vcl.
die übr.
cresc.
f
p
Kb.

176
1.gr. Fl.
1.Ob.
Englh.
dim.
p
B.-Kl.(B.)
dim.
mf
1.2.Fag.
p
1.2.H.(F)
p
dim.
pp
3.4.H.(F)
dim.
pp
3.Pos.
p
Tentb.(B.)
p
Bck.
pp
Hfe.
f
dim.
p
Dämpfer weg
1.Vl.
Br.Solo.
dim.
Solo.
Vlc.
die übr.
ff
pizz.
Kb.

179
2.Kl.(B)
B.-Kl.(B)
1.2.Fag.
3.Fag.
1.2.H.(F)
3.4.H.(F)
3.Trp.(D)
1.2.3.Pos.
Tentb.(B)
Btb.
Pk.
Bck.
2.Vl.
mit Dämpfer
Br.
mit Dämpfer
Solo.
Vlc.
die übrig.
2.3.4.5.Pult col ligno
Kb.

182
2.Kl.(B)
B.Kl.(B)
3.Fag.
3.Trp.(D)
Tentb.(B)
Pk.
2.Vl.
Br.
Solo. Vlc.
die übrig. col ligno 2.3.4.5.Pult.
gewöhnlich
184
poco accel.
(♩= 100.)
19
kl.Fl.
1.2.gr.Fl.
2.Kl.(B)
3.Fag.
3.Trp.(D)
Tentb.(B)
Btb.
3 erste Vl. Solo.
2.Vl.
Br.
Vlc.Solo.
cresc.

189
kl. Fl.
1.2. gr. Fl.
1.2. Ob.
Englh.
1. Kl. (B)
2. Kl. (B)
3. Fag.
Hörner (F)
1.2.
3.4.
5.6.
1.2. Trp. (D)
3. Trp. (D)
3. Pos.
Tentb. (B)
Btb.
Pk.
Bck.
Hfe.
glissando
3 erst Vl. Solo.
glissando
1. Vl.
2. Vl.
Br.
Solo Vlc.
die übr.

196
2. Kl. (B)
3. Fag.
3. Trp. (D)
Tentb. (B)
2. Vl.
Br.
Vlc. Solo
hervortretend
ausdrucksvoll
202
1. Kl. (B)
1. Fag.
4. H. (F.)
Solo Vlc.
die übrig.
geteilt
3 fach
207
1. 2. Ob.
Englh.
1. 2. Kl. (B)
1. Fag.
2. 3. Fag.
1. Trp. (D)
Pos.
Br.
Solo Vlc.
die übrig.
Kb.
espr.
dim.
arco

d) Variation II

220
langsam
1.2.gr.Fl.
1.2.Ob.
1.Kl.(B)
2.Kl.(Es)
muta in B
Hörner (F)
1. 2.
3. 4.
5. 6.
1.2.Trp.(D)
3.Trp.(D)
1.2.Pos.
3. Pos.
mit Dämpfer
Pk.
Bck.
1.Vl.
2.Vl.
Br.
1. Pult.
2. Pult.
trem.
3 Solo.
Vlc.
(geteilt)
die übrig.
Kb.

224
1. gr. Fl.
1. 2. Ob.
Englh.
1. 2. Kl. (B)
B.-Kl. (B)
1. Fag.
Hörner. (F) 1. 2.
3. 4.
5. 6.
1. 2. Trp. (D)
3. Trp. (D)
1. 2. Pos.
3. Pos.
1.
2.
Bratschen. 3.
4.
5.
6. Pult.
(hervortretend)
(hervortretend)
(hervortretend)
(hervortretend)
mit Dämpfer
mit Dämpfer
mit Dämpfer
mit Dämpfer

228
1.gr. Fl.
1.2. Ob.
Englh.
1.2. Kl. (B)
B-Kl. (B)
1. Fag.
Hörner. (F)
1.2.
3.4.
5.6.
1.2. Trp. (D)
3. Trp. (D)
1.2. Pos.
3. Pos.
Bratschen.
1.
2.
3.
4.
5.
6. Pult.
cresc.
p
p cresc.
sempre ppp senza cresc.

231
Wieder doppelt so schnell.
1.gr. Fl.
1.2. Ob.
Englh.
1.2. Kl. (B)
B.-Kl. (B)
1. Fag.
Hörner. (F)
1. 2.
3. 4.
5. 6.
1.2. Trp. (D)
3. Trp. (D)
1.2. Pos.
3. Pos.
Pk.
Bratschen.
1.
2.
3.
4.
5.
6. Pult.
Dämpfer weg
Dämpfer weg
Dämpfer weg
Dämpfer weg
3 Solo
Vlc.
die übrig.

234
1. gr. Fl.
1.2. Ob.
Englh.
1.2. Kl.(B)
B.-Kl.(B)
1. Fag.
Hörner (F)
1.2.
3.4.
5.6.
1.2.Trp.(D)
3.Trp.(D)
1. 2. Pos.
3. Pos.
Pk.
Bck.
1. Vl.
(pultweise
geteilt)
(am Frosch)
2. Vl.
(pultweise
geteilt
3 Solo.
Vlc.
die übrig.

238
1. 2. Ob.
1. 2. Kl.(B)
B. Kl.(B)
Hörner (F)
1. 2.
3. 4.
5. 6.
1.2.Trp.(D)
3.Trp.(D)
1. 2. Pos.
3. Pos.
Pk.
1. Vl.
(pultweise
geteilt)
2. Vl.
(pultweise
geteilt)
3 Solo
Vlc.
dim.
p
ff
Dämpfer weg.

242
kl. Fl.
1. 2. gr. Fl.
1. 2. Ob.
1. 2. Kl. (B)
Dämpfer weg.
1. 2. Trp. (D)
Pk.
Bck.
1. Vl. (pultweise geteilt)
2. Vl. (pultweise geteilt)
Br.
3 Solo.
Vlc.
die übrig.
(geteilt)
(nicht geteilt)
Kb.

245
etwas ruhiger werdend
kl. Fl.
1.2. gr. Fl.
1.2. Kl.(B)
B.-Kl.(B)
1.2. Fag.
Tentb.(B)
Pk.
p cresc.
langsamer!
Bck.
1. Vl.
2. Vl.
Br.
3 Solo.
Vlc.
die übrig.
Kb.
dim. molto

Igor Stravinsky (1882–1971)

Le Sacre du printemps (1913): *Danses des adolescentes*

15
Fl. picc. 1 2
Ob. 1 2
C. ing.
come sopra
Cl. picc. in Re
Cl. in Sib 2 3
Cor. in Fa 1.2 3.4 5.6 7.8
come sopra
Tr. in Do 1
Solo con sord.
15
pizz.
Vl. I
Vl. II
Vle.
Vc.
Cb.
16
1.2 a2
Ob. 1.2 3
C. ing.
Fag. 1 2
Tr. in Do 1
16
(pizz.)
Vl. I
Vl. II
Vle.
Vc.
pizz.
poco meno f
Cb.
pizz.
poco meno f

17
Fl. picc.
Fl. gr.
Fl. alto
Ob.
C. ing
Cl. picc. in Re
Cl. in La
Cl. in Sib
Fag.
Cor. in Fa
Tr. picc. in Re
Tr. in Do
Vl. I
Vl. II
Vle.
Vc.
Cb.
Flttzg.
sempre simile
1.2 a2
sim.
con sord.
pizz.
sf meno f
17

18
Fl. picc. 1 2
Fl. gr. 1 2
ff
Fl. alto
sim.
Ob. 1.2 3
1.2 a2
C. ing.
Cl. picc. in Re
sim.
muta in Mi♭
Cl. in La 1
muta in Si♭
Cl. in Si♭ 2 3
Fag. 1 2
tr
Cor. in Fa 1.2 3.4 5.6 7.8
4 senza sord.
sf sempre
Tr. picc. in Re
senza sord.
Tr. in Do 1.2 3.4
2.3.4
1.2.3.4
p
f
18
Vl. I
arco
f (non div.)
sempre sim.
ff
Vl. II
div.
unis.
mf
Vle.
come sopra
f (non div.)
Vc.
arco
Cb.

19
1.2 a2
Fag. 1.2 3
C. Fag. 1
Cor. in Fa 1.2 3.4 5.6 7.8
Vl. I
Vle.
Vc.
Cb.
f
p sub.
20
più f
Trbn. 1
mf

21
Ob. 1 2
Fag. 1.2 3
1.2 a2
C. Fag. 1
Vl. I
Vle.
Vc.
Cb.
p sub.
Fl. gr. 1
Ob. 1 2
Fag. 1.2 3
C. Fag. 1
più f
Cor. in Fa 1.5 2.6 3.7 4.8
1.5 a2
2.6 a2
3.7 a2
4.8 a2
Trbn. 1 2
Tbe. 1 2
Timp.
G.C.
Vl. I
Vl. II
Vle.
Vc.
Cb.
pizz.
arco

22
23
Fl. picc. 1 2
Fl. gr. 1
Ob. 1 2
C. ing.
Cl. in Sib 2 3
Fag. 2
Tr. picc. in Re
Tr. in Do 1
Trbn. 1 2
Vl. Solo
Vl. I
Vl. II
Vle.
Solo
stacc.
marc.
pizz.
arco
24
Solo
marc.
Fag. 1 2
2 Vl. Soli
sul Sol
col legno sino al segno
Vc.

25
C. ing.
Fag.
p sub.
p tr
p
p tr
Cor. in Fa
mp (mais en dehors)
Solo
p
25
2 Vl. Soli
p sub.
Vl. I
p
Vl. II
col legno al
mf
p sub.
Vle.
p sub.
Vc.
p sub.
Solo
Fl. gr.
p
Fag.
tr
Cor. in Fa
2 Vl. Soli
Vl. I
Vl. II
Vle.
Vc.

26
Soli
Ob. 1 2
Cl. in Sib 2 3
Fag. 1 2 3 4
Tr. in Do 1 2
Solo
Solo con sord.
senza sord.
2 Vl. Soli
Vl. I
Vl. II div.
Vle.
Vc.
27
Fl. gr. 2
Fl. alto
Solo
Cl. in Sib 2 3
Fag. 1 2 3 4
Cor. in Fa 5
Solo
2 Vl. Soli
Vl. I
Vl. II div.
Vle.
Vc.

28
Fl. gr.
Fl. alto
Cl. picc. in Mib
Cl. in Sib
Cl. bas. in Sib
Fag.
C. Fag.
Cor. in Fa 5
Trbn.
Timp.
2 Vl. Soli
Vl. I
Vl. II div.
Vle.
Vc.
Cb.
mf
f
pp
tr
pizz.

29
Fl. picc.
mf
Fl. gr.
Fl. alto
Ob.
f stacc.
Cl. picc. in Mib
Cl. in Sib
Cl. bas. in Sib
Fag.
C. Fag.
Tr. in Do
mp cantab.
Trbn.
Timp.
p
Triang.
bacch. di legno
ff
Cym. ant.
f
legg. 5.6 f
legg. 7.8 f
29
Tutti div.
Vl. I
Vl. II div.
Vle. div. a3
f
arco
marcatiss. e molto cantabile
3 Soli Vc.
gli altri
Cb

Fl. picc.
Fl. gr.
Fl. alto
Ob.
C. ing.
Cl. picc. in Mib
Cl. in Sib
Cl. bas. in Sib
Fag.
Cor. in Fa
Tr. in Do
Trbn.
Timp.
Triang.
Cym. ant.
Vl. I div.
Vl. II div.
Vle. div. a3
3 Soli
Vc.
gli altri
Cb.
mp
ff
p
f
sim.
C. ing. 2 muta in Ob. 4
Fag. 4 muta in C. Fag. 2

30
Cl. picc. in Mi♭
Cl. in Si♭ 1 2 3
Cl. bas. in Si♭
sempre sf
Vl. I div.
p sub. e stacc.
Vl. II div.
pizz.
p sub.
meno f
sul Sol
4 Sole
Vle.
le altre
3 Soli
Vc.
gli altri
Cb.
p sub.
31
Solo
mf grazioso
Fl. picc. 1
Ob. 1 2 3
C. ing.
muta in Re
C. Fag. 1 2
a 2
Cor in Fa 4
cresc.
(pizz.)
sim.
(sempre sim.)
Tutte pizz.
Tutti div.
sff

32
Fl. picc. 1
Fl. gr. 1 2
Fl. alto
Ob. 1 2 3 4
C. ing.
Cl. picc. in Re
Cl. in Si♭ 1 2 3
Fag. 3
C. Fag. 1 2
a2
(a2)
Cor. in Fa 1.2 3.4 5.6 7.8
Tr. in Do 1 3
Vl. I div.
Vl. II div.
Vle. div.
Vc. div.
Cb.
arco
unis. arco
mf cresc.
sff
sf
mf
f

Fl. picc. 1 2
Fl. gr. 1 2
Fl. alto
Ob. 1 2 3 4
C. ing.
Cl. picc. in Re
Cl. in Sib 1 2 3
Fag. 1 2 3
C. Fag. 1
Cor. in Fa 1.2 3.4 5.6 7.8
Tr. picc. in Re
Tr. in Do 1 2 3 4
Tbe. 1 2
Vl. I div.
Vl. II div.
Vle. div.
Vc.
Cb.
f sempre
sim.
Flttzg.
arco
mf cresc.

33
Fl. picc. 1 2
Fl. gr. 1 2
Fl. alto
Ob. 1 2 3 4
C. ing.
Cl. picc. in Re
Cl. in Sib 1 2 3
Fag. 1 2 3
C. Fag. 1 2
Cor. in Fa 1.2 3.4 5.6 7.8
Tr. picc. in Re
Tr. in Do 1 2 3 4
Tbe. 1 2
Vl. I div.
Vl. II div.
Vle. div.
Vc. div.
Cb.
Flttzg.
sempre sim.
stacc.
a 2
sim. sempre
pizz.

34
Fl. picc. 1 2
Fl. gr. 1 2
Fl. alto
Ob. 1 2 3 4
C. ing.
Cl. picc. in Re
Cl. in Sib 1 2 3
Cl. bas. in Sib
Fag. 1 2 3
C. Fag. 1 2
Cor. in Fa 1.2 3.4 5.6 7.8
Tr. picc. in Re
Tr. in Do 1.2 3.4
Trbn. 1 2 3
Tbe. 1 2
Vl. I div.
Vl. II div.
Vle. div.
Vc. div.
Cb. div.
a2
a3
ff
f
Flttzg.
stacc.
poco più
poco più f
f assai
ff
arco
sim.

35
Fl. picc. 1 2
a 2
Fl. gr. 1 2
Fl. alto
Ob. 1 2 3 4
C. ing.
Cl. picc. in Re
Cl. in Sib 1 2 3
Cl. bas. in Sib
Fag. 1 2 3
a 3
C. Fag. 1 2
Cor. in Fa 1.2 3.4 5.6 7.8
Tr. picc. in Re
Tr. in Do 1.2 3.4
Trbn. 1 2 3
Tbe. 1 2
Timp.
secco
come sopra
Vl. I div.
Vl. II div.
Vle.
unis.
div.
Vc. div.
Cb. div.
sff
ff
sf
f

36
Fl. picc. 1 2
Fl. gr. 1 2
Fl. alto
Ob. 1 2 3 4
C. ing.
Cl. picc. in Re
Cl. in Si♭ 1 2 3
Cl. bas. in Si♭
Fag. 1 2 3
C. Fag. 1 2
C. Fag. 2 muta in Fag. 4
Cor. in Fa 1 2 3 4 5.6 7.8
gliss.
Tr. picc. in Re
Tr. in Do 1.2 3.4
Trbn. 1 2 3
Tbe. 1 2
Timp.
36
Vl. I div.
Vl. II div.
Vle.
div.
unis.
Vc. div.
Cb. div.
sff

148

Arnold Schoenberg (1874–1951)
Variationen für Orchester, Opus 31 (1928): Theme and Variation VI

a) Theme

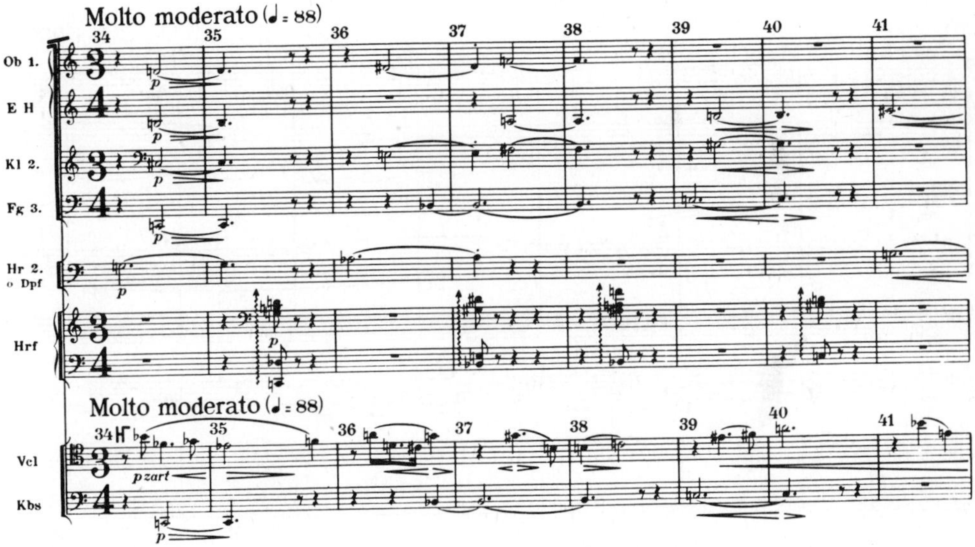

Reprinted from *Variationen für Orchester,* Opus 31, pp. 7–8, 36–38.

poco rit
Ob 1.
E H
Kl 2.
Bs Kl
Fg 3.
Hr 1.2.
Hrf
Vcl
Kbs
pp
p
mf
eventuell KFg
poco rit
I. Gg m Dpf
(m Dpf)
pp sehr ruhig
pp dolce
o Dpf

b) Variation VI

Fl 1.2.
E H
Kl 1.
Bs Kl
Fg 1.2.
Trp 1.2.3. m Dpf
Hrf
1. 2. Solo Br
1. Solo Vcl 2. 3.
1. Solo Kbs
molto stacc
molto stacc
pizz
arco
cresc
m Dpf
p dolce
Fl 1.2.
E H
Kl 1.
Fg 1.
Hr 1.
Trp 1.2.3. m Dpf
Pos 1.
I. Gg
II. Gg
1.2. Solo Br
Vcl
1. Solo Kbs
molto p
dim
pizz p
pizz
arco
alle pizz
1.2. Solo
3.4. Solo
1. Solo
alle übrigen
alle
dolce

rit. . . . . . .
232
233
234
235
236
237
1. Fl 2.
E H
Es Kl
Kl 1.
Fg 1.
Hr 1.
Hrf
Glsp
I. Gg
II. Gg
1. Solo Br die übr
1. 2. Solo Vcl 3. 4.
Vcl die übr
Kbs
dolce
arco
cresc
spring
alle get
1. allein
2. Solo
3. Solo

149

Anton Webern (1883–1945)
Symphonie, Opus 21 (1928): *Ruhig schreitend* (first movement)

Kl.
Bkl.
Hrn.
Hrf.
1. Gg.
2. Gg.
Br.
Vlc.
gedämpft
offen
pizz.
arco
calando
tempo
Dämpfer auf
m. Dpf.
dim.

rit.
tempo
rit.
tempo
Kl.
Bkl.
Hrn.
Hrf.
1. Gg.
2. Gg.
Br.
Vlc.
dim.
pp
p
Dämpfer auf
Solo
arco
Alle
pizz.
arco am Steg
Dämpfer ab
am Steg
Alle (m. Dpf.)
m. Dpf.
Alle (m. Dpf.)

Kl.
Bkl.
1.
Hrn.
2.
Hrf.
1.Gg.
2.Gg.
Br.
Vlc.
30
31
32
33
34
p
pp
dim.
ppp
am Steg
35
36
37
38
39
Solo

Kl.
Bkl.
1.
Hrn.
2.
Hrf.
1 Gg.
2. Gg.
Br.
Vlc.
m. Dpf.
Dämpfer ab
Dämpfer ab
Solo
o. Dpf.
Solo
Solo
Alle
Dämpfer ab
rit. tempo
rit. tempo
gedämpft
Alle (o. Dpf.)
Solo
Alle
Alle
Dämpfer ab
Alle
o. Dpf.
Dämpfer ab
Alle o. Dpf.
o. Dpf.

Kl.
Bkl.
1. Hrn. 2.
Hrf.
1. Gg.
2. Gg.
Br.
Vlc.
(o. Dpf.)
Dämpfer auf
Solo
Alle
Dämpfer auf

rit. tempo
59
60
61
Kl.
Bkl.
1.
Hrn.
2.
Hrf.
1. Gg.
2. Gg.
Br.
Vlc.
m. Dpf.
Dämpfer auf
Solo
m Dpf.
Alle
Dämpfer auf
Dämpfer auf
rit. tempo
62
63
rit. tempo
64
rit.
gedämpft
Solo
m. Dpf.
Solo
m Dpf

tempo
tempo
rit.
I.
II.
65a
66a
65b
66b
Kl.
Bkl.
1.
Hrn.
2.
Hrf.
1. Gg.
2. Gg.
Br.
Vlc.
pp
sf
Alle (m. Dpf.)
Alle (m. Dpf.)
m Dpf.
pp
pp
pp
pp

150

Aaron Copland (b. 1900)
Appalachian Spring (1944): "The Gift to be Simple"

a) Original Shaker melody and text

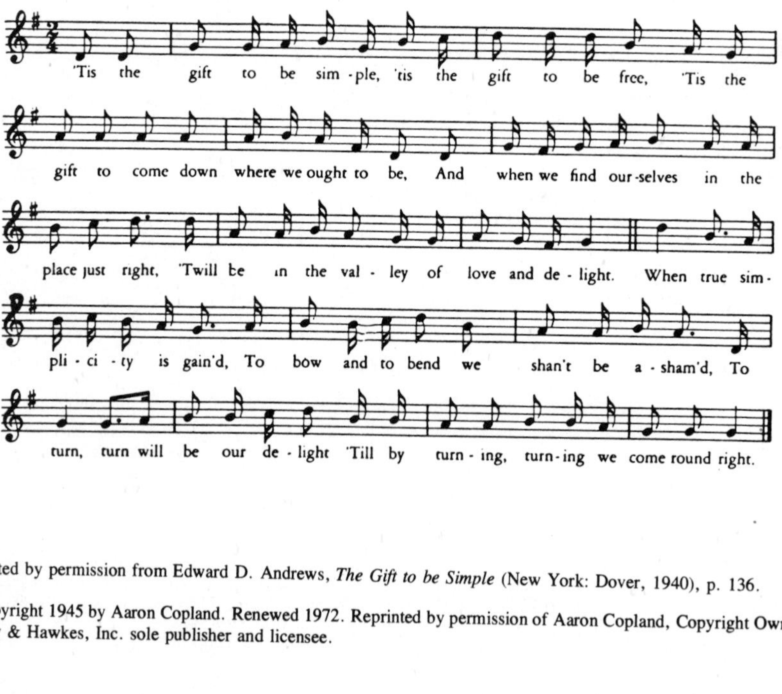

b) Copland's setting and variations

57
A trifle faster (♩= 80)
Fl. I
Picc.
Take Fl. II
Ob. I. II
II.
I. Solo
(In B♭) I.
Cl.
(In B♭) II
Solo
Fg. I. II
I. Solo
II. Solo
Tr. (B♭) I. II
con sord.
Arpa
58
I.
Fl.
II.
Ob. I. II
I.
a 2
(In B♭) I
Cl.
(In B♭) II
Fg. I. II
a 2
Cor. (F) I. II
(Open)
Tr. (B♭) I. II
Trl.

I.
Fl.
II
mf
mf
(a 2)
I. Solo
mf
Ob.
I. II
(in B♭) I
Cl.
(in B♭) II
mf
mf
(a 2)
Solo
Fg.
I. II
II.
mf
Cor. (F)
I. II
mf
Glock.
sounds 8va
p
8va
Arpa
p
8va
Pfte.
p
senza Ped.
Vl. I
div.
pizz.
Vl. II
p

59
I.
Fl.
II.
p leggiero
p leggiero
Ob.
I. II
p leggiero
(in B♭) I
Cl.
(in B♭) II
p leggiero
p leggiero
Fg.
I. II
p leggiero
con sord.
Cor. (F)
I. II
p
I. Solo cant.
Trb.
I. II
mf dolce
Glock.
sounds 8va
8va
Arpa
59 8va
Pfte.
59
Vl. I
Vl. II
Vla.
mf cant. dolce

60
I.
Fl.
II.
Ob. I. II
(in B♭) I
Cl.
(in B♭) II
Fg. I. II
Cor. (F) I. II
senza sord.
a 2
f cant.
Tr. (B♭) I. II
Trb. I. II
I.
a 2
Glock. sounds 8va
8va
Arpa
8va
Pfte.
cant. sonore
div.
f
Vl. I
Vl. II
Vla.
Vc. Cb.
f sonore

I.
Fl.
II.
Ob.
I. II
(in Bb) I
Cl.
(in Bb) II
Fg.
I. II
a 2
Cor. (F)
I. II
Tr. (Bb)
I. II
a 2
Trb.
I. II
Glock.
sounds 8va
8va
Arpa
8va
Pfte.
Vl. I
Vl. II
Vla.
Vc.
Cb.

I.
Fl.
II.
Ob. I. II
(In Bb) I
Cl.
(In Bb) II
Fg. I. II
a 2
Cor. (F) I. II
Tr. (Bb) I. II
a 2
Trb. I. II
Glock. sounds 8va
8va
Arpa
8va
Pfte.
Vl. I
Vl. II
Vla.
Vc. Cb.

I.
Fl.
II.
Ob.
I. II
(in B♭) I
Cl.
(in B♭) II
Fg.
I. II
Cor. (F)
I. II
Tr. (B♭)
I. II
Trb.
I. II
Glock.
sounds 8va
Arpa
Pfte.
Vl. I
Vl. II
Vla.
Vc.
Cb.
61
Solo
I. Solo
a 2
8va
arco
p sostenuto
pizz.

(♪ = ♩)
62 Doppio movimento.
Fl. I
Ob. I. II
(In Bb) I
Cl.
(In Bb) II
Fg. I. II
mf cresc.
non legato
Cor. (F) I. II
mf cresc.
Vigoroso e marc.
a 2
Tr. (Bb) I. II
mf cresc.
f
II.
Vigoroso e marc.
Trb. I. II
mf cresc.
f
(♪ = ♩)
62 Doppio movimento
div.
Vl. I
mf cresc.
Vl. II
f cresc.
Vla.
mf cresc.
Vc.
mf cresc.
a 2
Tr. (Bb) I. II
a 2
Trb. I. II
unis.
Vl. I
f
Vla.
f

63
Ob. I. II
a 2
f sf Vigoroso e marc.
(In Bb) I
Cl.
(In Bb) II
f sf Vigoroso e marc.
f sf Vigoroso e marc.
Cor. (F) I. II
a 2 sf
Tr. (Bb) I. II
a 2
sf
Trb. I. II
a 2 sf
Ob. I. II.
a 2
(In Bb) I
Cl.
(In Bb) II
Cor. (F) I. II
a 2
Tr. (Bb) I. II
a 2
Trb. I. II
a 2
Vl. I
Vla.

64 A trifle slower (♩= 66)
Ob I. II
I. Solo
(in B♭) I
Cl.
(in B♭) II
Solo
Fg. I. II
I. Solo
Tr. (B♭) I. II
a 2
Trb. I. II
a 2
64 A trifle slower (♩= 66)
Vl. I
Vla.
Vc. Cb.
arco
I.
Fl.
II.
Ob. I. II
I.
(in B♭) I
Cl.
(in B♭) II
Fg. I. II
I.
Vc. Cb.

(𝅗𝅥 = 𝅗𝅥) Broadly (in 2)
65
I.
Fl.
II.
fff legato e marc.
Ob. I. II
a 2
(in B♭) I.
Cl.
(in B♭) II
marc.
Fg. I. II
a 2
fff marc.
Cor. (F) I. II
Tr. (B♭) I. II
Trb. I. II
Timp.
Arpa
Pfte
8va
unis.
Vl. I
Vl. II
Vla.
Vc.
Cb.

66
I.
Fl.
II.
Ob.
I. II
a 2
(in Bb) I
Cl.
(in Bb) II
Fg.
I. II
Cor. (F)
I. II
Tr. (Bb)
I. II
Trb.
I. II
Timp.
Arpa
Pfte.
8va
Vl. I
Vl. II
Vla.
Vc.
Cb.
sf
p

Alexander Scryabin (1872–1915)

Vers la flamme, Poème pour piano, Opus 72 (1914)

32
sf poco
sf poco
38
avec une émotion naissante
pochiss.
pp
p
43
pp
p
avec une joie voilée
46
pp
49

53
56
59
de plus en plus animé
p
63
cresc.
poco
a
poco
avec une joie de plus en plus tumultueuse
66
p
cresc.
poco

69
a
poco
72
m.g.
75
m.g.
77
m.g.
m.d.
78

79
80
Eclatant, lumineux.
comme une fanfare
81
ff
ma dolce
82
83

84
m.d.
m.g.
85
m.g.
m.g.
f cresc.
88
3
3

91
92
m.d.
m.g.
93
m.g.
m.d.
94
m. g.
f cresc.

97
m.d.
f cresc.
100
102
p cresc.
104
p cresc.

107
m.g.
f
m.d.
110
113
116
8

120
125
m.d.
m.g.
ff
129
ff
133

152

Arnold Schoenberg

Pierrot lunaire, Opus 21 (1912) (No. 8 and No. 13)

a) No. 8, *Nacht*

B-Kl. (B)
Vcl.
Etwas rascher.
am Steg
(pp aber deutlich hörbar)
Flag.
gesungen (womöglich die tieferen Noten)
gesprochen
10
ruht der Ho - ri - zont,
verschwie - gen.
Aus dem Qualm ver - lor - ner
Flatterzunge
cresc.
pp dim.
ppp
stacc.
ohne Ped.
Tie - fen steigt ein Duft,
Erinnrung mordend!
Fin - stre, schwar - ze
I. Tempo
am Griffbrett
15
Rie - sen fal - ter tö - te - ten der Sonne Glanz.
dim.
Ped.

B-Kl. (B)
Vcl.
espress.
Flag.
Und vom Him - mel er - denwarts sen ken sich mit schwe - ren Schwin - gen
pp
molto legato
p
20
un - - sichtbar die Un - - ge - tü - me auf die Men - schen-
dim.
her - - zen nie - der...
fin - stre, schwar - ze
mf

b) No. 13, *Enthauptung*

B-Kl. (B)
Br.
Vcl.
p espress.
Sei_denkis_sen, ge_spen_stisch groß_dräut er hin_ab durch schmer_
sehr ruhig und gleichmäßig
pp sehr ruhig und gleichmäßig
pp sehr ruhig und gleichmäßig
10
_zens_dunk_le Nacht.
pizz.
arco
pizz.
Pier_rot irrt oh_ne Rast um_her und starrt empor in To_
pp sehr ruhig und gleichmäßig

B-Kl. (B)
Br.
Vcl.
arco
pizz.
15
des ängsten zum Mond dem blan ken Tür kenschwert auf einem schwar zen
rit.
Tempo
Sei denkis sen.
Es schlottern un ter ihm die Knie,
hervor
accel.
ohn mächtig bricht er jäh zusammen. Er wähnt: es sause strafend schon auf sei nen Sündenhals her

B-Kl. (B)
Br.
Vel.
G-Saite
gliss.
nie-der der Mond, das blan-ke Tür-kenschwert.
martellato
langsam (𝅗𝅥 ca 96-100)
Gr. Flote.
espress.
begleitend
nimmt Klarinette in A
Fl.
Kl. (A)
pizz.
arco
trem. am Steg
poco espress.

⌐ ⌐ bedeutet Hauptstimme.

Night

Finstre, schwarze Riesenfalter
Töteten der Sonne Glanz.
Ein geschlossnes Zauberbuch,
Ruht der Horizont—verschwiegen.

Aus dem Qualm verlorner Tiefen
Steigt ein Duft, Erinnrung mordend!
Finstre, schwarze Riesenfalter
Töteten der Sonne Glanz.

Und vom Himmel erdenwärts
Senken sich mit schweren Schwingen
Unsichtbar die Ungetüme
Auf die Menschenherzen nieder . . .
Finstre, schwarze Riesenfalter.

Gloomy, black bats
killed the radiant sun.
A sealed book of magic,
the horizon rests, taciturn.

From the vapor of forgotten depths
rises a fragrance, killing memory!
Gloomy, black bats
killed the radiant sun.

And from heaven earthwards
they sink with ponderous oscillations—
invisible, the monsters,
down to the hearts of men . . .
Gloomy, black bats.

Decapitation

Der Mond, ein blankes Türkenschwert,
Auf einen schwarzen Seidenkissen,
Gespenstisch gross—dräut er hinab
Durch schmerzensdunkle Nacht.

Pierrot irrt ohne Rast umher
Und starrt empor in Todesängsten
Zum Mond, dem blanken Türkenschwert
Auf einem schwarzen Seidenkissen.

Es schlottern unter ihm die Knie,
Ohnmächtig bricht er jäh zusammen.
Er wähnt: es sause strafend schon
Auf seinen Sündenhals hernieder
Der Mond, das blanke Türkenschwert.

The moon, a polished scimitar
set on a black silken cushion,
ghostly vast, menaces downwards
through pain's dark night.

Pierrot wanders about, restless,
and stares on high in death-agony
at the moon, a polished scimitar
set on a black silken cushion.

His knees knock together under him,
swooning, he collapses abruptly.
He fancies: let it whistle punishingly
already down on his guilty neck,
the moon, the polished scimitar.

ALBERT GIRAUD (1860–1929), translated from the French by ERICH HARTLEBEN (1860–1905)

Béla Bartók (1881–1945)

Music for Strings, Percussion, and Celesta (1936) Adagio (third movement)

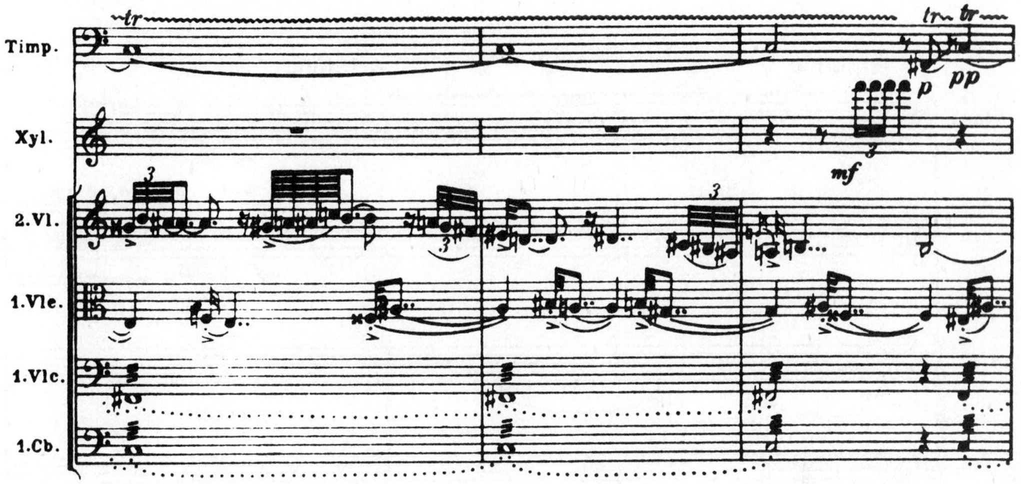

Timp.
Xyl.
2.Vl.
1.Vle.
1.Vlc.
1.Cb.
tr
p
pp
mf

15
poco ral -
Timp.
1.Vl.
2.Vl.
1.Vle.
1.Vlc.
1.Cb.
3.Vl.
4.Vl.
2.Vle.
2.Vlc.
tr
mf
p,espr.

lentando
a tempo
Timp.
dim.
p
mf
Xyl.
mf
p
1. Vl.
dim.
p
2. Vl.
dim.
p
1. Vle.
dim.
p
1. Vlc.
dim.
p
sul pont.
1. Cb.
dim.
pp
3. Vl.
dim.
p
4. Vl.
p
2. Vle.
dim.
p
sul pont.
2. Vlc.
dim.
p
pp
sul pont.
2. Cb.
pp

A
20 Più andante, ♩ ca 56
Gr. cassa
Tam-tam
Timp.
Xyl.
Cel.
Pfte.
1. Vl.
2 Soli
espr.
2. Vl. div.
con sord.
1. Vle.
1. Vlc.
1. Cb.
ord.
3. Vl.
div.
con sord.
4. Vl.
div.
con sord.
2. Vlc.
ord.
2. Cb.
ord.

25
Cel.
Pfte.
2 soli
1.Vl.
2.Vl.
div.
con sord
pp
1.Vle.
pp
II
1.Vlc.
pp
div.
3.Vl.
div.
4.Vl.

30
rallent. _ _ al Più lento, ♩ ca 46
Timp.
Xyl.
Cel.
Pfte.
1.Vl.
tutti
2.Vl. div.
1.Vle.
1.Vlc.
1.Cb.
3.Vl.
4.Vl.
2.Vlc.
2.Cb.

*) *Griffbezeichnung* / indique la manière de toucher

Timp.
p
Cel.
20
20
20
Arpa
Pfte.
gliss.
gliss.
gliss.
unis.
senza sord. flaut.
2.Vl.
pp
1.Vle.
flaut.
pp
1.Vlc.
flaut.
pp
senza sord.
flaut.
4.Vl.
pp
2.Vle.
flaut.
pp
flaut.
2.Vlc.
pp
2.Cb.

poco
Timp.
20
20
20
Cel.
Arpa
Pfte.
2.Vl.
1.Vle.
1.Vlc.
4.Vl.
2.Vle.
2.Vlc.
2.Cb.

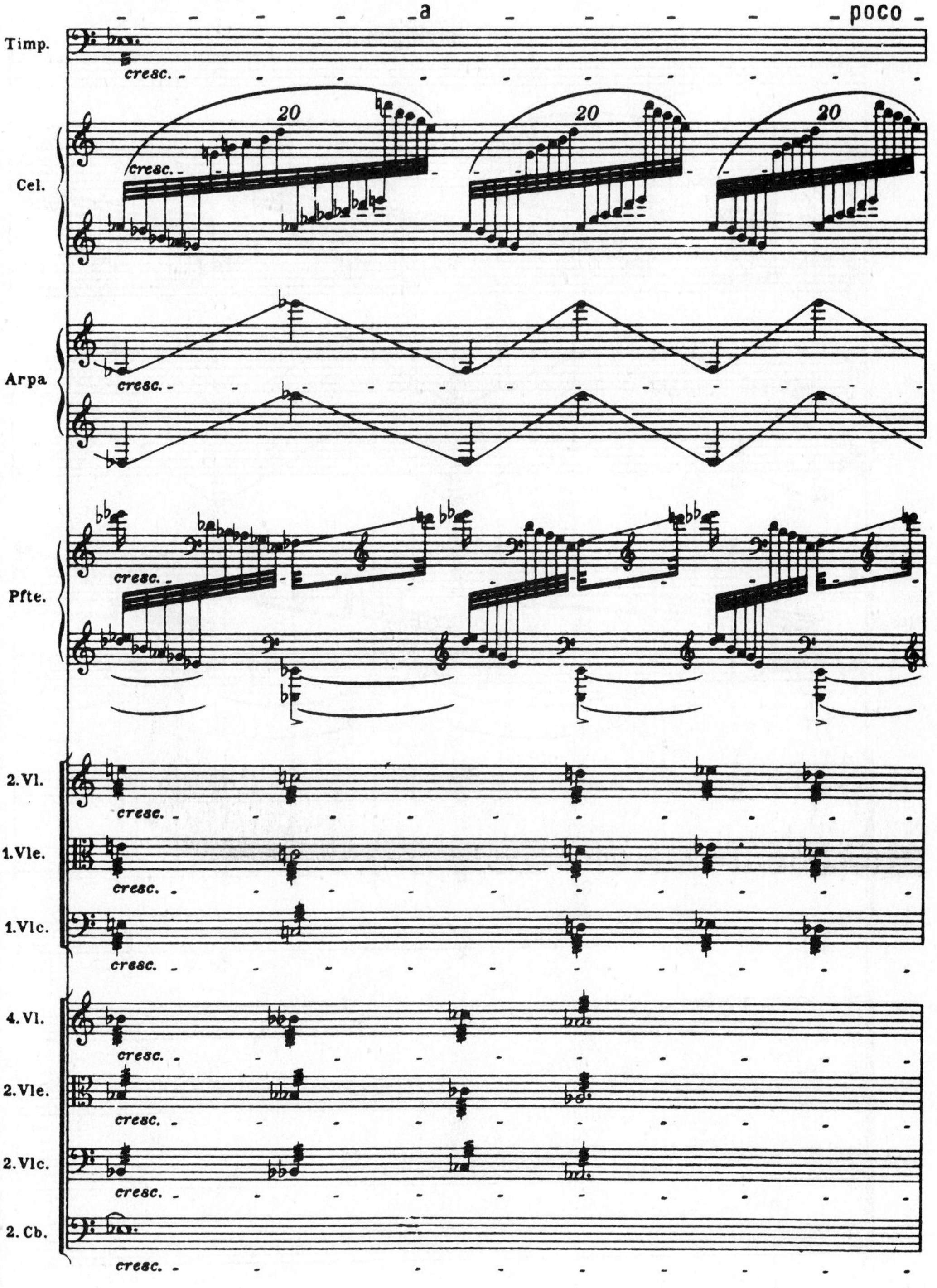
a
poco
Timp.
cresc.
Cel.
20
20
20
cresc.
Arpa
cresc.
Pfte.
cresc.
2. Vl.
cresc.
1. Vle.
cresc.
1. Vlc.
cresc.
4. Vl.
cresc.
2. Vle.
cresc.
2. Vlc.
cresc.
2. Cb.
cresc.

stringendo
Timp.
20
20
20
Cel.
Arpa
10
10
10
Pfte.
2. Vl.
1. Vle.
1. Vlc.
4. Vl.
2. Vle.
2. Vlc.
2. Cb.

40
imp.
el.
20
20
20
rpa
fte.
10
10
10
Vl.
Vle.
Vlc.
Vl.
Vle.
Vlc.
Cb.

Timp.
Cel.
f
5
Arpa
Pfte.
gliss.
10
(ord.)
1. Vl.
2. Vl.
1. Vle.
1. Vlc.
1. Cb.
4. Vl.
2. Vle.
2. Vlc.
2. Cb.
mp

Timp.
mf
Arpa
mf
Pfte.
10
10
10
f
1. Vl.
cresc.
2. Vl.
ord.
cresc.
1. Vle.
ord.
mf cresc.
1. Vlc.
ord.
mf cresc.
1. Cb.
mf
3. Vl.
senza sord.
(ord.)
mp cresc.
4. Vl.
ord.
mf cresc.
2. Vle.
ord.
mf cresc.
2. Vlc.
2. Cb.
mf

*) kleineres Instrument mit höherem Ton / *instrument plus petit au son plus clair*

*) kleineres Instrument / *instrument plus petit*

quasi a tempo, ♩ ca 80
Piatti
Timp.
Xyl.
Arpa
Pfte.
1. Vl.
2. Vl.
1. Vle.
1. Vlc.
1. Cb.
3. Vl.
4. Vl.
2. Vle.
2. Vlc.
2. Cb.
pizz.
arco

55 Allegretto, ♩ ca 104
Cel.
Arpa
Pfte.
1. Vl.
2. Vl.
1. Vle.
1. Vlc.
1. Cb.
3. Vl.
4. Vl.
2. Vle.
2 Vlc.
2. Cb.
mf
p
sempre stacc.
pizz.
div.
(non div.)

60
poco a poco rallent - - - D Meno mosso, ca 76
Pfte
p
1. Vl.
arco
pp, dolce
2. Vl.
pizz.
arco
pp, dolce
1. Vle.
arco
pp, dolce
1. Vlc.
1. Cb.
3. Vl.
arco
pp
4. Vl.
2. Vle.
arco
pp
2. Vlc.
2. Cb.

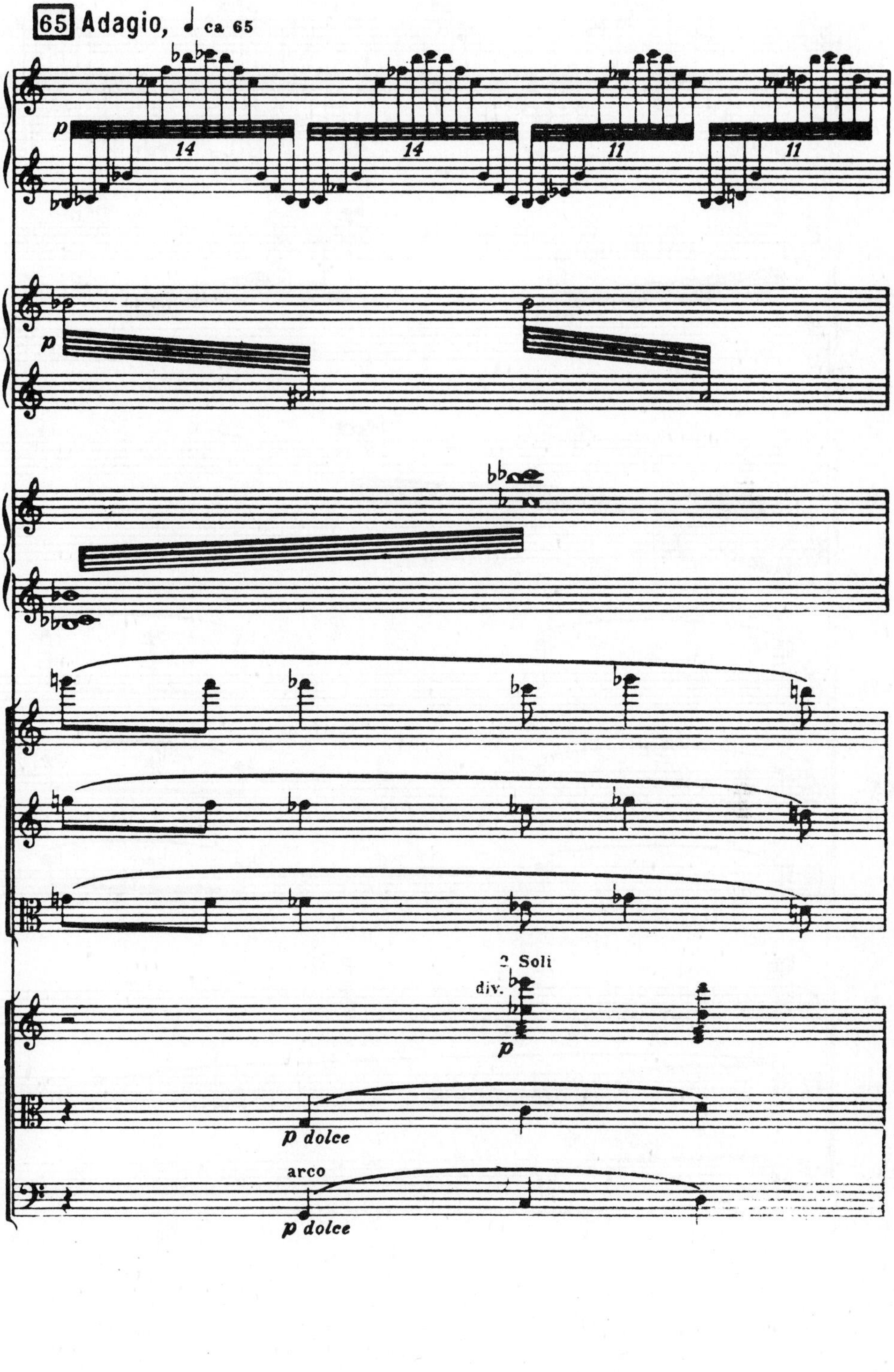
65 Adagio, ♩ ca 65
Cel.
p
14
14
11
11
Arpa
p
Pfte.
1. Vl.
2. Vl.
1. Vle.
2 Soli
div.
3. Vl.
p
2. Vle.
p dolce
arco
2. Vlc.
p dolce

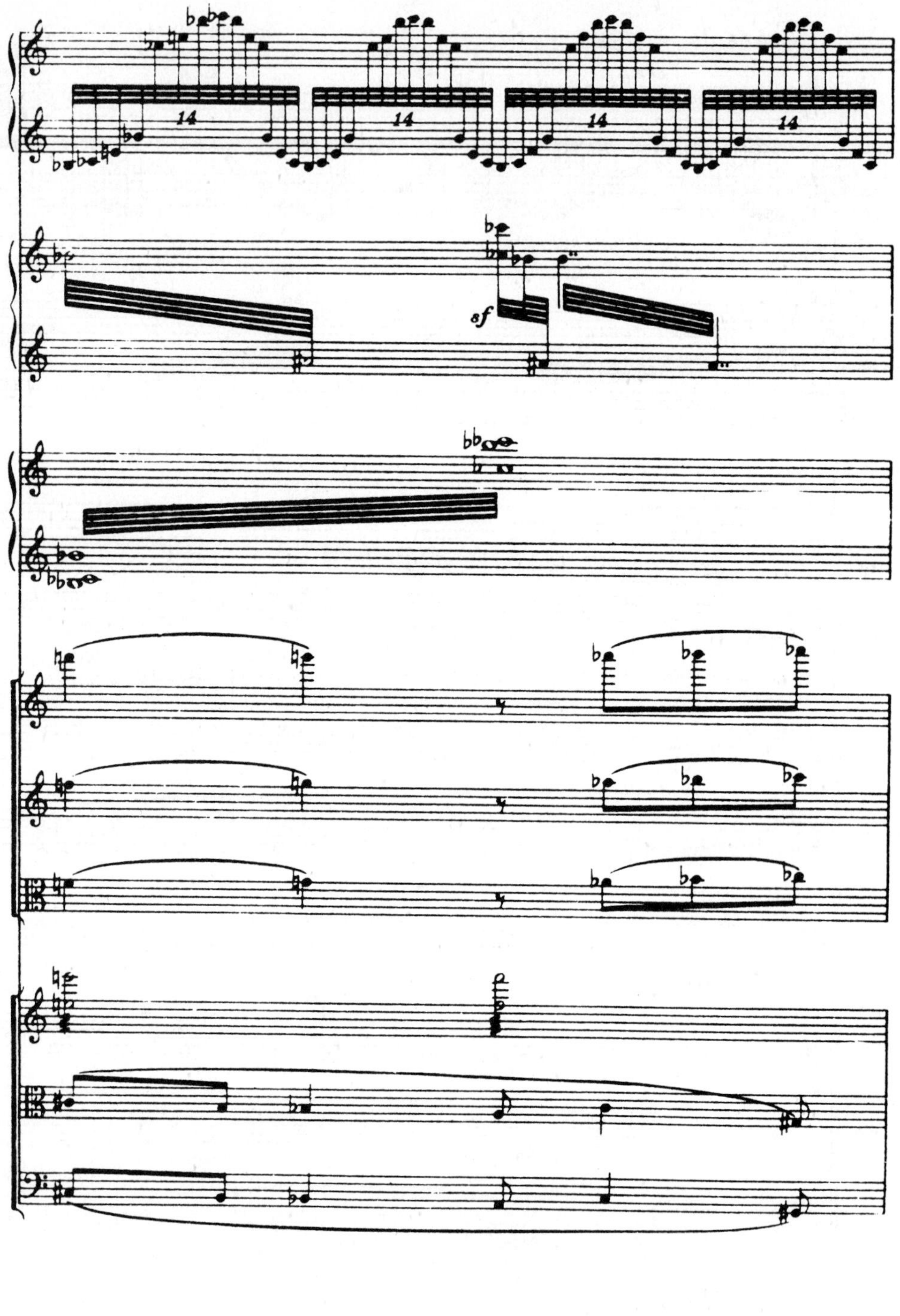
Cel.
14
14
14
14
Arpa
sf
Pfte.
1.Vl.
2.Vl.
1.Vle.
3.Vl.
2.Vle.
2.Vlc.

Cel.
14
14
14
14
Arpa
Pfte.
1. Vl.
2. Vl.
1. Vle.
3. Vl.
2. Vle.
2. Vlc.

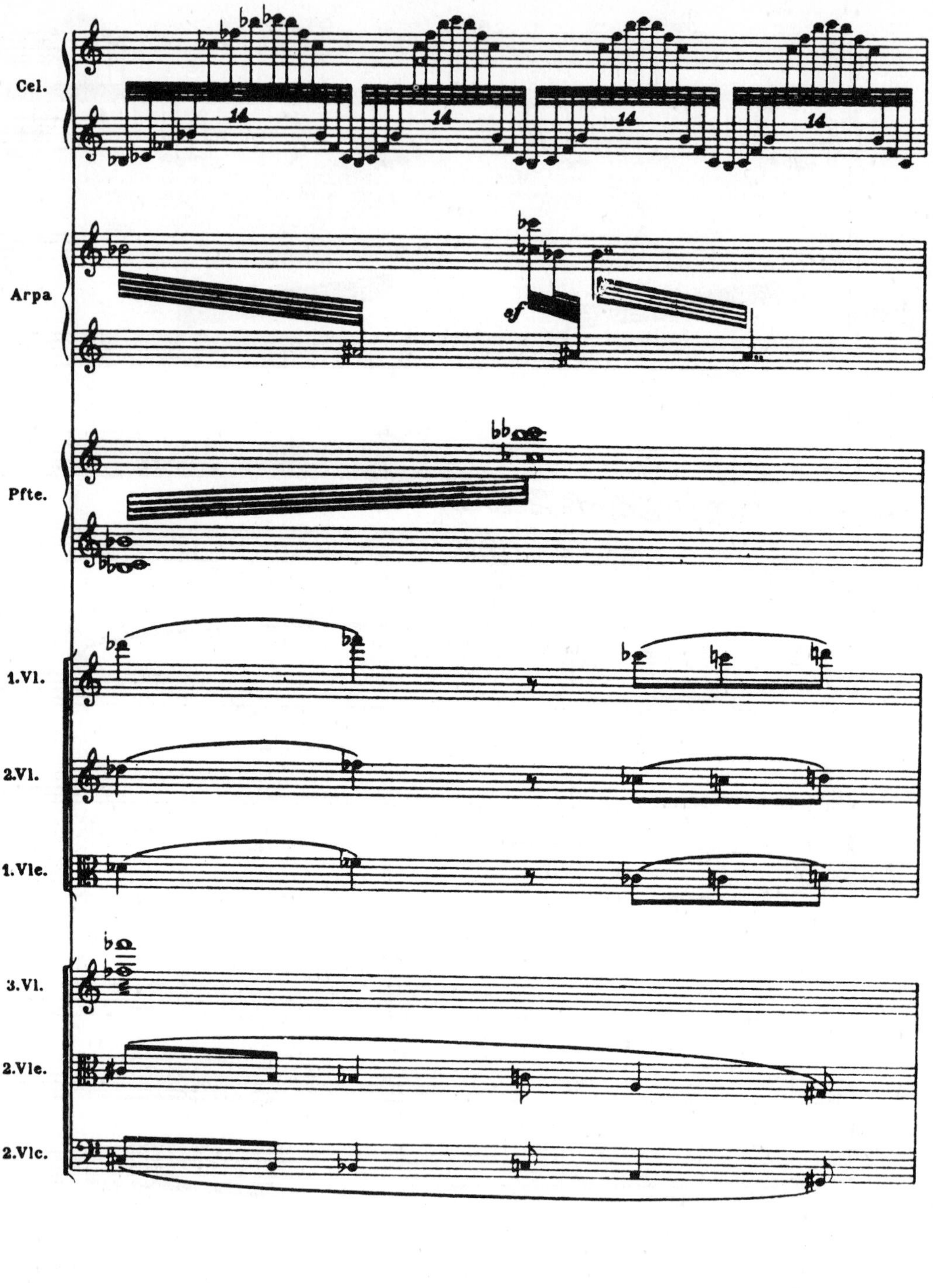
Cel.
14
14
14
14
Arpa
Pfte.
1.Vl.
2.Vl.
1.Vle.
3.Vl.
2.Vle.
2.Vlc.

Cel.
14
14
14
14
Arpa
sf
Pfte.
1.Vl.
2.Vl.
1.Vle.
3.Vl.
2.Vle.
2.Vlc.

rallen
70
Cel.
14
14
14
14
Arpa
sf
Pfte.
1. Vl.
2. Vl.
1. Vle.
3. Vl.
2. Vle.
2. Vlc.

tan
Cel.
14
14
14
14
Arpa
Pfte.
1. Vl.
2. Vl.
1. Vle.
3. Vl.
2.Vle.
2. Vlc.

do
Cel.
14
14
6
6
6
Arpa
Pfte.
1. Vl.
dim.
2. Vl.
dim.
1. Vle.
3. Vl.
2. Vle.
dim.
2. Vlc.
dim.

al ♪ ca 70
E Quasi a tempo
75 ♩ ca 50, rallent.
Cel.
pp
Arpa
ff près de la table
Pfte.
pp
1. Vl.
pizz.
ff
2. Vl.
1. Vle.
pizz.
f
1. Vlc.
pizz.
f
1. Cb.
pizz.
f
2. Vle.
pp
sul pont.
p
2. Vlc.
pp
f
arco
2. Cb.
f

Adagio molto, ♩ = 42
Timp.
tr
mf
arco
1. Vl.
p
2. Vl.
p
2. Vle.
2. Vlc.
p
II
2. Cb.
p

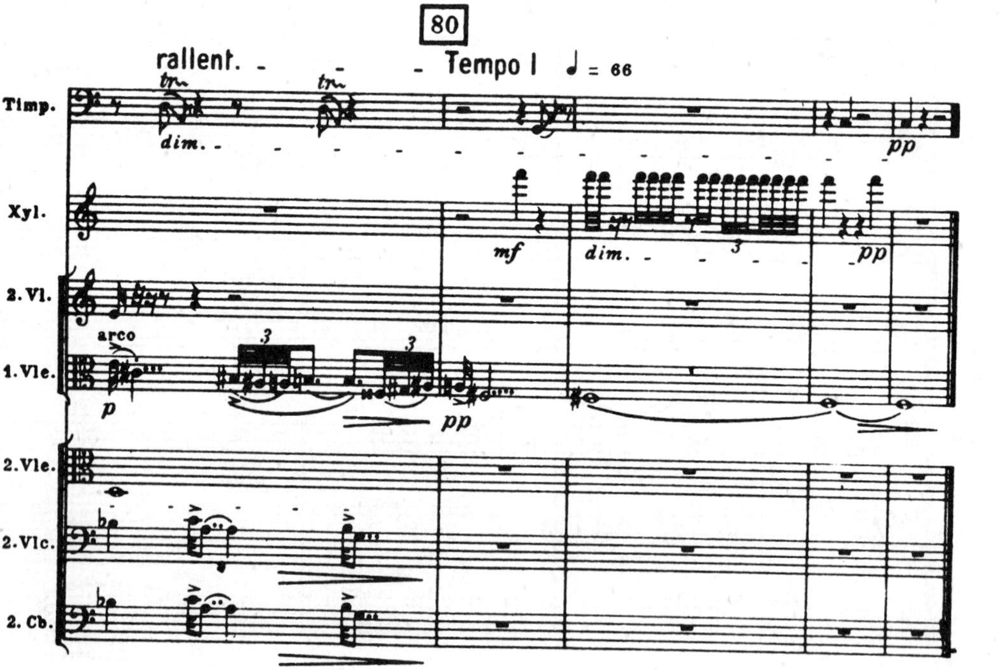
80
rallent.
Tempo I ♩ = 66
Timp.
tr
dim.
pp
Xyl.
mf
dim.
3
pp
2. Vl.
arco
1. Vle.
p
3
pp
2. Vle.
2. Vlc.
2. Cb.

George Crumb (b. 1929)
Black Angels, Thirteen Images from the Dark Land for Electric String Quartet (1970), Images 4 to 9

a) Devil-music

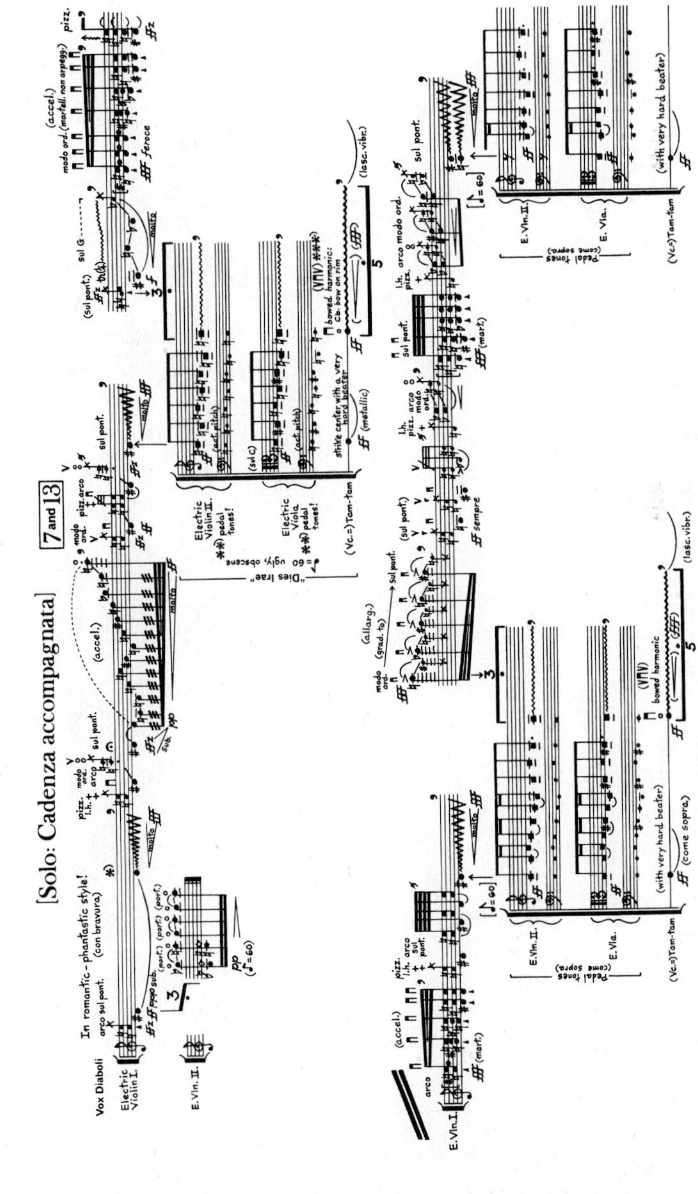

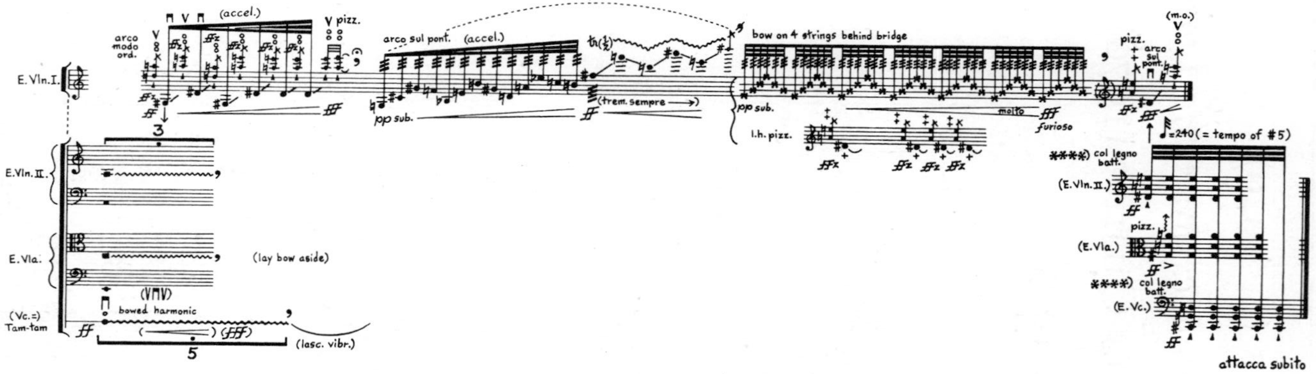

b) *Danse macabre*

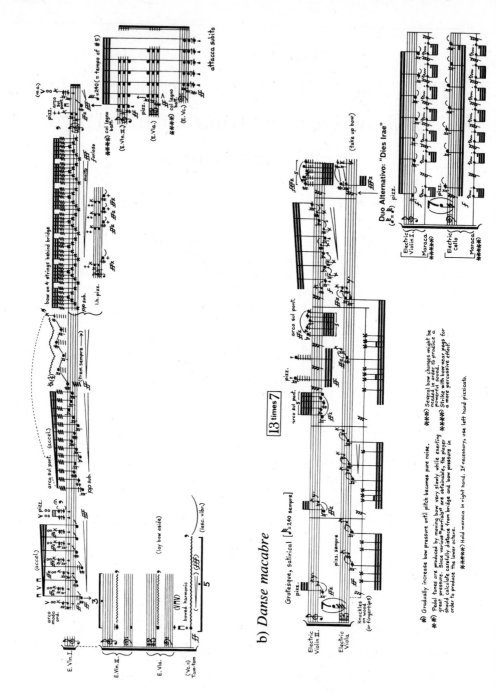

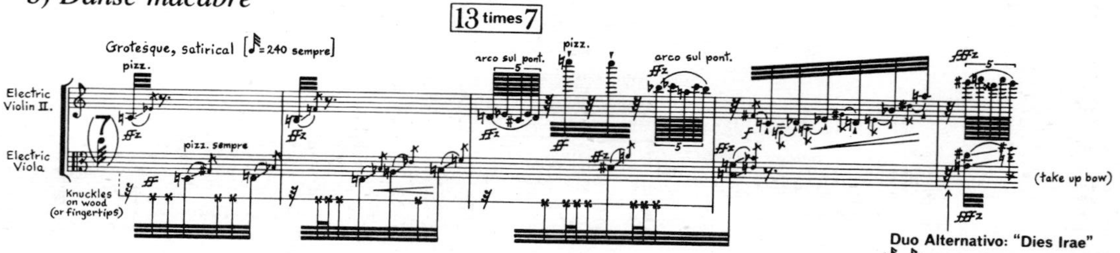

*) Gradually increase bow pressure until pitch becomes pure noise.

**) Pedal tones are produced by moving bow very slowly while exerting great pressure. Since various "partials" are obtainable, the player should calculate carefully distance from bridge and bow pressure in order to produce the lower octave.

***) Several bow changes might be needed in order to produce a powerful sound.

****) Strike with bow near pegs for a more percussive effect.

*****) Hold maraca in right hand. If necessary, use left hand pizzicato.

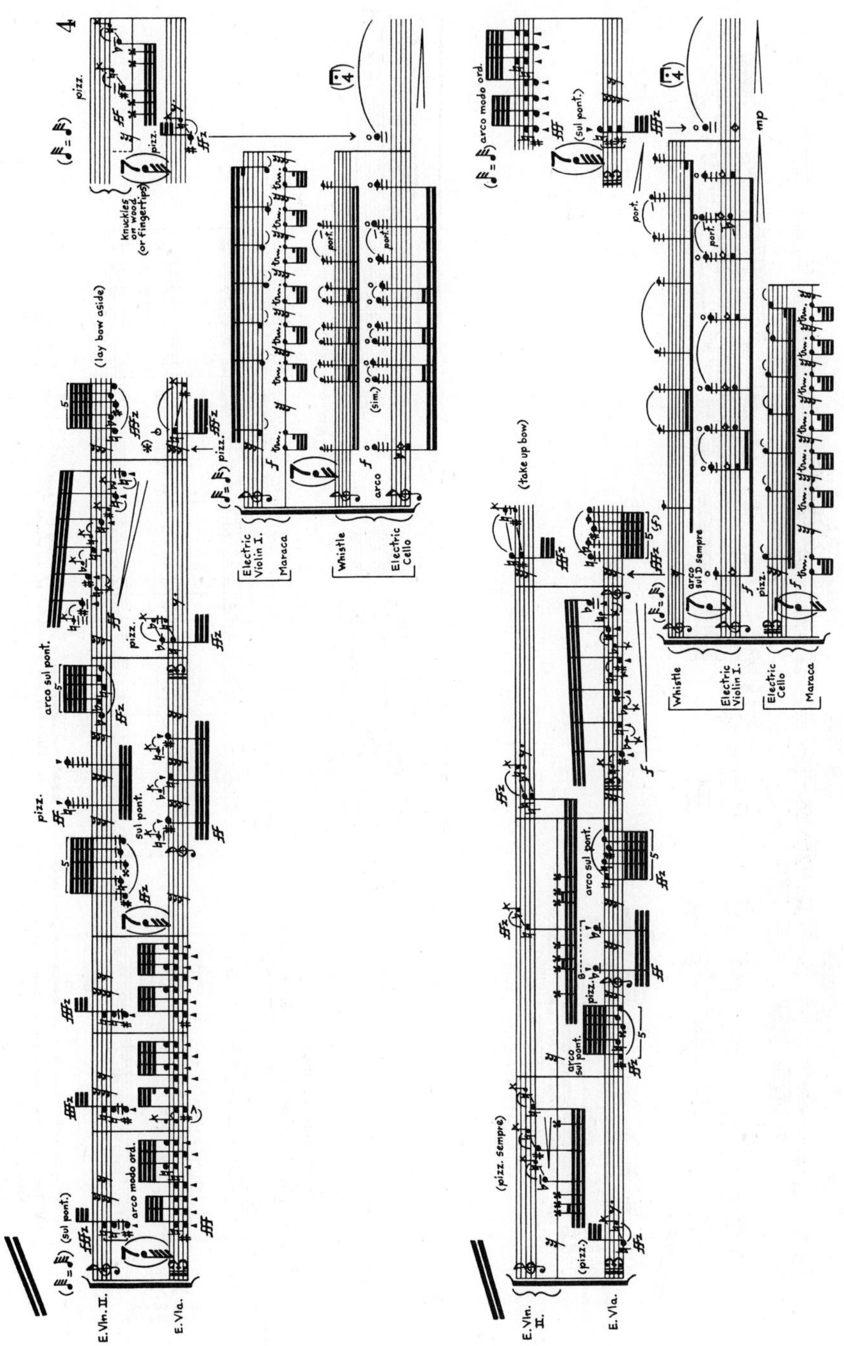
E. Vln. II.
E. Vla.
(sul pont.)
arco modo ord.
pizz.
arco sul pont.
(lay bow aside)
knuckles on wood (or fingertips)
Electric Violin I.
Maraca
Whistle
Electric Cello
(sim.)
port.
arco
(pizz. sempre)
(pizz.)
arco sul pont.
(take up bow)
(sul pont.)
arco sul D sempre
mp

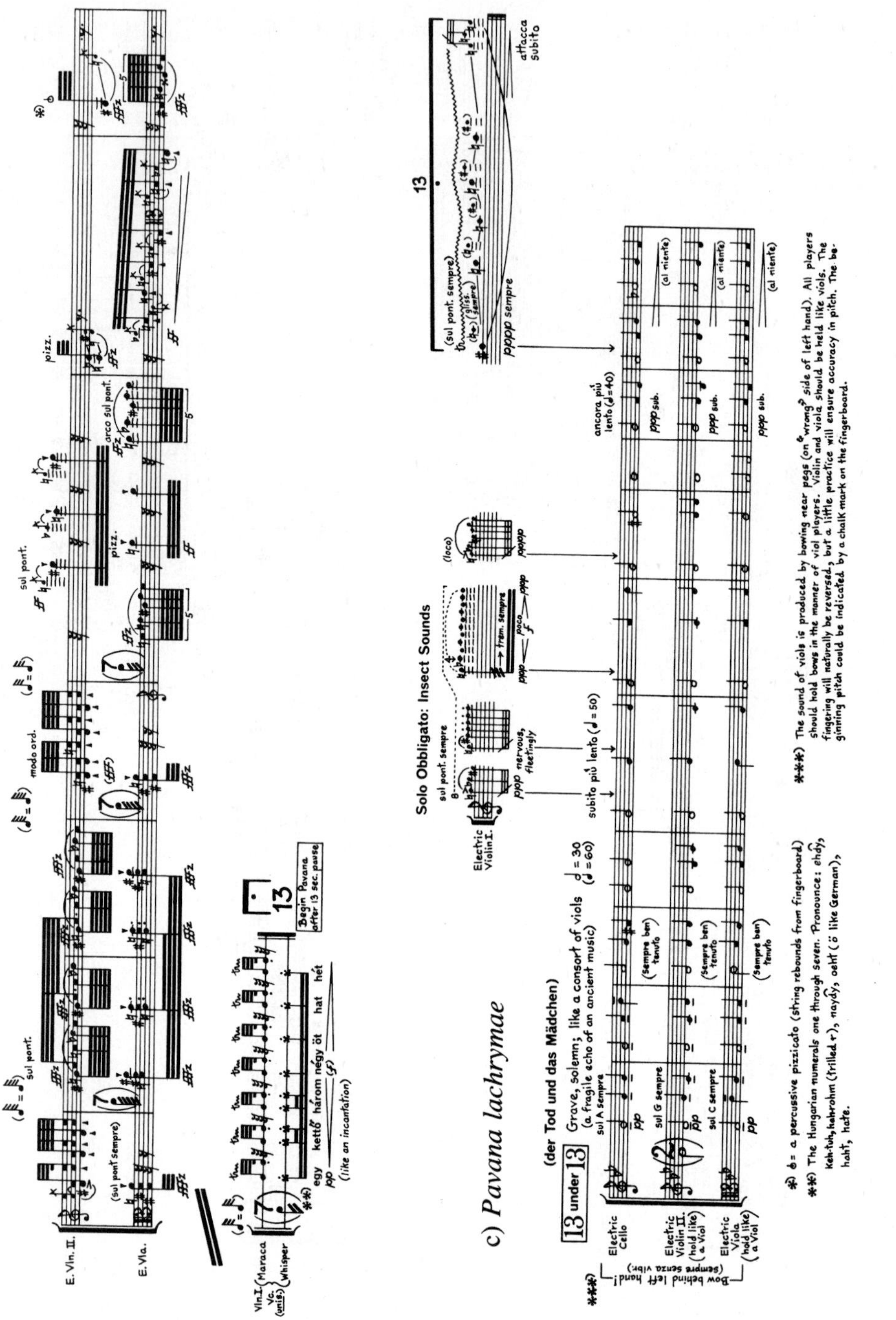
E. Vln. II
E. Vla.
sul pont.
(sul pont. sempre)
modo ord.
pizz.
arco sul pont.
Vln. I Maraca
Vc. (unis.) Whisper
egy kettő három négy öt hat hét
(like an incantation)
Begin Pavana after 13 sec. pause
c) Pavana lachrymae
(der Tod und das Mädchen)
13 under 13
Grave, solemn; like a consort of viols (a fragile echo of an ancient music)
sul A sempre
sul G sempre
sul C sempre
Electric Cello
Electric Violin II (hold like a Viol)
Electric Viola (hold like a Viol)
Bow behind left hand! (sempre senza vibr.)
(sempre ben tenuto)
subito più lento
ancora più lento
(al niente)
Solo Obbligato: Insect Sounds
Electric Violin I
sul pont. sempre
nervous, fleetingly
trem. sempre
(loco)
(sul pont. sempre)
attacca subito
*) ♭ = a percussive pizzicato (string rebounds from fingerboard)
**) The Hungarian numerals one through seven. Pronounce: ehdy, Keh-tuh, hahrohm (trilled r), naydy, oeht (ö like German), haht, hate.
***) The sound of viols is produced by bowing near pegs (on "wrong" side of left hand). All players should hold bows in the manner of viol players. Violin and viola should be held like viols. The fingering will naturally be reversed, but a little practice will ensure accuracy in pitch. The beginning pitch could be indicated by a chalk mark on the fingerboard.

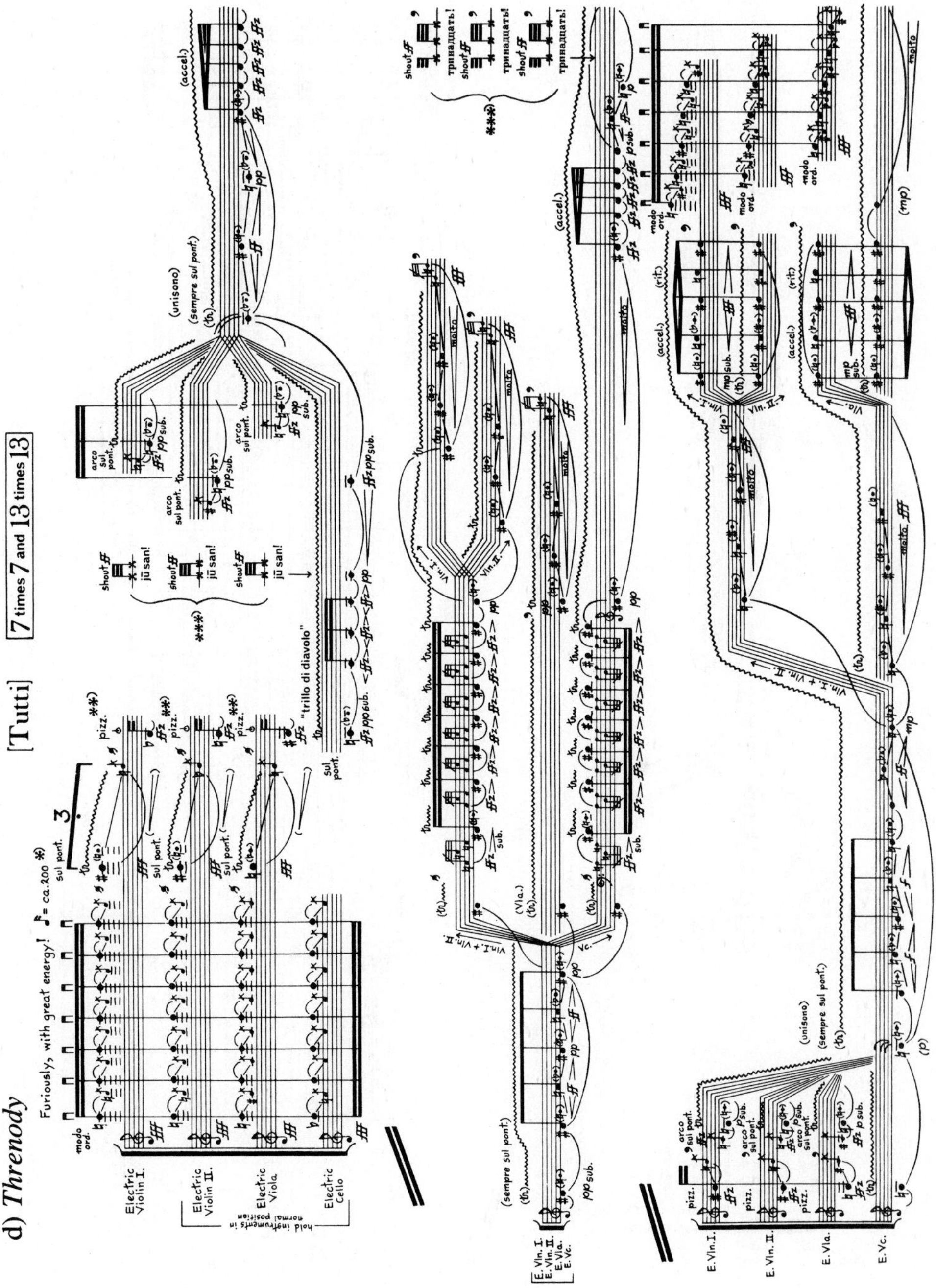
d) Threnody
[Tutti]
7 times 7 and 13 times 13
Furiouslys, with great energy!
♪ = ca. 200 *
modo ord.
sul pont.
pizz.
Electric Violin I.
Electric Violin II.
Electric Viola
Electric Cello
hold instruments in normal position
shout ff
jū san!
"trillo di diavolo"
arco sul pont.
pp sub.
(unisono)
(sempre sul pont.)
(accel.)
(rit.)
тринадцать!
E. Vln. I.
E. Vln. II.
E. Vla.
E. Vc.
Vln. I. + Vln. II.
(Vla.)
molto
E. Vln. I.
E. Vln. II.
E. Vla.
E. Vc.

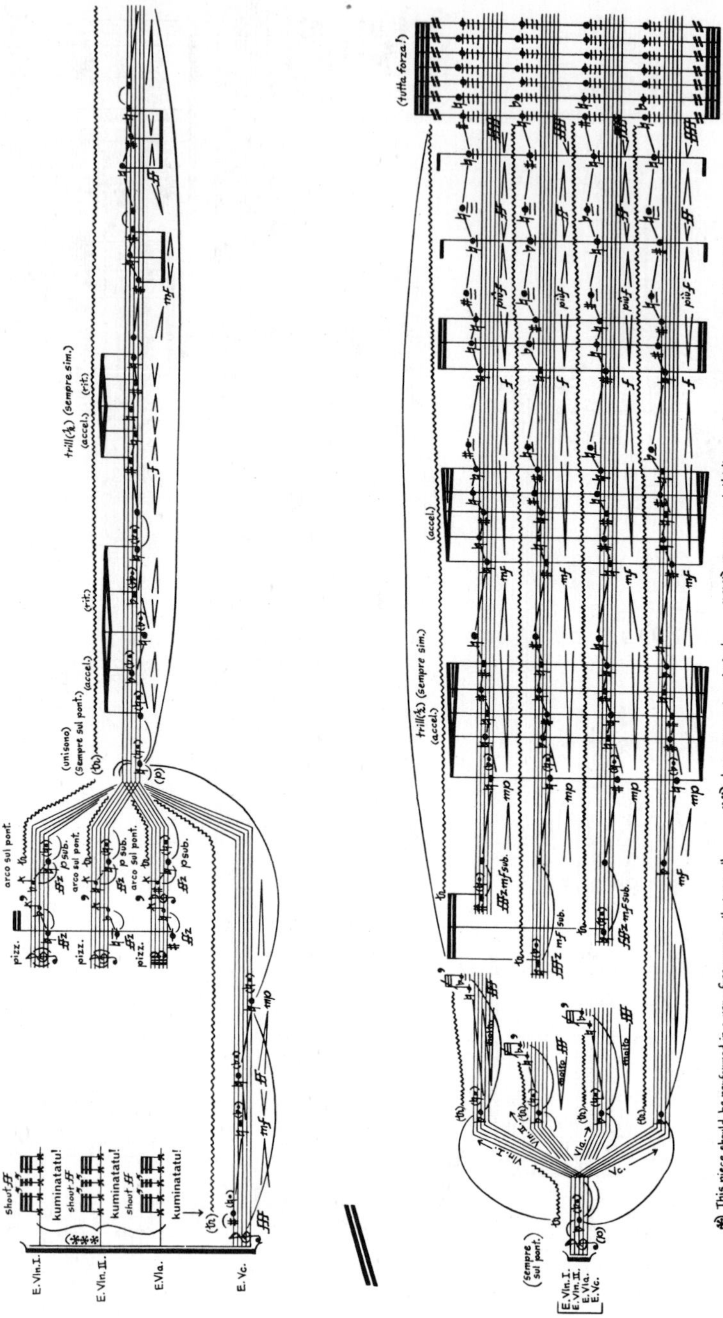

*) This piece should be performed in a very free manner. However, all precisely indicated durations should be approximately in tempo.

**) ♁ = a percussive pizzicato

***) The numeral thirteen in Japanese, Russian, and Swahili.
Pronounce: Joo-sahn, Tree-naht'-saht, Koo-me'nah'tah-too
(' = slight pause between syllables)

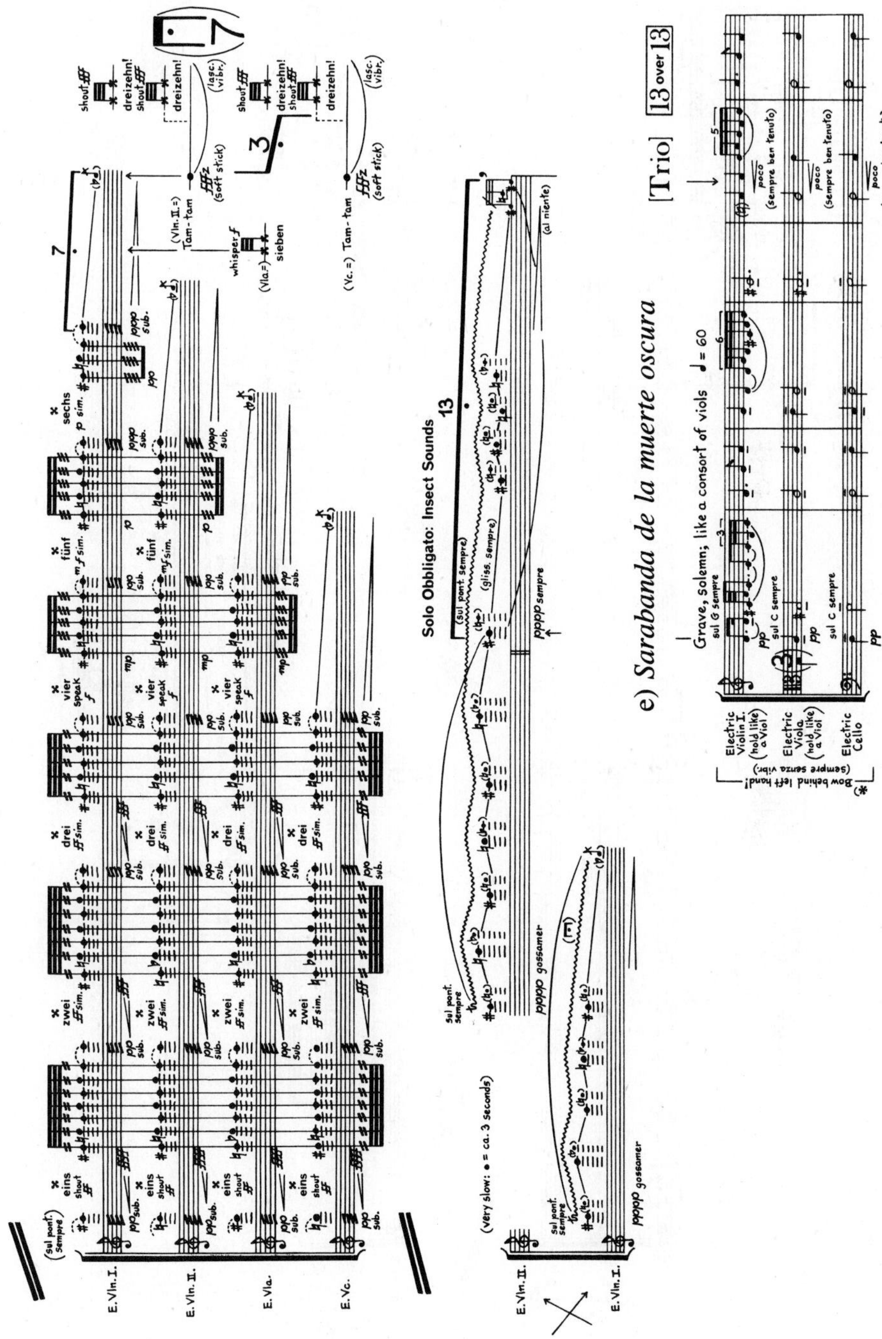
E. Vln. I.
E. Vln. II.
E. Vla.
E. Vc.
eins
zwei
drei
vier
fünf
sechs
sieben
dreizehn!
shout
speak
whisper
(sul pont. sempre)
Tam-tam
(soft stick)
(lasc. vibr.)
7
3
(very slow: ● = ca. 3 seconds)
Solo Obbligato: Insect Sounds
13
(sul pont. sempre)
(gliss. sempre)
pppp gossamer
pppp sempre
(al niente)
e) Sarabanda de la muerte oscura
[Trio] 13 over 13
Grave, solemn; like a consort of viols ♩ = 60
Electric Violin I. (hold like a Viol)
Electric Viola (hold like a Viol)
Electric Cello
sul G sempre
sul C sempre
poco
(sempre ben tenuto)
*) Bow behind left hand! (sempre senza vibr.)

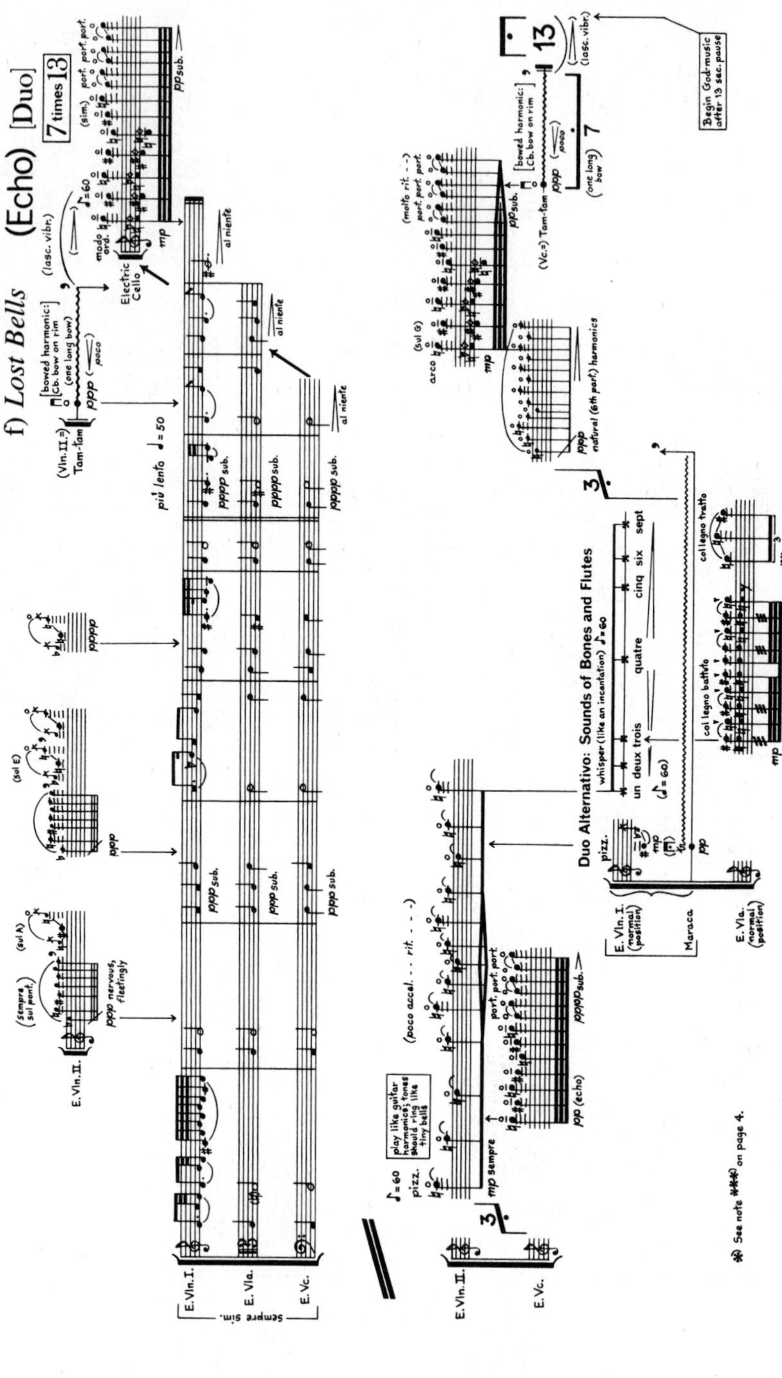
f) Lost Bells
(Echo) [Duo]
7 times 13
(Vln. II.=) Tam-tam
[bowed harmonic: Cb. bow on rim]
(one long bow)
(lasc. vibr.)
Electric Cello
modo ord.
pp sub.
E. Vln. II.
(sempre sul pont.)
ppp nervous, fleetingly
(sul A)
(sul E)
più lento ♪=50
ppp sub.
al niente
E. Vln. I.
E. Vla.
E. Vc.
sempre sim.
E. Vln. II.
E. Vc.
pizz.
mp sempre
play like guitar harmonics; tones should ring like tiny bells
(poco accel. - - rit. - - -)
port. port. port.
pp (echo)
pppp sub.
arco
(sul G)
(molto rit. - -)
natural (6th part.) harmonics
(Vc.=) Tam-tam
(one long bow)
Begin God-music after 13 sec. pause
Duo Alternativo: Sounds of Bones and Flutes
whisper (like an incantation)
un deux trois quatre cinq six sept
E. Vln. I. (normal position)
Maraca
E. Vla. (normal position)
col legno battuto
throw bow
col legno tratto
* See note *** on page 4.

Olivier Messiaen (b. 1908)

Méditations sur le mystère de la Sainte Trinité (1969): Vif (fourth movement)

All that we can know about God is summed up in these words at once so compact and simple: *he is;* words that we do not understand except in flashes, in rare and brief illuminations. Nearly all of this piece establishes a climate, preparing for the final vision. The strangeness of the bird calls chosen must evoke some unknown dimension . . . It is first of all the extraordinary cry of the Black Woodpecker (*Pic noir*), a rapid and discordant plaint that is heard in the forests of the Vosges or the high tops of the Larch trees and of the Piceas of the Dauphinese Alps. Two other primitive melodies: the call of the Ring Ouzel (*Merle à plastron*), and the little sad tolling bell in equal durations of the Tengmalm's Owl (*Chouette de Tengmalm*), heard in the Jura. Trilled clusters, a short trio passage evoking the Three Persons of the Holy Trinity. Then a long solo of the Song Thrush (*Grive musicienne*), with its thrice repeated themes on the *plein jeu* (principal chorus) and *clairon 4* (four-foot trumpet), and its changes of tone color and of attack (like pizzicato, water dropping, silk tearing). All of a sudden, towards the end of the piece, an organ fortissimo: chords in Iambic rhythm descending rapidly: this is the vision of Moses. ''And the Lord ('I am') passed by before him, and proclaimed, The Lord ('I am, I am!') (*Exodus* 34:6). Grand silence. The Tengmalm's Owl recedes, expressing our pettiness overwhelmed by the lightning flash of the Holy Scripture.

(Prefatory note by the composer)

Comb. 6 R: fonds 16,8 – bombarde 16, trp. 8 – < | Pos: fonds 16,8,4, mixtures, anches 16,8,4 < |
G: montre 8, prestant 4, plein jeu 5 rangs, cymbale 4 rangs – | Ped: fonds 16,8,32 – tir. R – |

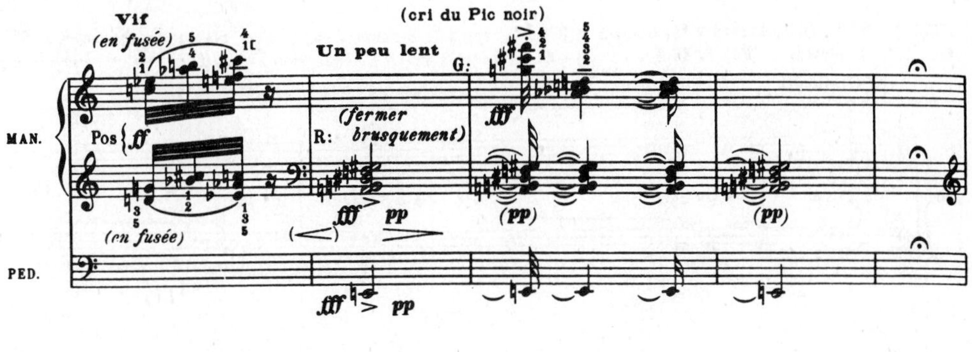

Éditions Musicales Alphonse Leduc, Paris, c 1973, pp. 29–36. Réproduit avec l'aimable autorisation de Alphonse Leduc & Cie., éditeurs et propriétaires en tous pays.

6

Comb. 1 R: fl., bourd., gambe > | Pos: cornet 5 rangs, cor de nuit 8 - < | G: fl. harm., bourdon 8, bourdon 16 - |

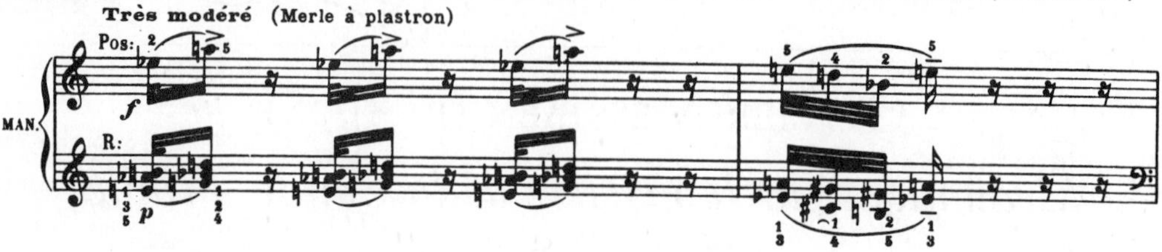

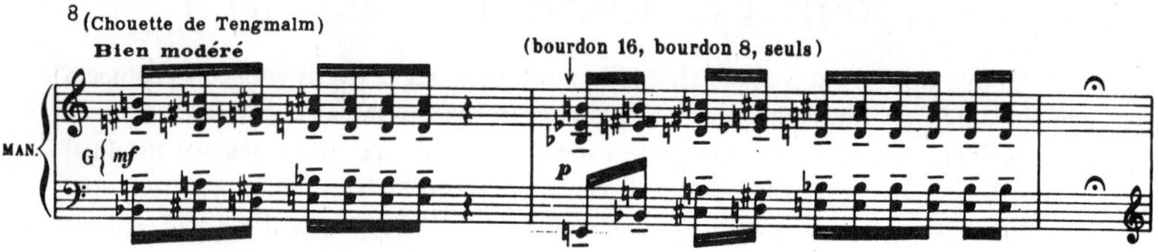

11

Comb. 6 R: fonds 16,8 - bombarde 16, trp. 8 - < | Pos: fonds 16, 8,4, mixtures, anches 16, 8,4 - < |
G: montre 8, prestant 4, plein jeu 5 rangs, cymbale 4 rangs - | Ped: fonds 16,8,32 - tir. R |

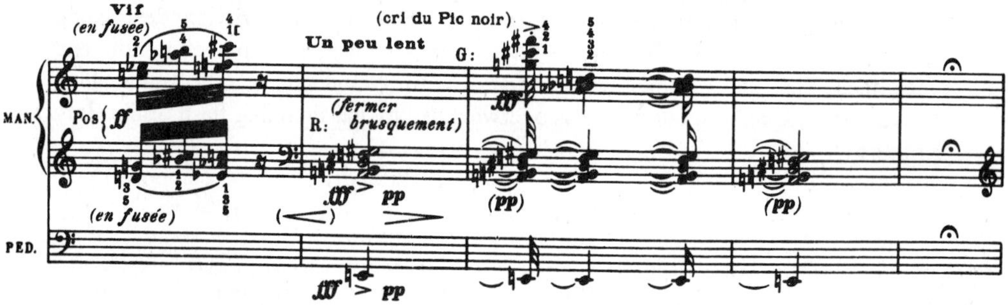

16

Comb. 8 R: fl. 4, nazard 2 2/3, octavin 2, 3ce 1 3/5, cymbale 3 rangs - < | Pos: clarinette, flageolet 2, 3ce 1 3/5,
piccolo 1 - Pos. en 16,8,4 - > | G: bourdon 8 seul - | Ped: violoncelle, flûte 4 - | →

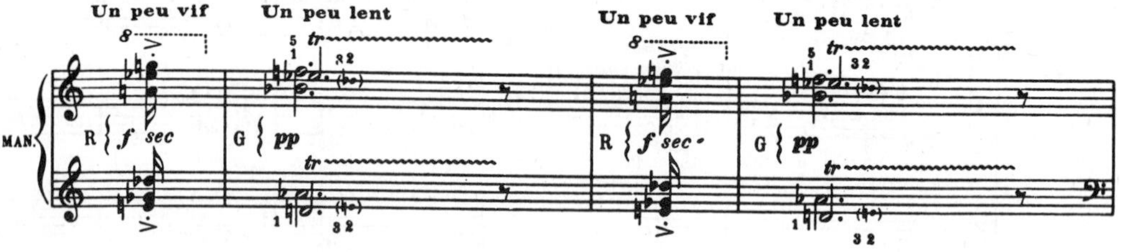

20
(Pos: clarinette, flageolet 2, 3ce 1 3/5, piccolo 1 - Pos. en 16, 8, 4 - >) (Ped: vcl., fl. 4 -)
Un peu lent
(Père)
legato
(râgavardhana)
MAN.
Pos { mf
(Fils)
legato
(pratâpaçekhara)
(Esprit)
PED.
legato
(simhavikrama)
mf
(R: fl. 4, nazard 2 2/3, octavin 2, 3ce 1 3/5, cymb. 3 rangs - <)
(G: bourdon 8 seul)
22
Un peu vif
Un peu lent
Un peu vif
R { f sec
G { pp
R { f sec
26
Un peu lent
Un peu vif
Un peu lent
G { pp
R { f sec
f sec
G { pp
(m.g. dessus)
Comb. 6
R: fonds 16, 8 - bombarde 16, trp. 8 - < | Pos: fonds 16,8,4, mixtures, anches 16,8,4 - < |
G: montre 8, prestant 4, plein jeu 5 rangs, cymbale 4 rangs - | Ped: fonds 16, 8, 32 - tir. R - |
29
Vif
(en fusée)
(cri du Pic noir)
Un peu lent
G:
fff
(fermer
R: brusquement)
Pos { ff
fff
pp
(pp)
(en fusée)
fff
pp

35
Comb. 5
R: bourdon 16, bourdon 8, nazard 2 2/3, octavin 2 - > | Pos: fl. 4, nazard 2 2/3, flageolet 2, 3ce 1 3/5, piccolo 1 - < | G: plein jeu 5 rangs - clairon 4 - |
Un peu vif
(éclatant)
MAN.
G ff
(grand solo de Grive musicienne)
Très modéré
R pp
(très sec, comme des pizzi)
38 Modéré
R f
Un peu vif
G ff
42 Modéré
R f
Modéré
Vif
Pos mf
(comme de la soie déchirée)
g. dessus
44 Très modéré
R pp
(très sec, comme des pizzi)
Un peu vif
G ff
Bien modéré
ff
48
Bien modéré
ff

52
Modéré
Un peu vif
MAN.
R pp
G ff
(comme des gouttes d'eau)
56
Modéré
Bien modéré
Modéré
Vif
ff
R f
Pos mf
(comme de la soie déchirée)
g. dessus
61
Un peu vif
d. dessus
G ff
g. dessus
64
Modéré
R f
f
66
Un peu lent
R f
pp
(très sec, comme des pizzi)

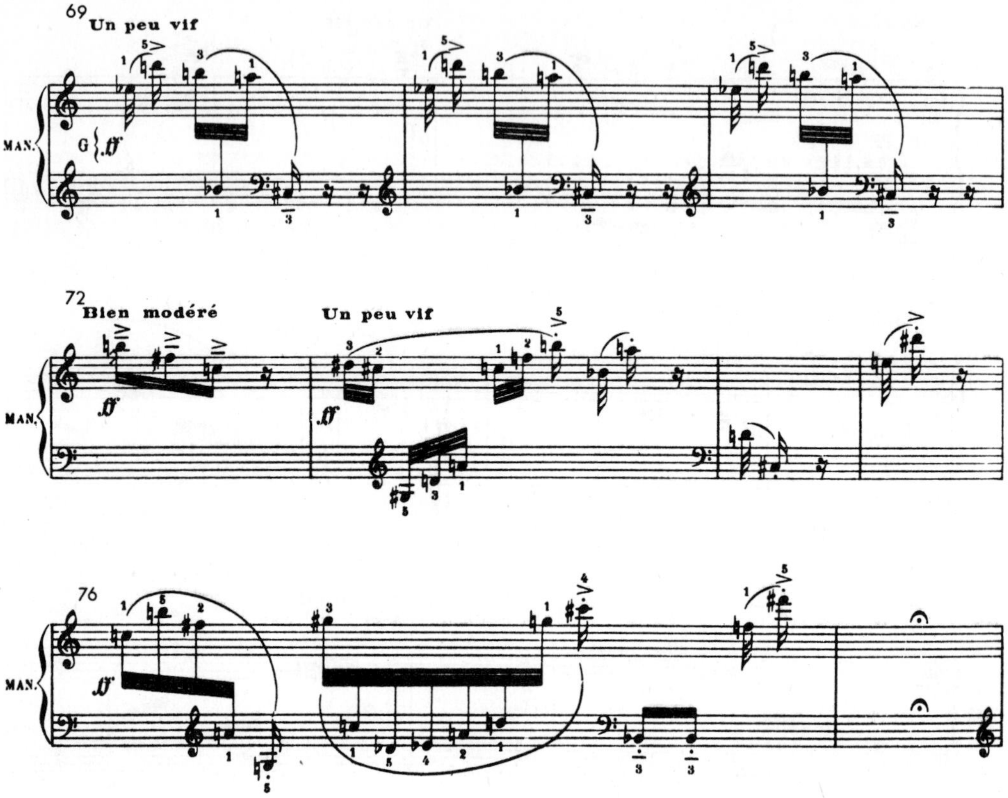

Comb. 6 R: fonds 16,8 – bombarde 16, trp. 8 – < | Pos: fonds 16, 8,4, mixtures, anches 16,8,4 < |
G: montre 8, prestant 4, plein jeu 5 rangs, cymbale 4 rangs – | Ped: fonds 16,8,32 – tir. R – |

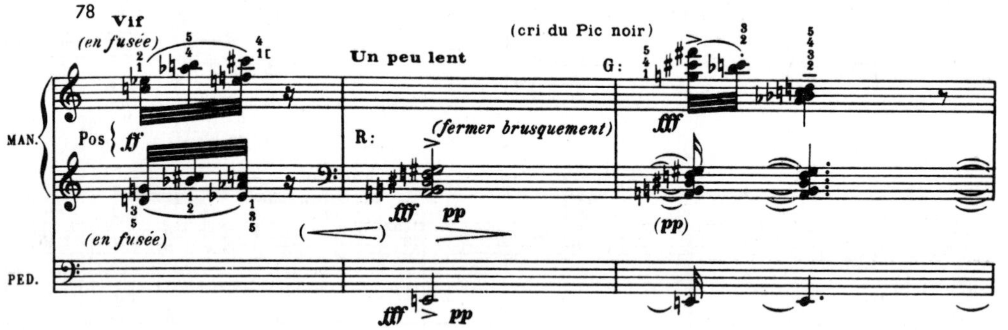

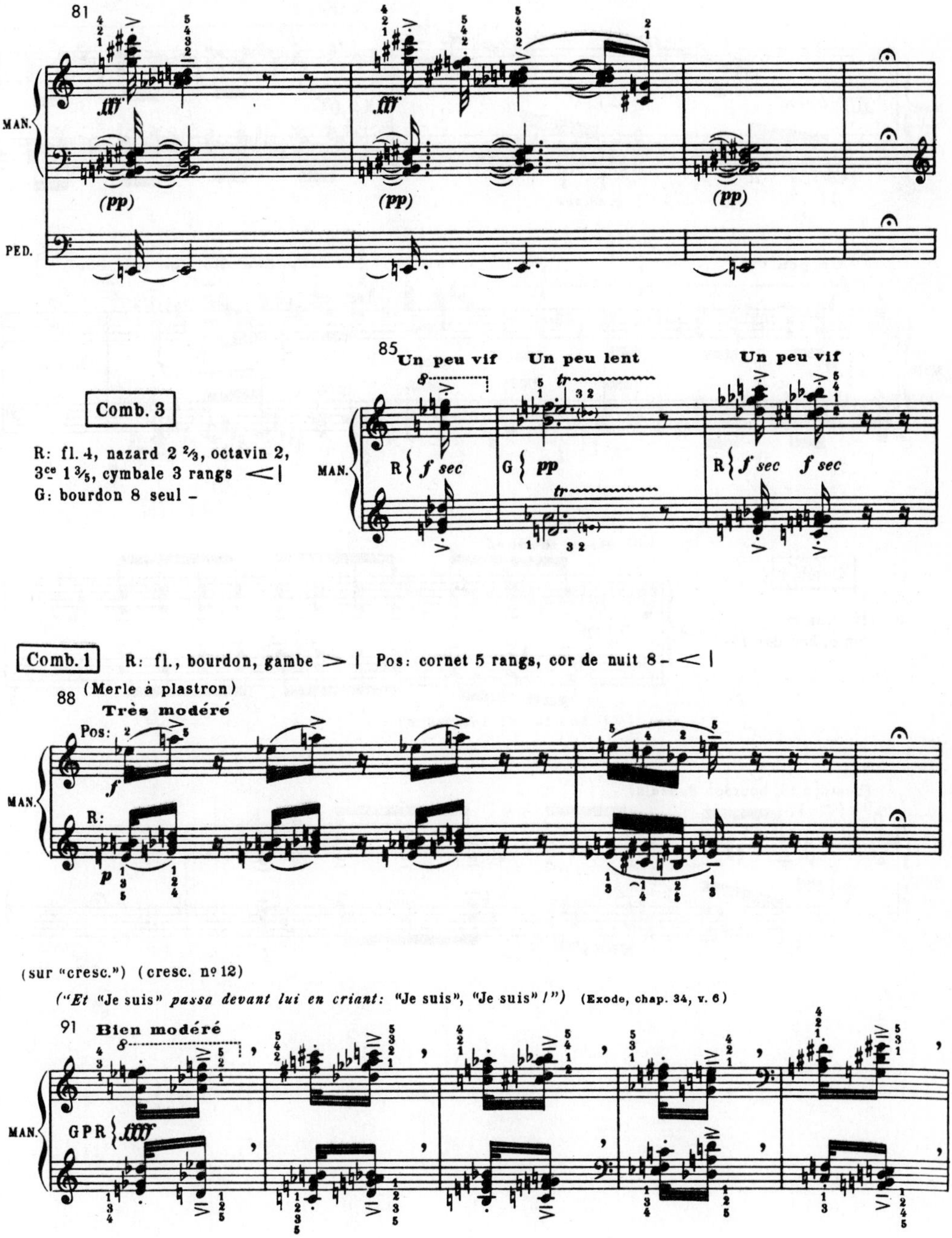
81
MAN.
(pp)
(pp)
(pp)
PED.
85
Un peu vif
Un peu lent
Un peu vif
Comb. 3
R: fl. 4, nazard 2 2/3, octavin 2,
3ce 1 3/5, cymbale 3 rangs
G: bourdon 8 seul –
MAN.
R { f sec
G { pp
R { f sec f sec
Comb. 1
R: fl., bourdon, gambe
Pos: cornet 5 rangs, cor de nuit 8 –
(Merle à plastron)
88
Très modéré
Pos:
MAN.
R:
(sur "cresc.") (cresc. nº 12)
("Et "Je suis" passa devant lui en criant: "Je suis", "Je suis" !") (Exode, chap. 34, v. 6)
91
Bien modéré
MAN.
GPR { ffff

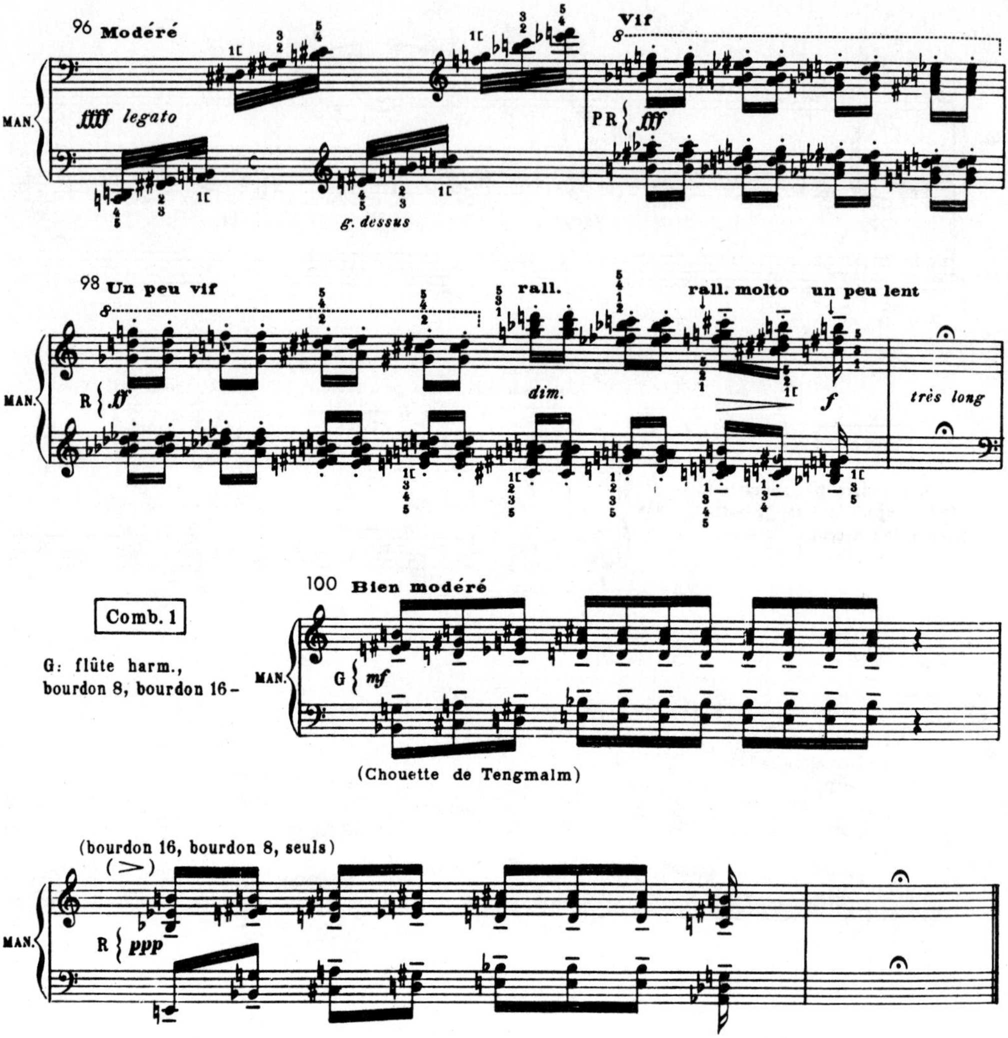
96 Modéré
fff legato
MAN.
g. dessus
Vif
PR { *fff*
98 Un peu vif
R { *ff*
rall.
dim.
rall. molto
un peu lent
f
très long
Comb. 1
G: flûte harm.,
bourdon 8, bourdon 16 –
100 Bien modéré
G { *mf*
(Chouette de Tengmalm)
(bourdon 16, bourdon 8, seuls)
R { *ppp*

156

Steve Reich (b. 1936)

Violin Phase (1979)

In the version for a single violinist and three-track tape, the performer first records bar 1 over and over again for one to five minutes. Then, after rewinding the tape, the violinist superimposes repetitions of the same pattern of notes, but now four eighth notes ahead of the first track, as at bar 7. The performer then rewinds the tape again and records the pattern four eighth notes ahead of track 2, as at bar 18. The best three to seven repetitions are made into a tape loop, resulting in the ostinato shown in bar 18, fourth staff from the top. The violinist performs the composition against this ostinato by playing at first in unison with the first track, then accelerating until he or she is one eighth note ahead of track 1, when the tempo is held for a number of repeats, after which the process of alternate acceleration and synchronization with the tape continues.

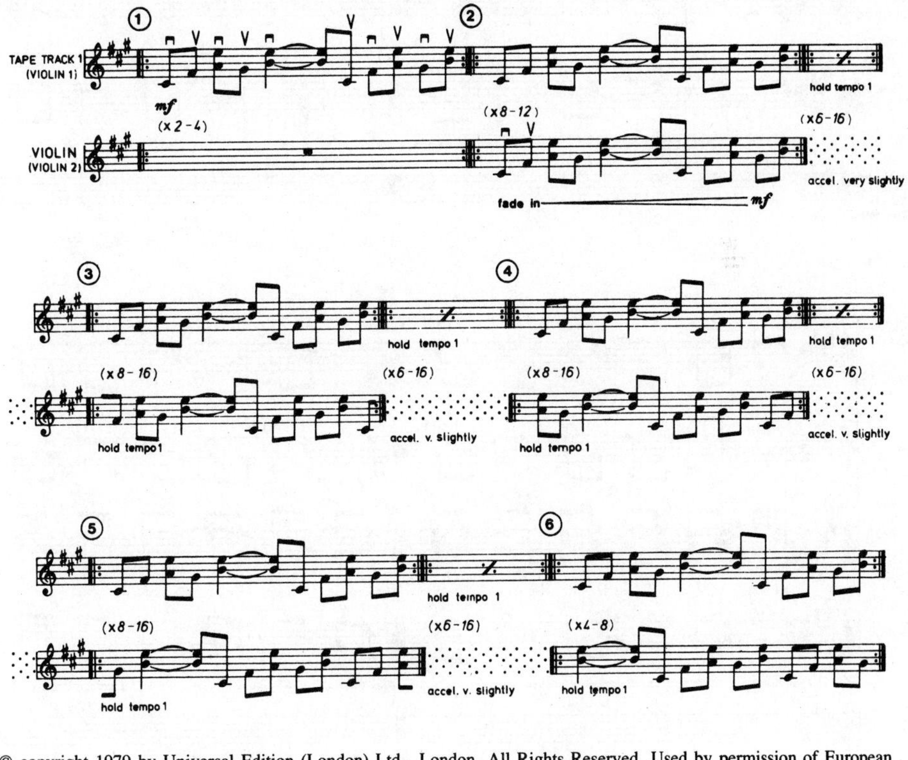

7
8
TAPE TRK 2
(VIOLIN 1)
x4-8
TAPE TRK. 2
(VIOLIN 3)
fade in
mf
(x4-8)
(x2-4)
VIOLIN
(VIOLIN 2)
fade out
9
9a
TAPE TRK. 2
(VIOLIN 1)
TAPE TRK. 2
(VIOLIN 3)
Result of
TAPE TRACK 2
(VIOLINS 1+3)
(x4-6)
(x4-6)
VIOLIN
(VIOLIN 2)
Fade in
f
Alternate
Resulting
Pattern
(see notes)
9b
10
(x4-6)
(x4-6)
Fade out
Fade in

10a
10b
TAPE TRK. 2
(VIOLIN 1)
TAPE TRK. 2
(VIOLIN 3)
Result of
TAPE TRK. 2
(VIOLINS 1+3)
(x4-6)
(x4-6)
VIOLIN
(VIOLIN 2)
f
Fade out
Alt. Res.
Pattern
(see notes)
11
(x3-5)
Fade in
11a
TAPE TRK. 2
(VIOLIN 1)
TAPE TRK. 2
(VIOLIN 3)
Result of
TAPE TRK. 2
(VIOLINS 1+3)
(x3-5)
VIOLIN
(VIOLIN 2)
f
Alt. Res.
Pattern
(see notes)

11b
(x3-6)
Fade out
12
13
TAPE TRK. 2
(VIOLIN 1)
hold tempo 1
hold tempo 1
TAPE TRK. 2
(VIOLIN 3)
hold tempo 1
hold tempo 1
(x8-12)
(x6-16)
(x8-16)
(x6-16)
VIOLIN
(VIOLIN 2)
accel. v. slightly
hold tempo 1
accel. v. slightly
Fade in
mf
14
15
hold tempo 1
hold tempo 1
hold tempo 1
hold tempo 1
(x8-16)
(x6-16)
(x8-16)
(x6-16)
hold tempo 1
accel. v. slightly
hold tempo 1
accel. v. slightly
16
17
TAPE TRACK 2
(VIOLIN 1)
TAPE TRACK 2
(VIOLIN 3)
(x4-8)
TAPE TRACK 1
(VIOLIN 4)
Fade in
mf
(x4-8)
(x4-8)
VIOLIN
(VIOLIN 2)
hold tempo 1
Fade out

18
19
TAPE TRK. 2 (VIOLIN 1)
TAPE TRK. 2 (VIOLIN 3)
TAPE TRK. 1 (VIOLIN 4)
Result of TAPE TRKS. 1+2 (VIOLINS 1+3+4)
VIOLIN (VIOLIN 2)
Alt. Res. Pattern (see notes)
hold tempo 1
tempo 1
(x4-8)
(x2-4)
(x2-6)
Fade in
f
accel. v. slightly
19a
19b
(x3-6)
19c
19d
Fade out

20
20a
TAPE TRK. 2 (VIOLIN 1)
TAPE TRK. 2 (VIOLIN 3)
TAPE TRK. 1 (VIOLIN 4)
Result of TAPE TRKS. 1+2 (VIOLINS 1+3+4)
VIOLIN (VIOLIN 2)
Alt. Res. Pattern (see notes)
hold tempo 1
tempo 1
(x2-4)
Fade in
f
accel. v. slightly
20b
20c
20d
21
(x3-6)
(x2-6)
Fade out

21a
21b
TAPE TRACK 2 (VIOLIN 1)
TAPE TRACK 2 (VIOLIN 3)
TAPE TRACK 1 (VIOLIN 4)
Result of TAPE TRKS. 1+2 (VIOLINS 1+3+4)
VIOLIN (VIOLIN 2)
Alt. Res. Pattern (see notes)
hold tempo 1
tempo 1
(x3-6)
(x2-6)
accel. v. slightly
21c
21d
Fade out
22
22a
TAPE TRK. 2 (VIOLIN 1)
TAPE TRK. 2 (VIOLIN 3)
TAPE TRK. 1 (VIOLIN 4)
Result of TAPE TRKS. 1+2 (VIOLINS 1+3+4)
VIOLIN (VIOLIN 2)
Alt. Res. Pattern (see notes)
(x3-5)
Fade in

22b
22c
(x3-5)
f
22d
22e
TAPE TRK. 2 (VIOLIN 1)
TAPE TRK. 2 (VIOLIN 3)
TAPE TRK. 1 (VIOLIN 4)
Result of TAPE TRKS.1+2 (VIOLINS 1+3+4)
VIOLIN (VIOLIN 2)
(x3-5)
fade out
Alt. Res. Pattern (see notes)
22f
22g

23
23a
TAPE TRK. 2 (VIOLIN 1)
TAPE TRK. 2 (VIOLIN 3)
TAPE TRK. 1 (VIOLIN 4)
Result of TAPE TRKS. 1+2 (VIOLINS 1·3·4)
(x3-6)
(x6-8)
CUE for End (see notes)
VIOLIN (VIOLIN 2)
Fade in
f

157

Gabriel Fauré (1845–1924)
La bonne chanson, Opus 61 (1892): No. 6, *Avant que tu ne t'en ailles*

12
thym!
rall.
Quasi Adagio. ♩= 68
15
dolce
Tour-ne devers le po - è - te dont les yeux sont pleins d'a-
pp
19
Allegro moderato. ♩= 96
-mour
pp
22
p
cresc.
L'a-lou - et - te mon-te au ciel a-vec le

25
f
jour!
f
rall.
28
Adagio. ♩= 68
p
Tour - ne ton re - gard que noi - e l'au - ro - re dans son a -
p
pp
32
-zur,
Allegro moderato. ♩= 96
pp
35
p
cresc.
Qu'el - le joi- - - - - e par -

38
-mi les champs de blé mûr
41
espressivo
sempre
44
Et fais lui-
48
-re ma pen-sé-e Là-bas bien
cresc.
52
loin! Oh! bien loin!

56
p
cresc.
La ro - sé - - e, gaîment, bril -
60
f
- le sur le foin!
cresc.
f
63
p
Dans le doux
f
pp
molto legato
66
rê - ve où s'a-gi-te ma mie en-dor-mie en - cor
69
cresc.
molto
Vi - te, vi - te,
cresc.
molto
f sempre

Avant que tu ne t'en ailles,
Pâle étoile du matin,
Mille cailles
Chantent, chantent dans le thym.

Tourne devers le poète,
Dont les yeux sont pleins d'amour,
L'alouette
Monte au ciel avec le jour.

Tourne ton regard que noie
L'aurore dans son azur;
Quelle joie
Parmi les champs de blé mûr!

Et fais luire ma pensée
Là-bas, bien loin, oh! bien loin!
La rosée
Gaîment brille sur le foin.

Dans le doux rêve où s'agite
Ma vie endormie encor . . .
Vite, vite,
Car voici le soleil d'or

PAUL VERLAINE (1844–96)

Before you go,
pale star of morning,
a thousand quails
sing, sing in the thyme.

Turn toward the poet,
whose eyes are filled with love,
the lark
climbs to the sky with the day.

Turn your gaze, that
the dawn drowns in its azure hue;
what joy
in the fields of ripe wheat!

Then make my thought shine
down there, quite far, o, quite far!
The dew
merrily sparkles in the hay.

In the sweet dream in which stirs
my life, still asleep . . .
quick, quick,
for here is the golden sun.

158

MODEST MUSORGSKY (1839–81)

Bez solntsa (Sunless; 1874): No. 3, *O konchen praedny* (The holidays are over)

See p. 540, Debussy, *Nuages,* where the accompaniment figure of measure 16 is borrowed. The present edition, based on that published by N. A. Rimsky-Korsakov in 1908, is identical musically to that printed by W. Bessel & Co., St. Petersburg, in 1874; the Russian text, omitted in 1908, has been restored.

спя.щу. ю ооъ. ем.лет. Но сон от глаз мо.их бе.жит И, при лу.
чах и.ной ден. ни.цы, Во.о.бра. же. ни. е вер.тит го
дов у.тра.чен.ных стра. ни.цы. Как буд.то вновь вды. ха. . я
яд Ве. сен. них, страст. ных
mf
pp

19
сно - ви - де - ний, В ду - ше я вос - кре - ша - ю ряд - на -
24 a tempo
вы, то при - зра - ки од - ни! Мне скуч - но с мерт - вой их тол - по - ю, И
p a tempo
22
poco ritard.
дежд, — по - ры - вов, за - блуж - де - ний... У -
pp poco ritard.
27
шум их ста - рой бол - тов - ни у - же не влас - тен на - до мно - ю. Лишь

31 Andante cantabile.
тень, од-на — из всех те-ней, я - ви-лась мне, ды-ша — лю-бо-вью. И,
m.s.
pp
33
вер-ный друг ми-нув-ших дней, Скло-ни-лась ти-хо к из-го-ло-вью. И
poco ritard.
35 a tempo
p
f
сме-ло от-дал ей сд-ной Всю ду-шу я — всле-

The holidays are over.
In the silence, all rest, all sleep.
The darkness of the May night slips through
the city,
but I cannot fall asleep . .
for in the rays of the aging hours,
my heart tarries as it leafs
through the pages of the deceased years,
and I breathe a slow poison.
Spring gone, ardors, extasies
return to my troubled heart.
Hope, dreams, fancies,
alas, all appeared to me.
I suffer as I see these phantoms.
They speak an ancient language,
to which my soul is deaf.
Here comes a shadow toward me;
with a gesture of tenderness
the faithful lover of yesteryears
bends over the bolster of my bed, mute;
with a bound, I extend to her my soul,
and a timid tear, silent, happy enough,
that for a long time I had held in.

159

CHARLES IVES (1874–1954)

In Flanders Fields (1917)

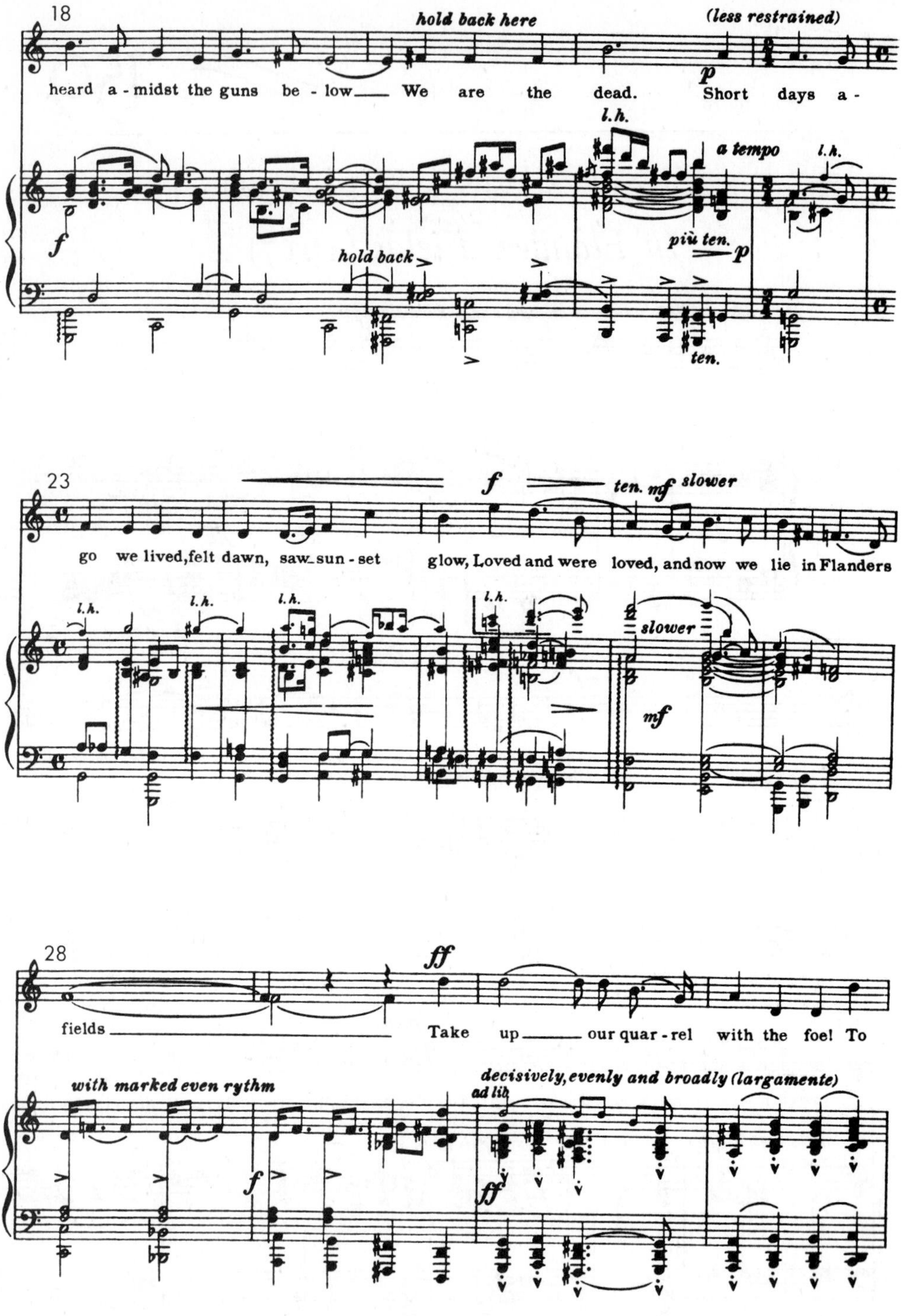
18
hold back here
(less restrained)
heard a-midst the guns be-low We are the dead. Short days a-
p
l.h.
a tempo
l.h.
f
hold back
più ten.
p
ten.
23
f
ten. mf slower
go we lived, felt dawn, saw sun-set glow, Loved and were loved, and now we lie in Flanders
l.h.
l.h.
l.h.
l.h.
slower
mf
28
ff
fields Take up our quar-rel with the foe! To
with marked even rythm
decisively, evenly and broadly (largamente)
ad lib
f
ff

Poem by JOHN MCCRAE

Alban Berg (1885–1935)

Wozzeck, Opus 7 (1917–22): Act III, Scene 3

140
Pk.
p
poco cresc.
Pianino
sempre ff
Wozz.
stürzt ein Glas Wein hinunter
dashes down a glass of wine
noch ein-mal der Teu-fel!
he'll fetch you. the Dev-il!
♩ = ♩ (𝅗𝅥 = daher 80)
145
1. 2. Kl. in B 3. 4.
p
1. 2. Hr. in F o. D. 3. 4.
mf
Pk.
kl. Tr.
f
mf
pp
Pianino
den Klavierspieler überschreiend
then, shouting down the pianist
Wozz.
f
Es rit-ten drei Rei-ter wohl an den Rhein, Bei ei-ner Frau Wir-tin da
Three horse-men came rid-ing up to the Rhine, And went to my host-ess to
♩ = ♩ (𝅗𝅥 = daher 80)
145
1. Vl.
pizz.
f
2. Vl.
Vla
Vlc.

etwas ruhiger (𝅗𝅥 = 70)
150
1. 2.
Kl. in B
3. 4.
1. 2.
Hr. in F
o. D.
3. 4.
Trgl
Hfe
p immer gebrochen
gleichsam versuchend, eine Begleitung für das Lied Wozzecks zu finden
149
150
Das Pianino a. d. Bühne
ff
p dolce
Wozz.
kehr_ten sie ein.
taste of her wine.
Mein Wein_ ist gut,
My wine_ is good,
mein Bier_ ist klar,
my ale_ is clear,
Mein Töch - ter-lein
my daugh - ter dear
etwas ruhiger (𝅗𝅥 = 70)
150
arco
1. 2. Solo
1. Vl.
3. 4. Solo
1. Vl.
d. Übrig.
2. Vl.
Vla
Vlc.

subito meno allegro (𝅗𝅥 = 60)
a tempo (♩ = ♩ = 160)
155
1. Hr. in F o. D.
2. Hr. in F o. D.
3.
3. Pos. o. D.
Btb. o. D.
gestopft
ff
fp
(o. Dpf.)
Pk.
f
Trgl
Hfe
nicht gebrochen
Pianino
Schnellpolka
verklingen lassen
quasi in den Tanz Wozzecks einfallend
Margret
mit Wozzeck tanzend
dancing with Wozzeck
Wozz.
sich unterbrechend
interrupts himself
springt auf
jumps up
tanzt mit Margret ein Paar Sprünge
dances a few steps with her
liegt auf der... Ver-dammt! Komm, Mar-gret!
lies on her... Be damned! Come, Mar-gret!
1. 2. Solo
1. Vl.
3. 4. Solo

rit. - - Wieder meno allegro
(ritardierte 𝅗𝅥 = neue 𝅗𝅥 = 60)
poco rit.
160
Englh.
die Singstimme fortsetzend
f
dimin.
nimmt 4. Ob.
1. 2. 3. Hr. in F o. D.
4.
gestopft
1.2. nehmen Dpf.
mf
3. o. D. Pos.
4. m. D.
nimmt Dpf.
m. Dpf.
Dpf. ab
Btb. o. D.
(ohne rit.) Plötzliche Unterbrechung
Pianino
Marg.
Wozz.
bleibt plötzlich stehen
then suddenly stops
führt sie an seinen Tisch und zieht sie auf seinen Schoß nieder
leads her to his table, and pulls her on his lap
Komm setz Dich her, Mar - gret!
Come, let's sit down, Mar - gret!
rit. - - Wieder meno allegro
poco rit.
160
get.
Griffbrett
arco
2. Vl.
ppp
fp
dimin.
Vla get.
Vlc.
(die Pos. nicht übertönend)
molto p
Kb.
(die Btb. nicht übertönend)

*) Triller ohne Nachschlag

165
168
1.2.Fl.
nehmen 1.u.2.Picc.
1.2.
Fg.
3.
Kfg.
1.2.Hr. in F
m.D.
Dpf.ab
1.
m.D.
Pos.
2.
o.D.
(m.Dpf.)
quasi Echo
(o.Dpf.)
mf
Hfe
nicht gebrochen
p
Die Margret begleitend
(♩=♩=120)
Das Pianino
a.d.Bühne
ff
m. d. Pianino
Marg.
In's
To
Wozz.
dolce
kalt
cold
wer - den!
al - so!
Kannst nicht sin - gen?
Can't you sing, girl?
1.Vl.
2.Vl.
Vla
Vlc.
Kb.
gewöhnlich

169
Hfe
170
Die neuen Viertel (im Pianino und Gesang der Margret) sind gleich den Vierteln der vorigen Triole (=120)
rall.
Pianino
mf
mit Pedal
übergreifen
Marg.
Schwa - ben - land, da magich nit, Und lan - ge Klei - der trag ich nit,
Swa - bi - a, I'll not go there And trail - ing dress - es I'll not wear,
hört dem Lied Margrets zu
listens to Margret's Song
Wozz.
1. Vl.
2. Vl.
Vla
Vlc.
Kb.
a tempo
175
rall.
Pianino
(f)
übergreifen
Marg.
Denn lan - ge Klei - der, spit - ze Schuh, Die kommen kei - ner Dienstmagd zu.
For point - ed shoes and powdered curls: They are no dress for ser-vant-girls!

plötzlich noch langsamer (♩ = 80)
180
1. 2.
Picc.
3. 4.
1. 2.
Ob.
3. 4.
a 2
1. 2.
Hr. in F
o. D.
3.
ff (f)
1. 3.
Trp. in F
m. D.
2. 4.
m. Dpf.
o. Dpf.
4. Pos.
o. D.
Btb.
o. D.
gr. Tr.
Xyl.
Hfe
auffahrend
flaming up
Wozz.
Nein! kei-ne Schuh, man kann auch bloß - fü-ßig in die Höll' geh'n! Ich möcht heut
No! wear no shoes, one can go bare - foot-ed down to hell - fire! I feel like
plötzlich noch langsamer (♩ = 80)
180
Doppelgriff
1. Vl.
2. Vl.

185
1.u.2. Picc. nehmen 1.u.2. Fl.
1.2. Picc. 3.4.
1.2. Ob. 3.4.
1.2. Kl. in B 3.4.
Echoton
pp
a 2
1. Fg. 2.3.
Kfg.
1.2.3. Hr. in F o.D.
1.2.3.4. Trp. in F m.D.
1.3. a 2
2.4. a 2
4. Pos. o.D.
subito p (Echo)
Btb. o.D.
Pk.
Xyl.
Cel.
f
Hfe
Marg.
mf
A - ber was hast Du
But what is that, there
Wozz.
rau - fen, rau - fen
fight - ing, fight - ing!
m. Dpf.
Solo m.D.
1. Vl. d. Übrig.
2. Vl.

kurzer Halt
poco Allegro (¢)
voriges ♩= neue 𝅗𝅥 (= 80)
1. 2.
Kl. in B
3. 4.
1.
Fg.
2. 3.
Kfg.
4. Pos. o. D.
(p)
Btb. o.D.
(p)
Pk.
Cel.
Hfe
p
Marg.
an der Hand?
on your hand?
p
Rot!
Red
Blut!
blood!
Wozz.
p
Ich?
Mine?
ich?
Mine?
poco Allegro (¢)
voriges ♩= neue 𝅗𝅥 (= 80)
kurzer Halt
Dpf. ab
Solo m.D. 1. Vl.
1. Solo Vlc. o.D.
o. Dpf.
col legno gestr.
pp
Solo Kb. o.D.
o. Dpf.
col legno gestr.
pp

190
195
1. Fg.
Kfg.
pp
p
Es stellen sich Leute um Margret u. Wozzeck
People gather round Margret and Wozzeck
Marg.
mf
Frei-lich
Blut.
Sure-ly
blood!
Wozz.
mp
Blut? Blut?
Blood? Blood?
Ich glaub; ich hab' mich
I think I must have
Solo Vla
gewöhnl. gestr.
(col legno gestr.)
1. Solo
Vlc.
2. Solo
Solo Kb.
200
1.2.3.4. Kl. in B
a 4
Bkl. in B
1. Fg. 2.3.
a 2
Kfg.
den Tonfall Wozzecks parodierend
imitating Wozzeck's tone of voice
Wie kommt's denn zum El- - len-bo-gen?
How comes it then on your el-bow?
ge-schnit-ten, da an der rech - ten Hand
I've cut it some-time on my right hand
Ich hab's
I've wiped

205
1.2.3.4.Kl. in B
a 4
Bkl. in B
1.2.3.Fg.
a 3
Kfg.
Hfe
ev. das Pianino a.d. Bühne
1. Ten. Solo
Chorauszug
Mit (der) rech - ten Hand am (rechten) Arm?
His (right) el - bow wiped with (his right) hand?
Marg.
Puh! Puh! Da
Pooh! Pooh! It
Wozz.
springt auf
jumping up
— dar - an ab - ge - wischt. Was wollt Ihr? Was gehts Euch an?
— my hand on it there. What mean - you? That's my af - fair.
Burschen
Ten.
1. Ten. Solo
Mit der rech - ten Hand am rech-ten Arm?
His right el - bow wiped with his right hand?
Baß
alle Violen
col legno gestr.
Vla
2 Soli gew. gestr.
2 Solo Vlc.
alle Kbs.
col legno gestr.
Kb.

1.2.3.4.Kl. in B
Bkl. in B
1.2.3.Fg.
Kfg.
Hfe
Soprane
Frei - lich da stinkt's nach
Sure - ly it smells of
ev. das Pianino a.d.Bühne
Blut Blood
1.Bässe
2.Ten.
2. Bässe Blut Blood
Marg.
stinkt's nach Men - schen - blut!
smells of hu - man blood!
Wozz.
Bin ich ein Mör - der? Platz! o - der es geht
Am I a murd' rer? Off! or else some - one
(alle Soprane)
Dirnen
Sopr.
Alt
Frei - lich da stinkt's nach
Sure - ly it smells of
Burschen
Ten.
Baß
1.Bässe Blut Blood
2.Ten. Blut Blood
2.Bässe Blut Blood
(col legno gestr.)
Vla
(gew.)
2 Soli
Vlc.
die Übrig.
(gew.)
get.
(col legno gestr.)
Kb.

210
1.2.Fl.
1.2.3.4.Kl. in B
Bkl. in B
1.2.3.Fg.
Kfg.
1.Hr.in F o.D.
1.3.Trp. in F m.D.
2.4.Pos. o.D.
Hfe
Pianino a.d.Bühne
Marg.
Wozz.
Dirnen
Sopr.
Alt
Burschen
Ten.
Baß
Vla
Vlc.
Kb.
mit den Sopranen und diese fortsetzend
a 2
a 4
a 3
menof
mit den Tenören und diese fortsetzend
(m.Dpf.) die Altstimme fortsetzend
(o.Dpf.) mit den Bässen und diese fortsetzend
Vorhang fällt rasch – Verwandlung
Quick curtain Change of scene
Men - schen - blut!
hum - an blood!
Blut
Blood
Frei - lich nach
Sure - ly of
Men - schen - blut!
hum - an blood!
Da
of
Alt
verhallend
Da stinkt's nach
of hum - an
Men - blood, of
Bässe
Men - - - schen - blut!
hum - - - an blood!
(ev. mit der Altstimme)
Frei - lich nach
Sure - ly of
Men - schen - blut!
hum - an blood!
stürzt hinaus
rushes out
wer zum Teu-fel!
pays the De-vil!
port.
(mit Flöten)
schon bei geschlossenem Vorhang
(get.) (mit Trp.)
1.Ten.
Blut!
Blood!
(m.1.Hr.)
2.Ten
Bässe (m.Pos.)
(col legno gestr.)
col legno geschlagen
get.(gew.gestr.)
(col legno gestr.)
mf
ff
f

215
3.4. Picc.
a 2
ff
1.2. Fl.
1.2.
Ob.
3.4.
a 2
ff
1.2.
Kl. in B
3.4.
a 2
ff
1.2.3. Fg.
a 3
ff
1.3. Trp.
inF m.D.
2.4. Pos.
o.D.
215
8
1. Vl.
fff
fp
2. Vl.
fff
gew. gestr.
Vla
fff
fp
Vlc.
get.
fff
fp
fff
fp
Kb.
gew. gestr.
fff
fp

etwas schwerer
(𝅗𝅥 = 50-60)
1.2.Fl.
1.2.3.4.Ob.
1.2.3.4.Kl. in B
Bkl. in B
1.2.3.Fg.
1.2.3.4.Hr. in F o.D.
2.4.Pos. o.D.
Btb. o.D.
kl.Tr. womöglich mehrere
a 2
a 4
a 3
fff
fp
nehmen Dpf.
sempre marc.
fp cresc.
1.Vl. get.
2.Vl.
Vla
Vlc. get.
col legno geschl.

Adapted by the composer from the play by GEORGE BUECHNER (1813-37)

161

Paul Hindemith (1895–1963)

Mathis der Maler (1934–35): Sechstes Bild

Very slow, free in measure
Sehr langsam, frei im Zeitmaß

Vorhang auf · Curtain
2
dim.
Whole bars
Ganze Takte (♩. etwa 80)
Mathis
Du wirst mich ver-lie-ren. Es ist zu lan-ge
her, daß ich so jung war wie du und so schnell.
3
M
in feverish haste
in fiebriger Hast
Regina
Laß uns doch wei-ter-lau-fen. Wer hat mir je ge-
M
Wo-hin willst du in der Nacht?

R
sagt, wo - hin der Weg geht?
4
mf
Noch im-mer
p
f
mf
f
p
R
drang-gen wir ins Un - be-kann te.
Mathis
p
Kei-ner jagt
calming down
beruhigen
Very slow,
Sehr langsam (♪ bis 66), aber stets erregt
but always agitated
R
Wie weißt du das?
Der lieb - ste Va-ter, er ver-
M
uns mehr.
calming down
beruhigen
Very slow,
Sehr langsam (♪ bis 66), aber stets erregt
but always agitated
R
stand mich oh - ne Wor-te,
er führ-te mich zart an der Hand.
5
cresc.
Und nur ein mal, zu-
pp

Moved
Bewegt (♩. bis 66)
letzt, ließ er mich al - lein zu - rück.
Seit ich ihn tot
holding back
Gehalten
lie - - gen sah, im Blu - te. mit off - nen Au - gen, die wie ein Wun-der des
6
holding back
Gehalten
Him-mels Schwär - - - - - ze an - starr - ten, mit den angst-voll ver-krall - ten
Calmer
Ruhiger
Hän - - - den, schüt-telt mich die Angst, daß der to - te Mann mir folgt.

accelerating
7 Vorangehen
R
Er holt mich ein, ist nah, er-greift mich.
leading into
einleiten
Very slow
Sehr langsam (♪ bis 66)
8
Und wie sehn - - lich wünschte ich, mein Herz bei ihm in Ru - he zu bet - ten.
Soll mich Sehn-sucht, soll mich Ent - set - - - zen läh-men? Sa-ge mir: wo ist er? Ver-

9
Again more vivacious
Wieder lebhafter (♩. 66)
R
sinkt ein To - ter, wird er er - ho - - - - - - - ben?— Laß mich nicht
pp
p
mf
R
al - lein!
Mathis
kisses her
küßt sie
Mein Töch - ter - lein, zu - sam - men blei - ben wir.
mp
p
10
M
Be - ru - - hi - ge dich. Le - ge dich zum Schlaf auf mei - nen Man - tel.
mf
He spreads his cloak for her to rest on, then beds her down and sits next to her.
Er bereitet ihr auf dem Mantel ein Lager, bettet sie und setzt sich tröstend neben sie.
M
Wie mür - be ist des Al - - ters Pein, maß - los das Leid der Ju - gend.
p
p
pp

B
Rather agitated semibreves
Ziemlich lebhafte Halbe (𝅗𝅥 108-112)
pp
11
mp
Mathis
pp
Al - te Mär - chen wo - ben uns from - - me Bil - der, die ein
pp
p
M
12
Wi - der - schei - nen des Hö - - - - he - ren sind.
mf
M
p
Ihr
f
p

leading into
einleiten
13
M
Sinn ist dir fern, du kannst ihn nur er-ah - - - - - nen.
p
A little calmer
Ein wenig ruhiger
Und frömmer noch re-den zu uns die Tö - - - - ne,
3
pp
14
wenn Mu-sik, in Einfalt hier ge - bo - - ren, die Spur
mp
mf
himm-li-scher Her - - - - - kunft trägt.

Principle measure
Im Hauptzeitmaß (♩ 108 - 112)
pp
15
Sieh, wie ei - ne Schar von En-geln e - wi-ge Bah - nen in ir - di-schen We-gen
p
pp
mp
ab-wandelt. Wie spürt man je - den ver - senkt in sein mil-des Amt. Der ei - ne
p
16
geigt mit wun - - - - der - sam ge - - sperr - tem Arm, den Bo-gen wägt er
mf
8
zart, da - mit nicht ei - nes we - ni - gen Schat - tens Rau - heit den lin - - den

17
f
M
Lauf trü - be. Ein and-rer streicht ge - hob - - nen Blicks aus
18
p
M
Sai - - - ten sei-ne Freu - - - - - - de. Ver - -
M
haf - - tet scheint der drit - te dem fer - nen Ge - läu - - te
M
sei - ner See - le und ach - - - - - - - -

M
pp
-tet leicht des Spiels.
pp
19
Regina
mf
Es sun-gen drei En-gel ein sü-ßen Ge-
M
mf
Wie be-reit er ist, zu-gleich zu
mf
R
sang, der weit in den ho-hen
M
hö-ren und zu

R
Him - mel er - klang.
M
die - nen.
pp
f
mp
20
Ihr Kleid selbst mu - si - ziert mit ih - nen. In
p markiert
schil - lern-den Fe - dern schwirrt der Tö - ne Ge - gen - spiel.
mf
Ein
mf
leich - ter Pan - zer un - ir - di - schen Me - talls er - glüht,

21
M
be - rührt vom Wo - gen des Klan - - - - - - - - ges wie vom
Be - ben be-weg-ten Her - - - zens. Und im Zu - - -
sam - - - - - - - - - - - men - klang viel bun - - ter
22
Lich - - ter - krei - - - se wird aus kaum ge -

Regina
f
Es eint sich mit ih-nen der himm-li-
M
f
hör-tem Lied auf wun-der-ba-re Art
8
ff
23
R
dim.
-sche Chor, sie sin-gen Gott und den
M
dim.
sicht-ba-res For-men-le-ben.
f
a little calmer
Ein wenig ruhiger
R
p
Es wird völlig Nacht.
Hei-li-gen vor. Night has fallen.
M
p
Wie die-se ihr klin-gen-des
a little calmer
Ein wenig ruhiger
mf
p

M
Werk ver - rich - - ten, so be - ten and - re.
24
mf
Mit wei-chen Fü-ßen tre-ten
sie auf_ die wei-che-ren Stu-fen der Tö - ne.
mf
Und du weißt nicht: mu-si-
zie - ren, die Ge - be - te dich - ten
p
o-der hörst du
25
Principal measure
Im Hauptzeitmaß
der Mu - si - kan - - ten Be - - ten. Ist so Mu - sik ___ Ge -

M
bet ge - - wor - den, hört lau - - - - - - -
p
26
pp
- - - schend zu Na - tur.
pp
Regina
falling asleep
einschlafend mp
dim.
Die Welt ist er - füllt von göt - li - chem Schall, im Her - - zen der
mp
dim.
Ein Rest des Schim - mers sol - cher Sphä - ren mög un - ser dunk - les
mp
p
dim.
calming down
beruhigen
pp
R
Men - - schen ein Wi - der - hall
M
Tun ver - klä - - ren.
calming down
beruhigen
pp
pp

Sixth Tableau

The Odenwald. A region with tall trees in the late twilight. Regina rushes in, Mathis close behind her.

MATHIS

Du wirst mich verlieren. Es ist zu lange her,	You almost lost me. It was too long ago
Dass ich so jung war wie du und so schnell.	that I was as young and as fast as you.

REGINA

Lass uns doch	Let us then
Weiterlaufen.	go on.

MATHIS

Wohin willst du in der Nacht?	Where would you go in the dark?

REGINA

Wer	Who could ever
Hat mir je gesagt, wohin der Weg geht? Noch	tell me where the path leads? Yet
Immer drangen wir ins Unbekannte.	we always hurry into the unknown.

MATHIS

Keiner jagt	No one chases
Uns mehr.	us any more.

REGINA

Wie weisst du das? Der liebste Vater, er verstand	How do you know that? My dearest father – he understood
Mich ohne Worte, er führte mich zart an der Hand.	me without words; he led me tenderly by the hand.
Und nur ein mal, zuletzt, liess er	And only once, for the last time, did he leave me
Mich allein zurück. Seit ich ihn tot liegen sah,	alone behind. For then I saw him lying dead
Im Blute, mit offnen Augen, die wie ein	in blood, with eyes open, as if
Wunder des Himmels Schwärze anstarrten, mit den angstvoll	he were staring at the mystery of heaven's darkness, his pained
Verkrallten Händen, schüttelt mich die Angst, dass der	hands twisted. I tremble with anxiety for fear
Tote Mann mir folgt. Er holt mich ein, ist nah,	the dead man is following me. He is overtaking me; he is nearby.
Ergreift mich. Und wie sehnlich wünschte ich, mein	He grabs me. How ardently I wish that
Herz bei ihm in Ruhe zu betten. Soll mich Sehnsucht, soll	He would put my heart to rest. Shall the longing
Mich Entsetzten lähmen? Sage mir: wo ist er?	and fear cripple me? Tell me: where is he?
Versinkt ein Toter, wird er erhoben?	A dead man sinks down; will he be lifted up?
Lass mich nicht allein!	Do not leave me alone.

MATHIS

Mein Töchterlein, zusammen bleiben wir.	My little daughter, we shall remain together.

(*he kisses her*)

Beruhige dich. Lege dich zum Schlaf auf meinen Mantel.	Now have a rest. Lie down to sleep on my cloak.

(He spreads his cloak to make a bed, settles her down, and comforting her, sits down beside her).

Wie mürbe ist des Alters Pein,	How weary is the pain of old age,
Masslos das Leid der Jugend.—Alte Märchen woben	boundless the sorrow of youth!—Old tales they wove:
Uns fromme Bilder, die ein Widerscheinen	to us innocent images that are a reflection
Des Höheren sind. Ihr Sinn ist dir	of higher things. Their sense
Fern, du kannst ihn nur erahnen.	eludes you; you can only surmise it.
Und frömmer noch reden	And more uncannily still do tones speak to us
Zu uns die Töne, wenn Musik, in Einfalt hier	
Geboren, die Spur himmlischer Herkunft trägt.	when music strikes up, bearing a sign of heavenly origin.
Sieh, wie ein Schar von Engeln ewige Bahnen	See how a troop of angels wanders through eternal paths
In irdischen Wegen abwandelt. Wie spürt man jeden	in an earthly direction. See how each one
Versenkt in sein mildes Amt. Der eine geigt	is engrossed in his tender task! One fiddles:
Mit wundersam gesperrtem Arm, den Bogen wägt	with wonderfully outstretched arm he balances the bow.
Er zart, damit nicht eines wenigen Schattens Rauheit	He fondles it so that not a shadow of coarseness
Den linden Lauf trübe. Ein andrer streicht	will disturb its gentle course. Another strokes
Gehobnen Blicks aus Saiten seine Freude.	uplifted glances from the strings of his joy.
Verhaftet scheint der dritte dem fernen Geläute	A third seems to listen to the ringing of bells
Seiner Seele und achtet leicht des Spiels. Wie bereit	in his soul. How ready
Er ist, zugleich zu hören und zu bedient.	he is both to hear and to serve.

REGINA

Es sungen drei Engel ein süssen Gesang,	Three angels sing a sweet song
Der weit in den hohen Himmel erklang.	that resounds widely through those high heavens.

MATHIS

Ihr Kleid selbst musiziert mit ihnen.	Even their garments make music
In schillernden Federn schwirrt der Töne Gegenspiel.	as their iridescent feathers whir a counter-voice.
Ein leichter Panzer unirdischen Metalls erglüht,	A light coat of mail of unearthly metal glows,
Berührt vom Wogen des Klanges wie vom Beben	shimmering with the waves of sound as with the trembling
Bewegten Herzens. Und im Zusammenklang viel	of an agitated heart. And through the harmony
Bunter Lichterkreise wird aus kaum gehörtem Lied	of countless bursts of color will form from a barely heard song
Auf wunderbare Art sichtbares Formenleben.	a wonderful kind of visible living form.

REGINA

Es eint sich mit ihnen der himmlische Chor,	Joining with them is the heavenly choir.
Sie singen Gott und den Heiligen vor.	They sing to God and the saints.

MATHIS

(*Light has fallen*).

Wie diese ihr klingendes Werk verrichten,
So beten andre. Mit weichen Füssen treten
Sie auf die weicheren Stufen der Töne. Und du
Weisst nicht: musizieren, die Gebete dichten
Oder hörst du der Musikanten Beten.
Ist so Musik Gebet geworden, hört lauschend zu
Natur. Ein Rest des Schimmers solcher Sphären
Mög unser dunkles Tun verklären.

While some attend to their sonorous duties,
others pray. With fleet feet they
descend the delicate steps of tones. And
you do not know whether, making music, they invent prayers
or whether you hear the musicians praying.
Has music, then, become prayer, as it imitates the harmony
of nature. A residue of splendor of those spheres
may brighten up our dark path.

REGINA

(*falling asleep*)

Die Welt ist erfüllt von göttlichem Schall,
Im Herzen der Menschen ein Widerhall.

The world is filled with a godly ringing
in the hearts of men sounds the echo.

162

Benjamin Britten (1913–76)

Peter Grimes, Opus 33 (1945): *To hell with all your mercy*

The voices are now close at hand and very distinct.
ritmico
Fog-horn
più f
poco a poco cresc.
impetuoso
P.
Do you hear them all shout-ing my name? D'you hear them? D'you hear them?
ritmico
Old Da-vy Jones shall ans wer: Come home! come
ritmico
S.
Peter Grimes! Peter Grimes!
A.
CHORUS (off)
T.
B. Grimes!
Peter Grimes! .... Peter Grimes!
Grimes!

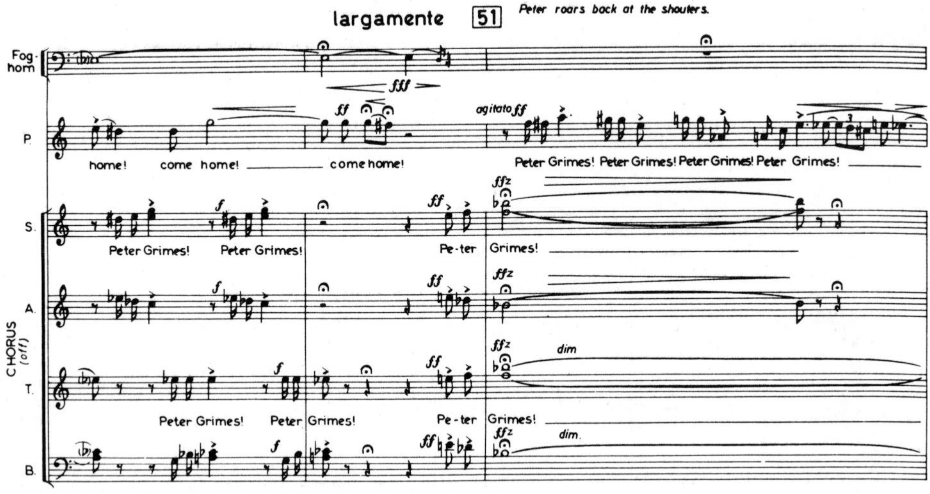
largamente 51 Peter roars back at the shouters.
Fog-horn
P.
agitato
home! come home! come home!
Peter Grimes! Peter Grimes! Peter Grimes! Peter Grimes!
S.
Peter Grimes! Peter Grimes! Pe-ter Grimes!
A.
CHORUS (off)
T.
Peter Grimes! Peter Grimes! Pe-ter Grimes!
dim
dim.
B.

poco a poco dim.
P.
Peter Grimes! Peter Grimes! Grimes! Grimes! Grimes! Peter Grimes! Peter Grimes! Peter Grimes!
(p) dim.
S.
Grimes!
(p) dim.
A.
CHORUS (off)
T.
B.
Ellen and Balstrode come in, and stand waiting till Peter has calmed.
Fog-horn
ppp
lento
pp
rall.
ppp
P.
Grimes! Pe-ter Grimes!
pp
ppp
S.
Grimes!
CHORUS (off)
pp
ppp
A.
ELLEN
Ellen goes up to Peter.
p
dolce
espress.
parlando
Pe-ter We've come to take you home. O come home out of this dreadful night! See, here's Balstrode.
Peter does not notice her. The voices are now very distant.
52 Andante comodo e molto tranquillo
E.
Pe-ter don't you hear me?
pp
S.
Grimes, Grimes, Grimes! Grimes!
pp
A.
CHORUS (off)
pp
T.
Pe-ter Grimes! Pe-ter! Pe-ter! Pe-ter! Pe-ter!
pp
B.

Fog-horn
colla parte
ppp
PETER
dolcissimo
What har - - - - bour shel - ters peace,
senza voce
a-way from ti - dal waves, a-way from storms!
S.
Grimes! Grimes!
CHORUS (off)
A.
T.
Pe - ter! Pe - ter! Pe - ter! Pe - ter! Grimes!
B.
Fog-horn
ppp
P.
cantando
What har - - bour can em - brace terrors and tragedies.
S.
pp
Grimes! Grimes! Grimes!
A.
pp
CHORUS (off)
T.
pp
Pe - ter! Pe - ter! Pe - ter! Pe - ter! Pe - ter! Grimes!
B.
pp
Fog-horn
P.
dim. poco a poco
Her breast is har - bour too Where night is turned
S.
pp
poco cresc.
dim.
Grimes! Grimes! Grimes! Grimes! Grimes!
A.
pp
poco cresc.
dim.
CHORUS (off)
T.
pp
poco cresc.
dim.
Pe-ter! Pe-ter! Pe - ter! Pe - ter! Pe - ter! Pe - ter! Pe - ter! Pe - ter! Pe - ter! Pe-ter!
B.
pp
poco cresc.
dim.

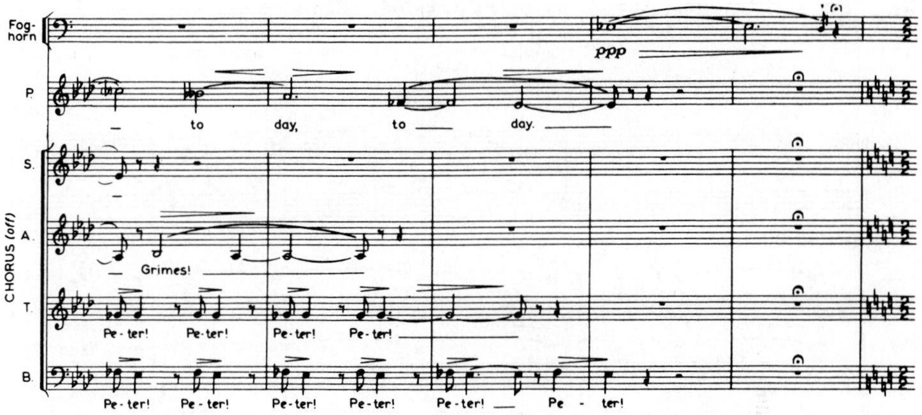

BALSTRODE: *(Crossing to lift Peter up)* Come on, I'll help you with the boat.
ELLEN: No!
BALSTRODE: Sail out till you lose sight of the Moot Hall. Then sink the boat. D'you hear? Sink her. Good-bye Peter.

There is a crunch of shingle as Balstrode leads Peter down to his boat, and helps him push it out. After a short pause, he returns, takes Ellen by the arm, and leads her away.

Dawn slowly begins and the Borough slowly comes to life. Some stragglers of the manhunt go

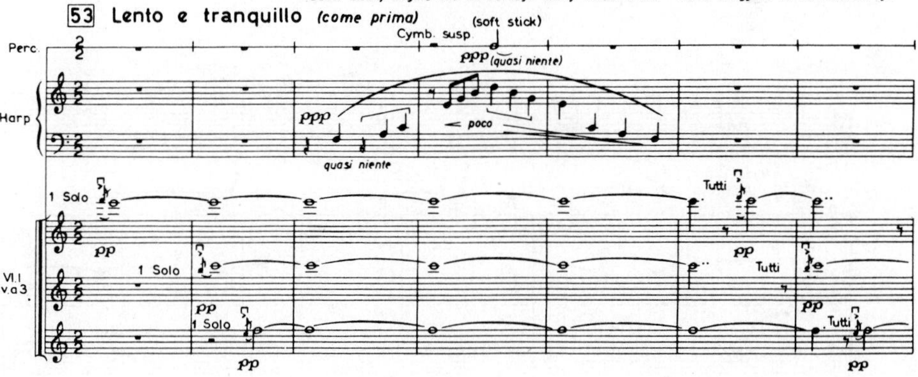

across the street to their houses. Shutters are drawn back.
Fl.
1. Solo
ppp poco a
Cl. in B♭
1. Solo
ppp
pp
Perc.
Cymb.
ppp
Harp
ppp
più
pp
Vl. Solo
f
pp
pp cresc.
Vl. I div. a 3
ppp
pp cresc.
Vl. II div. a 3
pp cresc.
Fl.
1.
poco e più espress.
f
tr
pp
Tutti
Vl. I div. a 3
pp cresc.
mf
dim.
Vl. II div. a 3
pp cresc.
mf
dim.

1.
a2
Fl.
pp sempre
a2
Cl. in B♭
pp
mf
pp
a2
Bsn.
ppp sempre
D. Bsn.
ppp sempre
1.2
Hn. in F
3.4
ppp sempre
ppp sempre
1.2
Tbn.
3
Tuba
ppp sempre
(in the Orchestra)
ppp sempre
tr
Timp.
ppp sempre
Cymb.
Perc.
pp
veloce
Harp
mf
pp
ppp
Vl. I. II
div. a 3
pp sempre
pp sempre
pp sempre
Sola
Vla.
div.
pp
mf
pp
mf
Vc.
pp sempre
Db.
pp sempre

54
Some women carry nets down to the shore
a2
Fl.
Cl.in B♭
Bsn.
D.Bsn.
1.2
Hn.in F
3.4
1.2
Tbn.
3
Tuba
Timp.
Perc.
Cymb.
Harp
SOPRANO
1st Solo (off)
distinto
Cho.
To those who pass, the Borough sounds be - tray
54
Vl.I.II
div.a 3
Vla.
div.
Vc.
Db.
pp
mf
ppp sost.
ppp

More and more of the Borough people come casually to their daily jobs.
Fl.
a2
Bsn.
a2
pp
D.Bsn.
pp
1.2
Hn. in F
3.4
dim.
Tr. 2 in C
ppp sost.
dim.
1.2
Tbn.
3
Tuba
pp
Timp.
(tr)
tr
pp
Perc.
B.D.
tr
p
ALL SOPRANOS
semplice
Cho.
(p)
The cold be-gin-ning of an-o-ther
(⊓) sim.
Vl. I. II div. a 3
Vla.
Vc.
pp
Db.
pp

55
Swallow comes in and speaks to some fishermen.
Fl.
a2
pp
poco cresc.
Cl. in B♭
mf
p
pp
Bsn.
ppp
poco cresc.
D. Bsn.
Hn. in F
1.2
3.4
Tbn.
3
Tuba
Timp.
tr
Perc.
Cymb.
più p
Harp
CHORUS
S.
A.
day.
pp sost.
And houses sleep - ing by the wa - ter side Wake,
f
Vl. I. II
div. a 3
mf dim.
Vla.
div.
Sola
Vc.
Db.

1. Solo
a2
Fl.
mf dim.
ppp
Cl. in B♭
1. Solo
ppp
a2
Bsn.
mf
D.Bsn.
mf
1.2
Hn. in F
3.4
mf
1.2
Tbn.
3
Tuba
mf
Timp.
(tr)
mf
Perc.
Cymb.
ppp
Harp
pp
SWALLOW
There's a boat sinking out at sea, Coastguard reports.
A FISHERMAN (BASS)
Within reach?
CHORUS
S.
dim.
— to the measured rip-ple of the tide.
A.
dim.
Vl. I. II div. a 3
mf dim.
ppp
Vla. div.
Sola
p
Vc.
Db.

56
Fl.
Cl. in B♭
Bsn.
D. Bsn.
Hn. in F 1.2 3.4
Tbn. 1.2 3 Tuba
Timp.
Perc.
Cymb.
Harp
Sw.
No!
Fisherman
f marc.
Let's have a look thro' the glasses.
CHORUS
TENOR
BASS
mf semplice
Or measured cadence of the lads who tow
Vl. I. II div. a 3
poco cresc.
Vla. div.
Sola
Tutte div.
Vc.
Db.
a2
ppp poco cresc.
1.
tr

Fl.
a2
p
p cresc.
Cl. in B♭
a2
p
f
mf
Bsn.
a2
pp
D. Bsn.
pp
1.2
Hn. in F
3.4
pp
1.2
Tbn.
3
Tuba
pp
Timp.
tr
pp
Perc.
Cymb.
mf
Harp
p
f
mf
CHORUS
T.
B.
Some en-tered hoy to fix her in her row.
(p)
Vl. I. II
div. a 3
p cresc.
(p) cresc.
(p) cresc.
Vla
div.
p
f
mf
Vc.
pp
Db.
pp

Auntie comes out of the pub door.
57
a2
Fl.
Ob.
Cl. in B♭
Bsn.
D.Bsn.
1.2
Hn. in F
3.4
1.2
Tbn.
3
Tuba
Timp.
Perc.
Cymb.
Harp
AUNTIE
What is it?
CHORUS
T.
B.
Or hol-low sound that from the passing bell To some de-part-ed spi-rits bids fare-well.
Vl. I. II div. a 3
trem.
Vla div.
Vc.
Db.

Fl.
Cl. in B♭
D. Bsn.
Hn. in F 1.2 3.4
Tr. 1.2 in C
Tbn. 1.2 3
Tuba
Timp.
Perc.
Cymb. (tr)
cresc.
B.D.
Harp
A.
BOLES
Nothing I can see.
One of these ru - mours!
TWO NIECES
AUNTIE and Mrs. SEDLEY
BOLES and RECTOR
KEENE
SWALLOW and HOBSON
In ceaseless motion
In cease-less motion
CHORUS S. A. T. B.
Vl. I. II div. a 3
cresc. molto
Vla. div.
Vc.
Db.

The stage is now filled with people singing at their daily work
a2
Fl.
Ob.
Cl. in B♭
Bsn.
D. Bsn.
1.2 Hn. in F 3.4
Tr. 1.2 in C
1.2 Tbn. 3 Tuba
Timp.
Cymb.
Perc.
B.D.
Harp
2 N.
comes and goes the tide. Flow - ing it fills the channel broad and wide,
A. & Mrs. S.
comes and goes the tide. Flow - ing it fills the channel broad and wide,
Bol. & Rec.
div. unis.
comes and goes the tide. Flow - ing it fills the channel broad and wide,
K.
comes and goes the tide. Flow - ing it fills the channel broad and wide,
Sw. & H.
comes and goes the tide. Flow - ing it fills the channel broad and wide
CHORUS S. A. T. B.
comes and goes the tide. Flow - ing it fills the channel broad and wide,
div. unis
comes and goes the tide. Flow - ing it fills the channel broad and wide,
Vl. I. II div. a 3
unis.
Vla.
Vc.
Db.

58
a2
Fl.
Ob.
Cl. in B♭
Bsn.
D. Bsn.
1.2 Hn. in F 3.4
1.2 Tr. in C 3
1.2 Tbn. 3 Tuba
Timp.
Cymb.
Perc.
B.D.
Harp
2 N.
A. & Mrs. S.
Bol. & Rec.
K.
Sw. & H.
S.
A.
T.
B.
CHORUS
Vl. I. II div. a 3
Vla.
Vc.
Db.
poco a poco dim.
sost.
meno f
Then back to sea with strong ma - jestic sweep It
(cambiare l'arco ad lib.)

SLOW CURTAIN
Fl.
Cl. in B♭
Bsn.
D. Bsn.
1.2 Hn. in F 3.4
1.2 Tr. in C 3
1.2 Tbn. 3 Tuba
Timp.
Perc.
B.D.
Cymb.
Harp
2 N.
rolls in ebb yet ter - ri-ble and deep.
A. & Mrs. S.
rolls in ebb yet ter - ri-ble and deep.
Bol. & Rec.
rolls in ebb yet ter - ri - ble, yet ter - ri - ble and deep.
K.
rolls in ebb yet ter - ri - ble, yet ter - ri - ble and deep.
Sw. & H.
rolls in ebb yet ter - ri - ble, yet ter - ri - ble and deep.
CHORUS
S.
rolls in ebb yet ter - ri-ble and deep.
A.
T.
rolls in ebb yet ter - ri - ble, yet ter - ri - ble and deep.
B.
meno f
ancora meno f
Vl. I, II div. a 3
Vla. div.
Vc.
Db.

Libretto by MONTAGU SLATER on a poem by GEORGE CRABBE

163

IGOR STRAVINSKY (1948–51)

The Rake's Progress (1951), Act III, Scene 2

PRELUDE

DUET

161
♪ = 84
Enter Rakewell and Shadow.
SOLI
Fl. I. II
SOLO
Cl. I in Sib
TUTTI
Vc.
ben articolato
Cb.
ben articolato
162
Rakewell
How dark, how dark, how dark and dreadful is this place.
TUTTI
mp
I Vl. II
TUTTI
mp
TUTTE
Vle.
mp ma espress.
Vc.
mf marc.
Cb.
mf marc.
163
Fl. I. II
come sopra
Cl. I in Sib
come sopra
R.
Why have you led me here?
163
I Vl. II
Vle.
Vc.
Cb.

164
R.
There's something, there's something, Sha - dow, in your face that
I
Vl.
II
come sopra
come sopra
Vle.
come sopra
Vc.
mf
Cb.
mf
165 ♩.=56
Timp.
p
R.
fills, that fills my soul with fear!
Shadow
A year and a day have
165
Vl.
div. pizz.
p
pizz.
p
Vle.
in harm.
mp marc.
Vc.
in harm.
mp marc.
Cb. div.
pizz.
p ma marc.
(arco)

166
Fl. I. II
mp
Timp.
Sh.
passed a - way Since first to you I came All
166
I
Vl.
II
Vle.
sim.
Vc.
sim.
Cb.
div.
167
Fl. I. II
Timp.
Sh.
things you bid, I du - ly did And now my wa - ges claim.
167
I
Vl.
II
Vle.
Vc.
Cb.
div.

168
♪=84
Rakewell
Sha - dow, good Sha - dow, be pa - tient;
arco
mp
arco
mp
mp ma espress.
mf
mf
I
Vl.
II
Vle.
Vc.
Cb. unis.
169
R.
I Am beg-gared as you know, But promise When I am
Cb.
rich a-gain to pay you, to pay you all I owe.

♩.:56
170
SOLO
Ob. I
mp
SOLA
Tr. I in Sib
mp
Timp.
171
Shadow
quasi messa voce
modo ordinario
'Tis not your mo-ney but your soul, — 'tis not your mo-ney but your soul Which I — this
170
♩.:56
171
pizz.
I Vl. II
pizz.
in harm. come sopra
Vle.
in harm. come sopra
Vc.
pizz.
Cb. div.
(arco)
172
Fl. I.II
mp
SOLO
Ob. I
mp
SOLA
Tr. I in Sib
mp
Timp.
quasi sotto voce
cresc.
Sh.
night re - quire. Look in my eyes, look in my eyes and re-cog - nise
172
I Vl. II
Vle.
Vc.
Cb. div.

173
174
Fl. I. II
Tr. I in Sib
Timp.
cant. espress.
Sh.
(pointing out grave)
Whom, Fool! you chose to hire. Be-hold,
I
Vl.
II
Vle.
Vc.
Cb. div.
arco
mf marc.
f ben articolato-marc.
(Taking objects mentioned out of his bag)
be-hold your wai - ting grave, be-hold Steel, hal - ter, poi - son, gun.
Cb. unis.

175
Fl. I. II
a 2
Cl. I. II in Sib
I.
Fag. I. II
Tr. I. II in Sib
I.
Cor. in Fa I
Cor. in Fa II
Timp.
Sh.
Make no ex-cuse: Your e-xit choose: Tom Rakewell's race is run.
175
Vl. I
Vl. II
Vle.
Vc.
pizz. div. arco unis.
Cb.
pizz. arco

176
♩.:84
Fl. I
Cl. I in Sib
Timp.
Rakewell
agitato ma tempo rigoroso
O let the wild hills
177
mf
sf
I
Vl.
II
Vle.
Vc.
Cb.
sf-mf sempre
sim.
mf sempre
Fl. I. II
R.
Sh.
178
I.
co-ver me or the a-boun-ding
The sins you did may not be hid. Think

179
I
Fl.
II
Cl. I in Sib
Fag. I
mf
R.
wave. O why did an un-cle I ne-ver
Sh.
not your soul to save. It plea-ses
179
I
Vl.
II
Vle.
Vc.
Cb.
sim.
sim.
180
Ob. I
knew Se-lect me for his heir?
well the damned in Hell to bring a-no-ther there.
180

181
allarg.
182 Lo stesso
I
Ob.
II
dolce
Fag.
Tr. I
in Sib
mf
Shadow
Mid-night is
Vl.
Vle.
Vc.
Cb.
f
Cor. I
in Fa
sf
marc.-articolato
Sh.
come; by rope or gun Or me-di-cine, or knife, On the stroke of twelve

183
Fl. I. II
a 2
Cl. I. II in Si♭
Fag. I. II
Tr. I. II in Si♭
I.
Cor. in Fa I II
Sh.
ten.
you shall slay your-self For forfeit is your life.
Vl. I II
Vle.
Vc.
pizz. div. arco unis.
Cb.
pizz. arco
184
(♩=42)
(A clock begins to strike)
Rakewell
Have mer-cy, have
Count one, count two, count three, count four, Count five, and
Bell off stage
real pitch
Shadow holds up his hand and the clock stops after the ninth stroke.
R.
mer-cy on me Hea-ven. Too late.
six and se-ven, Count eight; No, wait.
Bell

RECITATIVE

185
♩.= 69 circa
Shadow (urbanely)
Ve-ry well. Then__ my dear and good Tom, per-haps you im-pose a
Cemb.
Sh.
bit u-pon our friendship; but Nick, as you know, is a gent-le-man at heart,
Rakewell
A game?
for-gives your di-la-to-ri-ness and sug-gests a game.__
rubato
a tempo
rubato
R.
All
A game of chance to fi-nal-ly de-cide your fate. Have you a pack of cards?
sf
dolce

(taking a pack from his pocket)
186
a tempo
R.
that remains me of this world, and for the next.
Sh.
You jest. Fine, fine. Good spi-rits makes a game go
Cemb.
Sh.
well. I shall ex-plain. The rules are simple and the out-come simpler still: Nick will
Cemb.
(he points to the instruments of death)
Sh
cut three cards. If you can name them, you are free; if not,
Cemb.
(Rakewell nods)
Sh.
you choose the path to fol - low me. You un-der-stand. Let us be-gin.
Cemb.
pp
poco sf
pp
sf
sf

DUET

Shadow shuffles the cards, places the pack in the palm of his left hand and cuts with his right, holding then the portion with the exposed card towards the audience and away from Rakewell.

(aside)
(calmly)
R.
Anne!
My fear de-
Sh.
game instead of Sha-dow.
Cemb.
legato
R.
(dolce)
-parts; I name the Queen of Hearts.
(holding up the card towards Rakewell)
(he tosses it to one side)
Sh.
The Queen of Hearts. You see, it's quite a simple game.
(The clock strikes once)
Bell off stage
Cemb.
188
As Rakewell lifts his head in silent thanks, Shadow addresses the audience.
♩= 112
Sh.
To win at once in love or cards is dull, The gent-le-man loves sport, for
Cemb.
Sh.
sport is rare; The po-si-tive ap - pals him;
Cemb.

189
Sh.
He plays the pence of hope to yield the gui - neas
Cemb.
(turning back to Rakewell)
Sh.
of des - pair. A - gain, good Tom. You are my mas-ter yet.
Cemb.
Shadow repeats the routine of shuffling and cutting the cards.
190
Tempo I. (♪= 69)
Rakewell
What shall I trust in now? How throw the die,
Shadow
Come, try.
Cemb.
legato
R.
how throw the die to win, to win my soul, back, for my - self?
Sh.
Was
Cemb.

191
Sh.
For - tune not your mistress once? Be, be fair. Give her at least the se-cond chance to
Cemb.
The spade falls forward with a great crash.
Rakewell
(startled, cursing)
He looks at what fell.
The deuce!
Sh.
bare the hand of Sha-dow.
Cemb.
legato
(calmy)
R.
She lights the shades and shows the two of Spades.
Cemb.
192
(With scarcely contained anger, throwing the card aside).
Sh.
The two of Spades. Con-gra-tu-la-tions. The God-des still is faith-ful.
(the clock strikes once)
Bell off stage
Cemb.

Tempo I. (di recitativo) ♩=69 (circa)
(changing his tone)
Sh.
But we have one more, you know, the ve ry last.
Cemb.
sf sempre
Think for a while, my Tom, where you have come to, I would not want your last of chan-ces thought-less.
I am, you may have of-ten-times ob-served, real-ly com-pas-sio-nate. Think on your
♪=76
193
Shadow reaches deftly down, picks up one of the discarded cards and holds it up while he addresses the audience.
I
Fl.
II
p
cant.
Cl. in Si♭
Fag.
pp
Rakewell
dolce
O God — what hopes have I?
He covers his face in his arm and leans against the tomb.
hopes.

194
♩=126
Sh.
Cemb.
marc. scherzando
The simp - ler the trick, the simp-ler the de - ceit; That
there is no re-turn, I've taught him well, and re-pe-ti-tion
195
palls him: The Queen of Hearts a - gain shall be for him the
He slips the card into the deck and then turns to Rakewell.
meno mosso
Queen of Hell. Rouse, your-self, Tom, your tra-vail
sempre sf
p
(routine with cards)
soon will end. Come, try.
non stacc.
non f

196
♩.=♪=126
Rakewell
Now in his words I find no aid.
Sh.
Now in my words
Cemb.
p
R
Will For - tune give a-no-ther sign, will
Sh.
he'll find no aid and For - tune gives no o-ther sign, no o-ther sign, and
Cemb.
197
♩.=♩
Rakewell looks nervously about him.
Rakewell frightened looking away from the ground.
R
For - tune give a - no - ther sign?
Sh.
For - tune gives no o - ther sign. A-fraid, love-lu-cky Tom? Come, try!
Cemb.
pesante ma p
poco sf
non stacc.
poco marc.

sempre tempo rigoroso - non ad lib.
(stepping forward, agonized)
R.
Dear God, a track of cloven hooves.
Re - turn! and Love!
(sardonic)
Sh.
The knavish goats are back To crop the spring's re-turn.
Cemb.
Anne (off stage)
♪ = 84 (circa)
A Love That is sworn be-fore thee can
(he breaks off, startled, when he realizes he is singing with Anne)
The ba - nished words torment.
Re-turn, return! O Love!
(Shadow stands as though frozen)
You can - not now re-pent.
Rakewell (parlando) I wish for nothing else.
Anne off stage
plun - der Hell, can plun-der Hell of its prey.

198
♩=168
199
Rakewell (exalté)
Love,
I
Vl.
II
Vle.
Vc.
Cb.
f
R.
200
first and last as - sume e - ter - nal reign: Re - new, re - new my
As he sings "O Queen of Hearts again" he snatches the exposed half-deck from the still motionless Shadow.
The twelfth stroke strikes. With a cry of joy Rakewell sinks to the ground senseless.
Bell off stage
life, O Queen of Hearts, a - gain.

201
Tempo ♪ = 84
Fl. I. II
Ob. I. II
Cl. I. II in Sib
Fag. I. II
Cor. I. II in Fa
Timp
Shadow
1. I burn, I burn! I freeze! In shame I hear
2. De-feated, mocked, a-gain I sink In ice and flame,
201
Tempo ♪ = 84
I
Vl.
II
Vle.
Vc.
Cb.

202
Fl. I. II
a 2
Ob. I. II
Cl. I. II in Sib
Fag. I. II
Tr. I in Sib
f
Cor. I. II in Fa
Timp.
Sh.
— my fa — mished le - gions roar: — My — own — de-lay — lost
— in ice — and flame — to lie. — But — Hea - ven's will —
202
sim.
I
Vl.
II
Vle.
Vc.
Cb.

Fl. I. II
a 2
Ob. I. II
Cl. I. II in Sib
Fag. I II
Tr. I in Sib
Cor. I. II in Fa
Timp.
Sh.
me my prey And damns my- self the more.
I'll hate and till E-ter-ni-ty de-fy.
I Vl. II
Vle.
Vc
Cb.

203
(looking at Rakewell)
Sh.
Your sins, my foe, before I go give me some power to pain:
Vl. I
Vl. II
Vle.
Vc.
Cb.
ff
sempre sff
204
allargando
Cor. in Fa I
II
(with a magic gesture)
To rea-son blind shall be your mind; Hence-forth be you in
204
allargando

205
a tempo
Meno mosso (♪=66)
Fl. I.II
Ob. I.II
Cl. I.II in Sib
Fag. I.II
Tr. I.II in Sib
I. SOLA
Cor. I.II in Fa
Timp.
(slowly Shadow sinks into the grave)
Sh.
-sane.
205
a tempo
Meno mosso (♪=66)
I Vl. II
Vle.
Vc.
Cb.
p marc.
sim.
Tr. I.II in Sib
Timp.
p ma marc.
I Vl. II
Vle.
Vc.
Cb.

The dawn comes up. It is spring. The open grave is now covered with a green mound upon which Rakewell sits smiling putting grass on his head and singing to himself in a child-like voice.
♪ = 138
206
Fl. I
Ob. I
Cl. I in Sib
mp dolce
Cl. I.II in Sib
p
207
Rakewell
With ro - ses crowned, I sit on ground; A - do - nis
Cl. in Sib I II
208
R.
is my name The on - ly dear of Ve - nus

209
R.
fair:
Me - thinks it is no shame.
Fl. I
Ob. I
I
Cl. in Sib
II
210
Fl. I
Ob. I
Cl. I in Sib
SLOW CURTAIN
211
Fl. I
Ob. I
Cl. I in Sib
212
Fl. I
Ob. I
Cl. I in Sib
pp
pp
pp

Appendix A Instrument Names and Abbreviations

The following tables set forth the English, Italian, German, and French names used for the various musical instruments in these scores, and their respective abbreviations.

Woodwinds

English	*Italian*	*German*	*French*
Piccolo (Picc.)	Flauto piccolo (Fl. Picc.)	Kleine Flöte (Kl. Fl.)	Petite flûte
Flute (Fl.)	Flauto (Fl.); Flauto grande (Fl. gr.)	Grosse Flöte (Fl. gr.)	Flûte (Fl.)
Alto flute	Flauto contralto (fl.c-alto)	Altflöte	Flûte en sol
Oboe (Ob.)	Oboe (Ob.)	Hoboe (Hb.); Oboe (Ob.)	Hautbois (Hb.)
English horn (E. H.)	Corno inglese (C. or Cor. ingl., C.i.)	Englisches Horn	Cor anglais (C. A.)
Sopranino clarinet	Clarinetto piccolo (clar. picc.)		
Clarinet (C., Cl., Clt., Clar.)	Clarinetto (Cl. Clar.)	Klarinette (Kl.)	Clarinette (Cl.)
Bass clarinet (B. Cl.)	Clarinetto basso (Cl. b., Cl. basso, Clar. basso)	Bass Klarinette (Bkl.)	Clarinette basse (Cl. bs.)
Bassoon (Bsn., Bssn.)	Fagotto (Fag., Fg.)	Fagott (Fag., Fg.)	Basson (Bssn.)
Contrabassoon (C. Bsn.)	Contrafagotto (Cfg., C. Fag., Cont. F.)	Kontrafagott (Kfg.)	Contrebasson (C. bssn.)

Brass

English	*Italian*	*German*	*French*
French horn (Hr., Hn.)	Corno (Cor., C.)	Horn (Hr.) [*pl.* Hörner (Hrn.)}	Cor; Cor à pistons
Trumpet (Tpt., Trpt., Trp., Tr.)	Tromba (Tr.)	Trompete (Tr., Trp.)	Trompette (Tr.)

English	*Italian*	*German*	*French*
Trumpet in D	Tromba piccola (Tr. picc.)		
Cornet	Cornetta	Kornett	Cornet à pistons (C. à p., Pist.)
Trombone (Tr., Tbe., Trb., Trm., Trbe.)	Trombone [*pl.* Tromboni (Tbni., Trni.)]	Posaune (Ps., Pos.)	Trombone (Tr.)
Tuba (Tb.)	Tuba (Tb, Tba.)	Tuba (Tb.)	Tuba (Tb.)

PERCUSSION

English	*Italian*	*German*	*French*
Percussion (Perc.)	Percussione	Schlagzeug (Schlag.)	Batterie (Batt.)
Kettledrums (K. D.)	Timpani (Timp., Tp.)	Pauken (Pk.)	Timbales (Timb.)
Snare drum (S. D.)	Tamburo piccolo (Tamb. picc.) Tamburo militare (Tamb. milit.)	Kleine Trommel (Kl. Tr.)	Caisse claire (C. cl.), Caisse roulante Tambour militaire (Tamb. milit.)
Bass drum (B. drum)	Gran cassa (Gr. Cassa, Gr. C., G. C.)	Grosse Trommel (Gr. Tr.)	Grosse caisse (Gr. c.)
Cymbals (Cym., Cymb.)	Piatti (P., Ptti., Piat.)	Becken (Beck.)	Cymbales (Cym.)
Tam-Tam (Tam-T.)			
Tambourine (Tamb.)	Tamburino (Tamb.)	Schellentrommel, Tamburin	Tambour de Basque (T. de B., Tamb. de Basque)
Triangle (Trgl., Tri.)	Triangolo (Trgl.)	Triangel	Triangle (Triang.)
Glockenspiel (Glocken.)	Campanelli (Cmp.)	Glockenspiel	Carillon
Bells (Chimes)	Campane (Cmp.)	Glocken	Cloches
Antique Cymbals	Crotali Piatti antichi	Antiken Zimbeln	Cymbales antiques
Sleigh Bells	Sonagli (Son.)	Schellen	Grelots
Xylophone (Xyl.)	Xilofono	Xylophon	Xylophone

Strings

English	*Italian*	*German*	*French*
Violin (V., Vl., Vln, Vi.)	Violino (V., Vl., Vln.)	Violine (V., Vl., Vln.) Geige (Gg.)	Violon (V., Vl., Vln.)
Viola (Va., Vl., *pl.* Vas.)	Viola (Va., Vla.) *pl.* Viole (Vle.)	Bratsche (Br.)	Alto (A.)
Violoncello, Cello (Vcl., Vc.)	Violoncello (Vc., Vlc., Vcllo.)	Violoncell (Vc., Vlc.)	Violoncelle (Vc.)
Double bass (D. Bs.)	Contrabasso (Cb., C. B.) *pl.* Contrabassi or Bassi (C. Bassi, Bi.)	Kontrabass (Kb.)	Contrebasse (C. B.)

Other Instruments

English	*Italian*	*German*	*French*
Harp (Hp., Hrp.)	Arpa (A., Arp.)	Harfe (Hrf.)	Harpe (Hp.)
Piano	Pianoforte (P.-f., Pft.)	Klavier	Piano
Celesta (Cel.)			
Harpsichord	Cembalo	Cembalo	Clavecin
Harmonium (Harmon.)			
Organ (Org.)	Organo	Orgel	Orgue

Appendix B Glossary

a. The phrases *a 2, a 3* (etc.) indicate that the part is to be played in unison by 2, 3 (etc.) players; when a simple number (1., 2., etc.) is placed over a part, it indicates that only the first (second, etc.) player in that group should play.
abdämpfen. To mute.
aber. But.
accelerando (*acc.*). Growing faster.
accompagnato (*accomp.*). In a continuo part, this indicates that the chord-playing instrument resumes (*cf. tasto solo*).
adagio. Slow, leisurely.
a demi-jeu. Half-organ; i.e., softer registration.
ad libitum (*ad lib.*). An indication giving the performer liberty to: (1) vary from strict tempo; (2) include or omit the part of some voice or instrument; (3) include a cadenza of his own invention.
agitato. Agitated, excited.
alla breve. A time signature (𝄵) indicating, in the sixteenth century, a single breve per two-beat measure; in later music, the half note rather than the quarter is the unit of beat.
allargando (*allarg.*). Growing broader.
alle, alles. All, every, each.
allegretto. A moderately fast tempo (between allegro and andante).
allegro. A rapid tempo (between allegretto and presto).
alto, altus (*A.*). The deeper of the two main divisions of women's (or boys') voices.
am Frosch. At the heel (of a bow).
am Griffbrett. Play near, or above, the fingerboard of a string instrument.
amoroso. Loving, amorous.
am Steg. On the bridge (of a string instrument).
ancora. Again.
andante. A moderately slow tempo (between adagio and allegretto).
animato,animé. Animated.
a piacere. The execution of the passage is left to the performer's discretion.
arco. Played with the bow.
arpeggiando, arpeggiato (*arpeg.*). Played in harp style, i.e. the notes of the chord played in quick succession rather than simultaneously.
assai. Very.
a tempo. At the (basic) tempo.
attacca. Begin what follows without pausing.
auf dem. On the (as in *auf dem G,* on the G string).
Auftritt. Scene.
Ausdruck. Expression.
ausdrucksvoll. With expression.
Auszug. Arrangement.

baguettes. Drumsticks (*baguettes de bois, baguettes timbales de bois,* wooden drumsticks or kettledrum sticks; *baguettes d'éponge,* sponge-headed drumsticks; *baguettes midures,* semi-hard drumsticks; *baguettes dures,* hard drumsticks; *baguettes timbales en feutre,* felt-headed kettledrum sticks).
bariton. Brass instrument.
bass, basso, bassus (*B.*). The lowest male voice.
Begleitung. Accompaniment.
belebt. Animated.
beruhigen. To calm, to quiet.
bewegt. Agitated.
bewegter. More agitated.
bien. Very.
breit. Broadly.
breiter. More broadly.
Bühne. Stage.

cadenza. An extended passage for solo instrument in free, improvisatory style.
calando. Diminishing in volume and speed.
cambiare. To change.
cantabile (*cant.*). In a singing style.
cantando. In a singing manner.
canto. Voice (as in *col canto,* a direction for the accompaniment to follow the solo part in tempo and expression).
cantus. An older designation for the highest part in a vocal work.
chiuso. Stopped, in horn playing.
col, colla, coll'. With the.
come prima, come sopra. As at first; as previously.
come. Like, as.
comodo. Comfortable, easy.
con. With.
Continuo (*Con.*). A method of indicating an accompanying part by the bass notes only, together with figures designating the chords to be played above them. In general practice, the chords are played on a lute, harpsichord or

organ, while, often, a viola da gamba or cello doubles the bass notes.
contratenor. In earlier music, the name given to the third voice part which was added to the basic two voice texture of discant and tenor, having the same range as the tenor which it frequently crosses.
corda. String; for example, *seconda* (*2a*) *corda* is the second string (the A string on the violin).
coro. Chorus.
coryphée. Leader of a ballet or chorus.
countertenor. Male alto, derived from *contratenor altus*.
crescendo (*cresc.*). Increasing in volume.

da capo (*D.C.*). Repeat from the beginning, usually up to the indication *Fine* (end).
daher. From there.
dal segno. Repeat from the sign.
Dämpfer (*Dpf.*). Mute.
decrescendo (*decresc., decr.*). Decreasing in volume.
delicato. Delicate, soft.
dessus. Treble.
détaché. With a broad, vigorous bow stroke, each note bowed singly.
deutlich. Distinctly.
diminuendo, diminuer (*dim., dimin.*). Decreasing in volume.
discantus. Improvised counterpoint to an existing melody.
divisés, divisi (*div.*). Divided; indicates that the instrumental group should be divided into two or more parts to play the passage in question.
dolce. Sweet and soft.
dolcemente. Sweetly.
dolcissimo (*dolciss.*). Very sweet.
Doppelgriff. Double stop.
doppelt. Twice.
doppio movimento. Twice as fast.
doux. Sweet.
drängend. Pressing on.

e. And.
Echoton. Like an echo.
éclatant. Sparkling, brilliant.
einleiten. To lead into.
Encore. Again.
en dehors. Emphasized.
en fusée. Dissolving in.
erschütterung. A violent shaking, deep emotion.
espressione intensa. Intense expression.
espressivo (*espress., espr.*). Expressive.
et. And
etwas. Somewhat, rather.
expressif (*express.*). Expressive.

falsetto. Male singing voice in which notes above the ordinary range are obtained artificially.
falsobordone. Four-part harmonization of psalm tones with mainly root-position chords.
fauxbourdon (*faulx bourdon*). Three-part harmony in which the chant melody in the treble is accompanied by two lower voices, one in parallel sixths, and the other improvised a fourth below the melody.
fermer brusquement. To close abruptly.
fine. End, close.
flatterzunge, flutter-tongue. A special tonguing technique for wind instruments, producing a rapid trill-like sound.
flüchtig. Fleeting, transient.
fois. Time (as in *premier fois*, first time).
forte (*f*). Loud.
fortissimo (*ff*). Very loud (*fff* indicates a still louder dynamic).
fortsetzend. Continuing.
forza. Force.
frei. Free.
fugato. A section of a composition fugally treated.
funebre. Funereal, mournful.
fuoco. Fire, spirit.
furioso. Furious.

ganz. Entirely, altogether.
gebrochen. Broken.
gedehnt. Held back.
gemächlich. Comfortable.
Generalpause (*G.P.*). Rest for the complete orchestra.
geschlagen. Struck.
geschwinder. More rapid, swift.
gesprochen. Spoken.
gesteigert. Intensified.
gestopft (*chiuso*). Stopped; for the notes of a horn obtained by placing the hand in the bell.

gestrichen (*gestr.*). Bowed.
gesungen. Sung.
geteilt (*get.*). Divided; indicates that the instrumental group should be divided into two parts to play the passage in question.
gewöhnlich (*gew., gewöhnl.*). Usual, customary.
giusto. Moderate.
gleichmässig. Equal, symmetrical.
gli altri. The others.
glissando (*gliss.*). Rapidly gliding over strings or keys, producing a scale run.
grande. Large, great.
grave. Slow, solemn; deep, low.
gravement. Gravely, solemnly.
grazioso. Graceful.
grossem. Large, big.

H⌐. *Hauptstimme*, the most important voice in the texture.
Halbe. Half.
Halt. Stop, hold.
harmonic (*harm.*). A flute-like sound produced on a

string instrument by lightly touching the string with the finger instead of pressing it down.
Hauptzeitmass. Original tempo.
heftiger. More passionate, violent.
hervortretend. Prominently.
Holz. Woodwinds.
hörbar. Audible.

immer. Always.
impetuoso. Impetuous, violent.
istesso tempo. The same tempo, as when the duration of the beat remains unaltered despite meter change.

klagend. Lamenting.
klangvoll. Sonorous, full-sounding.
klingen lassen. Allow to sound.
kräftig. Strong, forceful.
kurz. Short.
kurzer. Shorter.

laissez vibrer. Let vibrate; an indication to the player of a harp, cymbal, etc., that the sound must not be damped.
langsam. Slow.
langsamer. Slower.
largamente. Broadly.
larghetto. Slightly faster than largo.
largo. A very slow tempo.
lebhaft. Lively.
legato. Performed without any perceptible interruption between notes.
leggéro, leggiero (*legg*.). Light and graceful.
legno. The wood of the bow (*col legno tratto*, bowed with the wood; *col legno battuto*, tapped with the wood; *col legno gestrich*, played with the wood).
leidenschaftlich. Passionate, vehement.
lent. Slow.
lentamente. Slowly.
lento. A slow tempo (between andante and largo).
l.h. Abbreviation for "left hand."
lié. Tied.

ma. But.
maestoso. Majestic.
maggiore. Major key.
main. Hand (*droite*, right; *gauche*, left).
marcatissimo (*marcatiss*.). With very marked emphasis.
marcato (*marc*.). Marked, with emphasis.
marcia. March.
marqué. Marked, with emphasis.
mässig. Moderate.
mean. Middle part of a polyphonic composition.
meno. Less.
mezza voce. With half the voice power.
mezzo forte (*mf*). Moderately loud.
mezzo piano (*mp*). Moderately soft.
minore. In the minor mode.
minuetto. Minuet.
mit. With
M. M. Metronome; followed by an indication of the setting for the correct tempo.
moderato, modéré. At a moderate tempo.
molto. Very, much.
mosso. Rapid.
motetus. In medieval polyphonic music, a voice part above the tenor; generally, the first additional part to be composed.
moto. Motion.
muta, mutano. Change the tuning of the instrument as specified.

N⌐. *Nebenstimme*, the second most important voice in the texture.
Nachslag. Auxiliary note (at end of trill).
nehmen (*nimmt*). To take.
neue. New.
nicht, non. Not.
noch. Still, yet.

octava (*okt*., *8va*). Octave; if not otherwise qualified, means the notes marked should be played an octave higher than written.
ohne (*o*.). Without.
open. In brass instruments, the opposite of muted. In string instruments, refers to the unstopped string (i.e. sounding at its full length).
ordinario, ordinairement (*ordin*., *ord*.). In the usual way (generally cancelling an instruction to play using some special technique).
ôtez les sourdines. Remove the mutes.

parlando. A singing style with the voice approximating speech.
parte. Part (*colla parte*, the accompaniment is to follow the soloist in tempo).
passione. Passion.
pause. Rest.
pedal (*ped*., *P*.). In piano music, indicates that the damper pedal should be depressed; an asterisk indicates the point of release (brackets below the music are also used to indicate pedalling). On an organ, the pedals are a keyboard played with the feet.
perdendosi. Gradually dying away.
peu. Little, a little.
pianissimo (*pp*). Very soft (*ppp* indicates a still softer dynamic).
piano (*p*). Soft.
più. More.
pizzicato (*pizz*.). The string plucked with the finger.
plötzlich. Suddenly, immediately.
plus. More.
pochissimo (*pochiss*.). Very little.
poco. Little, a little.
poco a poco. Little by little.

ponticello (*pont.*). The bridge (of a string instrument).
portato. Performance manner between legato and staccato.
prenez. Take up.
près de la table. On the harp, the plucking of the strings near the soundboard.
prestissimo. Very fast.
presto. A very quick tempo (faster than allegro).
prima. First.
principale (*pr.*). Principal, solo.

quasi. Almost, as if.
quasi niente. Almost nothing, i.e. as softly as possible.
quintus. An older designation for the fifth part in a vocal work.

rallentando (*rall., rallent.*). Growing slower.
rasch. Quick.
recitative (*recit.*). A vocal style designed to imitate and emphasize the natural inflections of speech.
rinforzando (rinf.). Sudden accent on a single note or chord.
ritardando (*rit., ritard.*). Gradually slackening in speed.
ritmico. Rhythmical.
rubato. A certain elasticity and flexibility of tempo, speeding up and slowing down, according to the requirements of the music.
ruhig. Calm.
ruhiger. More calmly.

saltando (*salt.*). An indication to the string player to bounce the bow off the string by playing with short, quick bow-strokes.
sans. Without.
scherzando (*scherz.*). Playfully.
schleppend. Dragging.
schnell. Fast.
schneller. Faster.
schon. Already.
schwerer. Heavier, more difficult.
schwermütig. Dejected, sad.
sec., secco. Dry, simple.
segno. Sign in form of :S: indicating the beginning and end of a section to be repeated.
segue. (1) Continue to the next movement without pausing; (2) continue in the same manner.
sehr. Very.
semplice. Simple, in a simple manner.
sempre. Always, continually.
senza. Without.
senza mis[*ura*]. Free of regular meter.
serpent. Bass of the cornett family.
seulement. Only.
sforzando, sforzato (*sfz, sf*). With sudden emphasis.
simile. In a similar manner.
sino al . . . Up to the . . . (usually followed by a new tempo marking, or by a dotted line indicating a terminal point).
sombre. Dark, somber.
son. Sound.
sonore. Sonorous, with full tone.
sopra. Above; in piano music, used to indicate that one hand must pass above the other.
soprano (*Sop., S.*) The voice with the highest range.
sordino (*sord.*). Mute.
sostenendo, sostenuto (*sost.*). Sustained.
sotto voce. In an undertone, subdued, under the breath.
sourdine. Mute.
soutenu. Sustained.
spiccato. With a light bouncing motion of the bow.
spiritoso. Lively, witty.
sprechstimme (*sprechst.*). Speaking voice.
staccato (*stacc.*). Detached, separated, abruptly disconnected.
stentando, stentato (*stent.*). Delaying, retarding.
Stimme. Voice.
strepitoso, strepito. Noisy, boisterous.
stretto. In a non-fugal composition, indicates a concluding section at an increased speed.
stringendo (*string.*). Quickening.
subito (*sub.*). Suddenly, immediately.
sul. On the (as in *sul G*, on the G string).
suono. Sound, tone.
superius. The uppermost part.
sur. On.

Takt. Bar, beat.
tasto solo. In a continuo part, this indicates that only the string instrument plays; the chord-playing instrument is silent.
tempo primo (*tempo I*). At the original tempo.
tendrement. Tenderly.
tenerezza. Tenderness.
tenor, tenore (*T., ten.*). High male voice or part.
tenuto (*ten.*). Held, sustained.
touche. Fingerboard or fret (of a string instrument).
tranquillo. Quiet, calm.
trauernd. Mournfully.
treble. Soprano voice or range.
tremolo (*trem*). On string instruments, a quick reiteration of the same tone, produced by a rapid up-and-down movement of the bow; also a rapid alteration between two different notes.
très. Very.
trill (*tr.*). The rapid alternation of a given note with the note above it. In a drum part it indicates rapid alternating strokes with two drumsticks.
triplum. In medieval polyphonic music, a second voice part added above the tenor or chant.
tristement. Sadly.
troppo. Too much.
tutti. Literally, "all"; usually means all the instru-

ments in a given category as distinct from a solo part.

übertönend. Drowning out.
unison (*unis.*). The same notes or melody played by several instruments at the same pitch. Often used to emphasize that a phrase is not to be divided among several players.
Unterbrechung. Interruption, suspension.

veloce. Fast.
verhalten. Restrained, held back.
verklingen lassen. To let die away.
Verwandlung. Change of scene.
verzweiflungsvoll. Full of despair.
vibrato. Slight fluctuation of pitch around a sustained tone.
vif. Lively.
vigoroso. Vigorous, strong.
vivace. Quick, lively.
voce. Voice.
volti. Turn over (the page).
Vorhang auf. Curtain up.
Vorhang fällt, Vorhang zu. Curtain down.
voriges. Preceding.
vorwärts. Forward, onward.

weg. Away, beyond.
wieder. Again.
wie oben. As above, as before.

zart. Tenderly, delicately.
ziemlich. Suitable, fit.
zurückhaltend. Slackening in speed.
zurückkehrend zum. Return to, go back to.

Index of Composers

Index of Titles

Index of Forms and Genres

Index of NAWM references in Grout-Palisca, *A History of Western Music,* 4th, ed.